Lecture Notes in Computer

Edited by G. Goos, J. Hartmanis and J.

Advisory Board: W. Brauer   D. Grie

Springer

Berlin
Heidelberg
New York
Barcelona
Budapest
Hong Kong
London
Milan
Paris
Tokyo

Manfred Meyer (Ed.)

Constraint Processing

Selected Papers

 Springer

Series Editors

Gerhard Goos
Universität Karlsruhe
Vincenz-Priessnitz-Straße 3, D-76128 Karlsruhe, Germany

Juris Hartmanis
Department of Computer Science, Cornell University
4130 Upson Hall, Ithaca, NY 14853, USA

Jan van Leeuwen
Department of Computer Science, Utrecht University
Padualaan 14, 3584 CH Utrecht, The Netherlands

Volume Editor

Manfred Meyer
software design & management GmbH & Co KG
Am Schimmersfeld 7a, D-40880 Ratingen, Germany

CR Subject Classification (1991): D.1, D.3.2-3, I.2.3-4, F.3.2, F.4.1, I.2.8, H.3.3

ISBN 3-540-59479-5 Springer-Verlag Berlin Heidelberg New York

CIP data applied for

© Springer-Verlag Berlin Heidelberg 1995
Printed in Germany

Typesetting: Camera-ready by author
SPIN: 10485943   06/3142-543210 - Printed on acid-free paper

Preface

An increasing number of researchers all over the world are now dealing with different aspects of constraint processing regarded as a general paradigm of computation. However, the constraint processing community still appears to be very heterogeneous: Researchers from logic programming, knowledge representation, expert systems, theoretical computer science, operations research and other related fields are investigating the use of constraint processing methods, their foundations, and their applications to real-life problems.

Thus, the need became obvious to bring together researchers from different areas dealing with various aspects of constraint processing. Therefore, in July 1993 we organized a two-day international workshop on Constraint Processing in conjunction with the International Congress on Computer Systems and Applied Mathematics (CSAM'93) in St. Petersburg which aimed at exchanging, comparing and contrasting research results in all areas of constraint processing regarded as a general paradigm of computation. For this workshop, papers were submitted by authors working on various aspects of constraint processing at different sites in Austria, England, France, Germany, The Netherlands, Russia, Slovenia, Switzerland, and the United States. From these, 19 papers were accepted for presentation at the workshop together with an invited talk given by Andreas Podelski.

Among the conclusions drawn at the closing round-table discussion of this meeting, a common desire was expressed for more communication and cross-fertilization between the various research communities. Consequently, during the winter 1993/94 we started the formal process for the creation of a new Internet newsgroup named *comp.constraints*, the first international forum for discussion of all aspects of constraint processing. The most impressive result of 501 vs. 13 votes for the creation of this newsgroup again showed the need to bring together people working on or interested in constraint processing from different viewpoints.

Consequently, in 1994 we organized a successor workshop on Constraint Processing, this time in conjunction with the European Conference on Artificial Intelligence (ECAI'94) held in Amsterdam. The increasing interest in this topic again became obvious as we received a total number of 43 submissions to the workshop from which 10 papers were selected for long presentations at the workshop. An invited talk given by Gene Freuder, short presentations of another 5 papers, together with a final panel discussion organized by Hans Guesgen then concluded the workshop program.

This book now contains revised and extended versions of the best papers and the invited talks presented at both workshops.

- Chapter 1 by Andreas Podelski and Peter van Roy is based on the invited talk given at the St. Petersburg workshop in 1993. They present the "Beauty-and-the-Beast" algorithm for testing guards over feature trees which is needed in constraint logic programming with entailment-based coroutining and in concurrent constraint programming.

- Christian and Philippe Codognet then present a framework for abstract interpretation of concurrent constraint languages that is based on their denotational semantics and the notion of abstraction between constraint systems (Chapter 2).

- Chapter 3 by Anton Ertl and Andreas Krall discusses how to extend constraint logic programming languages by incorporating high-level constraints, i.e. predicates with additional control information, in order to achieve fine-grained control over the tradeoff between pruning power and execution time.

- Jérôme Gensel presents the TROPES system, an object-based knowledge representation system in which constraints are integrated as objects. They provide a declarative means for expressing relations both inside and between objects while constraint maintenance offers an inference mechanism based on value propagation (Chapter 4).

- The section based on papers presented at the St. Petersburg workshop is then concluded by Chapter 5 where Patrice Boizumault, Yves Delon and Laurent Péridy discuss how to use the constraint logic programming system CHIP to solve examination planning problems.

- The 1994 workshop at ECAI started with an invited talk on "The many paths to Satisfaction" where Eugene Freuder gave an overview about various ways to represent and solve constraint satisfaction problems. A collection of illustrations from his talk is also included as Chapter 6 where he takes a simple coloring problem as a kind of Rosetta stone for constraint satisfaction which is then represented in many different ways.

- The issue of overconstrained problems is then tackled by Richard Wallace in Chapter 7 who describes a family of strategies based on directed arc-consistency testing during preprocessing.

- In Chapter 8, Barbara Smith investigates exceptionally difficult problems in the context of binary constraint satisfaction problems and identifies three possible reasons for their occurrence. She addresses, e.g., the question of how problems which are difficult to solve can arise in a region where most problems are easy to solve.

- The AC-6 algorithm by Bessière and Cordier is claimed to be optimal in time for achieving arc-consistency in arbitrary constraint networks. In the following two chapters, Christian Bessière and Jean-Charles Régin (Chapter 9) as well as Eugene Freuder (Chapter 10) both present extensions and improvements to the AC-6 algorithm, named AC6++ and AC-7 respectively, that are based on making use of the bidirectionality of constraints.

- The contribution by Patrick Prosser (Chapter 11) discusses the FC-BM algorithm, a combination of the forward-checking (FC) and backmarking (BM) routines, that aims at minimizing the number of nodes visited while avoiding redundant consistency checks.

- Francesca Rossi then studies finite domain constraint problems with hidden variables, i.e. variables that are not visible from the outside. She proposes several sufficient conditions for hidden variable redundancy and presents algorithms for removing the variables found to be redundant (Chapter 12).

- The constraint logic programming language CHIP is revisited by Gilberto Filé, Giuseppe Nardiello, and Adriano Tirabosco in Chapter 13 where they discuss some semantic properties of a significant subset of CHIP covering the finite domain operations.

- Chapter 14 by Dan Vlasie then applies a combination of forward-checking and hill-climbing to checking the consistency of disjunctive constraint sets. He also gives a qualitative model that allows one to predict the average-case advantages of the combined method compared with standard forward-checking.

- The presentation and discussion of various aspects in constraint processing is then completed by Chapter 15, where Ágoston Eiben, Paul-Erik Raué and Zsófia Ruttkay finally discuss the possibilities of also applying genetic algorithms for solving constraint satisfaction problems.

Finally, I would like to thank all the people who have helped in the realization of this book. I am most grateful to Philippe Codognet, Hans Guesgen, and Walter Hower who helped organizing the ECAI workshop and also to the numerous referees for contributing to the difficult task of paper selection and for recommending paper revisions. My thanks also

4

extend to the organizers of the CSAM'93 congress, Dimitrij Shiriaev and Sergej Voitenko, and to the ECAI'94 workshop organizers, Frances Brazier and Jan Treur, for their local support. Last but not least, I want to sincerely thank the authors of the papers presented here for their contribution to the workshops and for revising their papers for inclusion in this book.

Kaiserslautern, March 1995   Manfred Meyer

Contents

8

1

A Detailed Algorithm Testing Guards over Feature Trees

Andreas Podelski[1]
Peter Van Roy[2]

ABSTRACT We give the detailed formulation of an algorithm testing guards over feature trees. Such an algorithm is needed in constraint logic programming with entailment-based coroutining and in concurrent constraint programming; feature-tree constraint systems model extensible record descriptions (for example, in LIFE). We call this algorithm "Beauty-and-Beast" algorithm because it uses, for each variable X and for each guard test being suspended on X, a special-purpose data structure (the "beast") which encodes the data relevant for that guard test (essentially, a unifier). A variable X has a multiple-binding list where each of its bindings to a beast is indexed by the particular guard test. This is how we achieve that the algorithm is incremental when it is applied for repeated resumptions of suspended tests. Its online time complexity is almost-linear (which is the same as for the best existing offline algorithms for the problem). Our implementation technique of multiple-bindings is applicable to all constraint systems over trees (finite trees, rational trees, etc.); the beast construction is motivated in particular by the implementation of record-descriptions with extensible lookup-tables.

1.1 Introduction

We consider the tests of guards as they are needed for the delay mechanisms in (constraint) logic programming languages and concurrent constraint programming languages, cf., [5, 6, 7, 9, 12, 13, 15, 16, 19, 20, 21, 22]. They are also used for solving inequations, i.e., constraints with negation [8]. We study these tests for the case of the feature-tree constraint systems which are related to Prolog-II's rational-tree constraint system and which

---

[1]Max-Planck-Institut für Informatik, Im Stadtwald, D-66123 Saarbrücken, podelski@mpi-sb.mpg.de

[2]German Research Center for Artificial Intelligence (DFKI), Stuhlsatzen-hausweg 3, D-66123 Saarbrücken, vanroy@dfki.uni-sb.de.
This work was done while both authors were at Digital Paris Research Laboratory. A short description appeared in [17].

are used, for example, in LIFE [5] in order to model extensible record descriptions.

The formal conditions of a guard test are entailment and disentailment of one constraint by another (which is matching and non-unifiability of terms, respectively). These two conditions are tested simultaneously and (possibly) repeatedly. For example, assume the tests are applied to the constraint part γ of the global resolvent (the "actual parameter", *e.g.* the predicate's arguments) and the local constraint φ (the "formal parameter", *e.g.* the guard). If both tests fail, *i.e.*, γ neither entails nor disentails φ, then after each modification of the resolvent (yielding the sequence $\gamma, \gamma_1, \gamma_2, \ldots$) the tests will be applied on γ_1 and φ, γ_2 and φ, ..., until one of them succeeds. Modification of a resolvent means instantiating the predicate's arguments; logically it means adding a conjunct to its constraint part (*i.e.*, $\gamma_i = \gamma_{i-1} \& C_i$).

Therefore, an important aspect of an efficient implementation of the two tests is its *incrementality*. This means, intuitively, its ability to reuse work done in previous resumptions of the tests. We define *true incrementality: The complexity of the entailment and disentailment tests is the same whether the resolvent is given at once, or whether it is built up step by step (and the tests are applied at each step).* More formally, given the sequence $\gamma, \gamma_1, \gamma_2, \ldots$, the time complexity of the two tests applied to γ_n and φ equals the total time complexity of the n applications of the two tests applied to γ and φ, γ_1 and φ, ..., and γ_n and φ, for any n.

This article contains the detailed presentation of such an algorithm that does the simultaneous tests of entailment and disentailment in almost-linear time[3] with true incrementality. That is, an online algorithm with the same complexity as the best known offline algorithm. A short presentation of this "Beauty-and-Beast" algorithm appeared in [17].

The algorithm consists of two parts. The first one is the "wavefront algorithm" which performs a depth-first pattern matching on the actual and the formal term. If the actual term is not enough instantiated to match the formal one, then its leave variables X correspond to positions in the formal term (that we designate by local variables U). These positions form a "wavefront" which gets pushed down upon further instantiation of the actual term. The global variable X gets a binding (in a multiple-bindings list for X) to the local variable U which is indexed by the guard test being invoked.

If, during the partial traversal of the formal term, no incompatibility of the formal with the actual term is detected, then in certain cases the disentailment test must be delayed. As an example of such a case, the

---

[3] "Almost-linear" time is standard terminology for a Union-Find algorithm, whose execution time is $O(n\alpha(n))$ where $\alpha(n)$ is the inverse Ackermann function. The usual implementation of variable-variable unification is as a Union-Find algorithm.

constraint corresponding to the term $f(X, Y)$ does not entail nor disentail the one for the term $f(g(a), h(U))$. Here, our algorithm just checks the compatibility of the respective root function symbols and then stops at the roots of the two subterms $g(a)$ and $h(U)$; it will resume the tests from there upon reactivation.

The solution outlined above is always sufficient for testing entailment over feature trees. It is not, however, sufficient for disentailment, namely if there is variable aliasing (*i.e.*, if there are no multiple occurrences of the same variable, or, logically, if there are no equality constraints). For example, $f(a, b)$ disentails $f(X, X)$ and $f(X, X)$ disentails $f(a, b)$. This case can get rather complex; testing $f(t_1, t_2, \ldots, t_n)$ against $f(U, U, \ldots, U)$ must yield a result as soon as either $t_1, t_2, \ldots, t_n$ are all "the same" or all together they are incompatible.

Our algorithm accounts for the case of variable aliasing by creating a special-purpose data structure (from now on referred to as the "beast") that represents the most general unifier of *all* the terms, actual or formal, whose compatibility has to be compared in order to check disentailment. For example, when testing $f(t_1, t_2)$ against $f(U, U)$ where $t_1 = g(s_1, s_2, X_3)$ and $t_2 = g(s_1', X_2, s_3)$, the corresponding beast represents the term $g(s_1'', U_2, U_3)$ where s_1'' represents the unifier of s_1 and s_1' and U_2 and U_3 point to the terms s_2 and s_3, respectively.

In our representation, we always associate the term $f(t_1, t_2)$ with some (global) variable X and the beast with some (new local) variable V. Then, X has a binding (in its multiple-bindings list) to V which is indexed by the guard test being invoked. So has X_2, namely to U_2, and so on.

If, for example, X_2 gets more instantiated to $X_2 = s_2'$, then the guard test is resumed. This means that one accesses U_2 (through the multiple-bindings list of X_2) and augments the beast with the unifier of s_2 and s_2',

This algorithm is the first one with almost-linear online complexity (and, thus, true incrementality). An early description of an implementation of the entailment and disentailment tests for rational trees can be found in [8]. The implementation in the AKL system [12] is formalized and proven correct in [23]. In that approach one effectuates the two tests by first unifying the actual and formal terms and then checking whether any modifications were done to the actual parameters. Accommodating the case where neither of the two tests succeeds is expensive in that one needs to first trail all such modifications and then undo them after the unification. This leads to quadratic online complexity; for a worst-case example, see [17].

Order-Sorted Feature Constraints. The problem of incrementality becomes even more important if the constraints are finer grained than the ones corresponding to Prolog terms. We have in mind the order-sorted feature constraints that correspond to ψ-terms, the data structures of LIFE [5]. Roughly, the Prolog term $X = f(X_1, \ldots, X_n)$ is refined into a conjunction of the sort constraint $X : f$, that is, "X is of sort f", and the n feature constraints $X.i=X_i$, that is, "argument number i of X has value X_i" where $i = 1, \ldots, n$. Since in LIFE any combination of these constraints may occur, each constraint has to be taken into account *individually*.

In addition to the finer granularity of the constraints, there is also the fact that the structure for sorts can be richer than for function symbols (or constructor symbols). Whereas function symbols in Prolog are either the same or incompatible, the sort symbols that take their place in ψ-terms are partially ordered. More precisely, they form a partial order that admits greatest lower bounds (glb's); *i.e.*, a lower semi-lattice. This semi-lattice has a most general element, top (denoted "$\top$"), and a most specific element, bottom (denoted "$\bot$"). The unification of two sort symbols is their glb. In the AKL implementation, this would be yet another datum to put on the trail. If the result of the glb is $\bot$ then the unification fails.

It is this particular constraint system that motivates the use of the special-purpose data structure that we name the beast. Namely, the implementation of a ψ-term with an extensible lookup-table seems more economical when such a table is allocated for every guard test being invoked. Also, the glb of all variables being compared during one guard test has to be stored somewhere. For Prolog-terms (and the interpretation of term equations over rational or finite trees) the technique of multiple-bindings lists is sufficient to achieve a truly incremental implementation [18].

Structure of the Paper In this introduction we have introduced the problem and put it in context with other work in the field. Section 1.2 gives a precise statement of the problem. Section 1.3 gives an overview of the algorithm. Section 1.4 gives a precise description of the algorithm written in pseudocode. Section 1.5 gives some example executions of the algorithm to help explain the pseudocode. Section 1.6 contains a proof of correctness. In the conclusion, we indicate further work.

1.2   The Problem

The problems of matching and unification of terms can be treated elegantly and concisely when viewed in the constraint framework. We will first define atomic constraints and then show how terms can be represented as conjunctions of these. After we have defined entailment and disentailment with respect to a theory, we can give a general and concise statement of the problem.

1.2.1   THE ATOMIC CONSTRAINTS

Consider the three disjoint sets *Vars*, *Sorts*, and *Features* of variable symbols, sort symbols (for function- or constructor symbols or tree-node labels) , and feature symbols (for argument selectors or subterm positions), respectively. We impose a partial order $\leq$ and a greatest-lower-bound op-

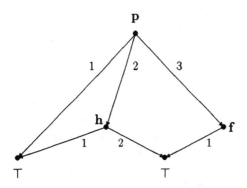

FIGURE 1.1. Representing the Prolog term $p(Z, h(Z, W), f(W))$ as a graph

eration glb on $Sorts$. In Prolog, the partial order is equality of the functor symbols and the glb of two functor symbols is $\bot$ iff they are different (and $glb(f, f)$ is f). We consider atomic constraints C of three kinds as follows:

$$C = \begin{cases} V : s & V \in Vars, \ s \in Sorts \\ V_1.f = V_2 & V_1, V_2 \in Vars, \ f \in Features \\ V_1 = V_2 & V_1, V_2 \in Vars \end{cases}$$

We call these a $sort$ constraint, a $feature$ constraint, and an $equality$ constraint, respectively.

We partition $Vars$ into the two subsets $GlobVars$ and $LocVars$, the sets of global variables and local variables (occurring in the actual and formal parameter), respectively.

1.2.2 TERMS AS CONJUNCTIONS OF ATOMIC CONSTRAINTS

We represent a term as a conjunction of atomic constraints in close correspondence to its graphical representation ($cf.$, figure 1.1). Here, a sort constraint "translates" node-labeling, and a feature constraint "translates" an edge together with its label which indicates the subterm position. We will next indicate how to derive such a representation by first $flattening$ and then $dissolving$ the terms.

For example, the Prolog term $X_1 = p(Z, h(Z, W), f(W))$ can be flattened into the conjunction ($cf.$, [1]):

$$(X_1 = p(X_2, X_3, X_4)) \wedge (X_2 = Z) \wedge$$
$$(X_3 = h(X_2, X_5)) \wedge (X_4 = f(X_5)) \wedge (X_5 = W).$$

By dissolving the term equations $V = f(V_1, ..., V_n)$, one obtains the representation of the above term as the conjunction of atomic constraints:

$$(X_1 : p) \land$$
$$(X_1.1 = X_2) \land (X_1.2 = X_3) \land (X_1.3 = X_4) \land$$
$$(X_2 : \top) \land (X_2 = Z) \land (X_3 : h) \land$$
$$(X_3.1 = X_6) \land (X_3.2 = X_7) \land (X_4 : f) \land$$
$$(X_4.1 = X_5) \land (X_5 : \top) \land (X_5 = W) \land$$
$$(X_6 = Z) \land (X_7 = W).$$

Notice that (1) the functor/arguments constraint $V = f(V_1, \ldots, V_n)$ is dissolved into one sort constraint $(V : f)$ and n feature constraints $(V.i = V_i)$, and (2) all equality constraints are explicit. We may assume that all variables occur at most once on the right-hand side of a feature or equality constraint.

From now on we will assume that the actual and formal parameters are represented by constraints which are conjunctions of atomic constraints following the above form and representing one or several terms. Often we will refer to them as γ and φ, respectively.

1.2.3 ENTAILMENT AND DISENTAILMENT OF CONSTRAINTS

Entailment and disentailment of constraints are defined relative to a given *constraint theory* Δ. A *theory* consists of all the logical formulas ϕ that are "valid;" *i.e.*, such that $\Delta \models \phi$. It characterizes a particular domain on which we want to compute, for example the Herbrand universe in the case of the theory given by Clark's equality axioms.

Given a constraint theory Δ and the two constraints γ and φ, we say that γ *entails* φ if and only if:

$$\Delta \models (\gamma \to \varphi)$$

That is, the implication of φ by γ is valid in Δ. We say that γ *disentails* φ if and only if:

$$\Delta \models (\gamma \to \neg\varphi)$$

Entailment [Disentailment] corresponds to matching [non-unifiability] of the terms represented by the constraints [15]. Namely, the term t with the variables $X_1, \ldots, X_n$ matches the term s with the variables $U_1, \ldots, U_m$ iff $\Delta \models X = t \to (\exists \ldots) \, X = s$, and t is non-unifiable with s iff $\Delta \models X = t \to \neg \, (\exists \ldots) \, X = s$, the "local" variables $U_1, \ldots, U_m$ being existentially quantified (and the others, "global" ones universally quantified).

Several constraint theories have been proposed for, *e.g.*, finite trees (as in Prolog with occurs check), infinite trees (as in Prolog-II [8], AKL [12], *etc.*.), feature trees (as in FT or CFT [2, 23]), and order-sorted feature trees as in LIFE [3]. The explicit formulation of the algorithm given in this paper is for the theory of order-sorted feature trees. It would have to be modified (usually simplified) to accommodate the other theories.

In certain constraint theories over infinite trees, such as Prolog-II [8], AKL [12] and CFT [23], the algorithm requires memoization. For example, the constraints $X = f(X, Y)$ and $Y = f(X, Y)$ together entail $X = Y$ in these theories. The proof that an equality is entailed by γ although it is not present explicitly in γ works roughly as follows (cf., [23]): Each variable equality to be tested for entailment (here $X = Y$) is memoized upon its first encounter. The proof completes if it completes for each of the corresponding subterm equalities (which are, in the example, $X = Y$ and $Y = Y$). This recursion terminates if an equality is encountered a second time (here, the memoized equality $X = Y$). Now, it turns out that this memoizing is implemented already by the construction of the beast. Namely, the equality $X = Y$ is memoized iff both X and Y point to the same beast W. In the notation of section 1.4, both $X.F$ and $Y.F$ contain the same $(beast, W)$ object. Thus, the modification for the above mentioned constraint theories can be readily implemented.

1.2.4   STATEMENT OF THE PROBLEM

Consider the statically known constraint φ representing the formal parameter and the sequence of constraints $\gamma_0, \gamma_1, \gamma_2, \ldots$ representing the actual parameter (that is, the *context*, which is the constraint part of the resolvent). We assume that $\gamma_{i+1} = \gamma_i \wedge C_i$ where C_i is an atomic constraint. The problem is to find the least index i such that γ_i entails or disentails φ.

From this statement, we see that the algorithm has two phases:

- an *initialization phase*, corresponding to the entailment and disentailment checks of γ_0 with φ;

- an *incremental phase*, corresponding to the sequential feeding of the constraints C_0, C_1, C_2, etc., to the algorithm, and the successive entailment and disentailment checks of γ_i with φ.

Splitting the algorithm into an initialization phase and an incremental phase is essential for highest performance. One might argue that the constraints in γ_0 could also be added incrementally, thus rendering superfluous the initialization phase. Indeed, since the algorithm is truly incremental this will have the same execution time complexity. The absolute execution time, however, will in general increase. For example, if γ_0 represents the actual term $f(X, Y)$ together with the equality constraint $X = Y$ and ϕ represents the formal term $f(U, U)$, then in a version without the initialization phase a beast would be created (unnecessarily, of course). Note that, if X and Y are bound to big terms and the equality $X = Y$ is added incrementally, then a beast is constructed which is the unification of X and Y. But even this case is in agreement with our claim of true incrementality, since our implementation is still almost-linear in the size of the input terms.

1.3   Overview of the Algorithm

The algorithm has three possible results, namely *entailment*, *disentailment*, and *suspension*. The first two imply that the algorithm has terminated. The third implies that the algorithm has not yet terminated, but may terminate if information is added to the arguments. Therefore the algorithm must store enough state to be able to resume execution if global variables are refined (that is, if constraints are added to the globals). This state is stored in a distributed manner, attached to the globals (in suspension lists) and indexed by an identifier that is unique for each invocation of the algorithm.

Entailment and disentailment are handled by independent mechanisms. These mechanisms are described in the following two sections. Entailment is handled by maintaining a count of the number of delayed constraints. Disentailment is handled by constructing a "beast".

1.3.1   TERMINOLOGY

A variable in an actual argument γ (the call) is referred to as a *global* variable. A variable in a formal argument φ (the definition) is referred to as a *local* variable. In the terminology of logical entailment, we consider the implication $\gamma \rightarrow \varphi$. During program execution, global variables exist as data in memory. Local variables may exist as data in memory, however, if they are known at compile time they may instead exist as executable code. This distinction is crucial for an efficient implementation, but it has no effect on the correctness or completeness of the algorithm. When relevant, the distinction is marked in the pseudocode definition of the algorithm.

An *equality set* S_x is the set of occurrences in the formal arguments that are linked by equality constraints. For example, the term $f(U, f(U, U)$ is considered as $f(U_1, f(U_2, U_3)$ with the equality set $S_x = \{U_1, U_2, U_3\}$.

1.3.2   WAVEFRONT

We described in Section 1.2.2 how a term is represented as a conjunction of atomic contraints. Now, for representing a formal term, we want to add control flow information. The atomic contraints are tree-like interdependent; the tree correspondends to the term up to the fact that each sort and each equality contraint forms an own subtree. Thus, *e.g.*, $V = f(U, U)$ yields a constraint tree with one subtree formed by $V : f$, one rooted in $V.1 = U_1$ with subtree $U1 \in S_x$, and a third one rooted in $V.2 = U_2$ with subtree $U2 \in S_x$.

The wavefront algorithm consists of traversing this constraint tree such that as many entailed constraints as possible are encountered. If a constraint is reached which is not entailed, then it is *delayed*. That is, it becomes part of the wavefront. The constraints in the subtree below it are not tested. The traversal is depth-first except that the constraints below the wavefront are skipped.

Each delayed position is kept in the suspension list of the corresponding global variable (which is not instantiated enough...). Upon its further instantiation, the algorithm will resume from that delayed position and possibly push the wavefront further down. It will not, however, resume the depth-first traversal (i.e., jump to a neighboring subtree). For example, when matching $f(X_1, X_2)$ against $f(g(t_1), h(t_2))$, the wavefront will consist of the two sort constraints for g and for h. When X_1 gets instantiated, say, to $X_1 = g(Y)$, then the wavefront will be pushed down to the constraints for t_1; the sort constraint for h remains delayed. For another, visualized example, cf. the figure on page 21.

All very well and good, but how is this compiled into static code? The constraint tree which presents the formal terms is itself presented as a linear code sequence. This sequence is obtained by a depth-first traversal of the constraint tree. It has two key properties: (1) Each subtree is represented by a contiguous sequence $C_i, \ldots, C_{i+j}$ of constraints; (2) The root C_i of each subtree is the first constraint in the code sequence for that subtree. The constraints are macro-expanded to native code (with a granularity similar to WAM instructions).

The code for each subtree t of the constraint tree ensures that (1) if C_i is not entailed, a *residuation point* is set up and the constraints $C_{i+1}, \ldots, C_{i+j}$ are skipped, and (2) upon reactivation of that residuation point, only the relevant subtree (i.e., the constraints $C_i, \ldots, C_{i+j}$) are executed. This is achieved by using a single global register R and by giving each subtree a unique identifier l; if $R = l$, one jumps out of the code sequence for that subtree. In fact, we do not even need a unique identifier for each subtree, but can choose for l the nesting level of the subtree.

1.3.3 ENTAILMENT

The result is 'entailment' if all the constraints in the formal arguments are entailed. The algorithm maintains a count of the number of constraints in the wavefront, which is exactly the set of delayed constraints. At the start of the initialization phase the count is set to zero, the initial size of the wavefront. It is incremented whenever a constraint is delayed and decremented when a delayed constraint is entailed. If the value is zero after executing all formal constraints without any disentailment occurring, then the algorithm returns with entailment.

1.3.4 DISENTAILMENT

The result is 'disentailment' if at least one constraint in a formal argument is disentailed. The disentailment of sort constraints is easy to detect: the glb of the actual and formal arguments is $\perp$ (bottom). In Prolog, this means simply that the function symbols are different. The disentailment of terms linked by equality constraints is more difficult. In essence, the algorithm maintains a local term (the "beast") for each equality set. The beast represents their unifier. If the unification ever fails, then an equality constraint belonging to the set is disentailed.

The intuition behind this idea is straightforward. To implement it practically and efficiently, however, introduces difficulties. First, one is not allowed to modify the global variables, because doing so would destroy true incrementality. Second, there may be any number of function invocations in varying stages of completion. These must not interact. Third, the algorithm must run in almost-linear time in the total complexity of the input terms, otherwise it is not practical. That is, disentailment must be detected immediately. Fourth, equality constraints may be introduced dynamically, which means that the equality sets are only partially known at compile time. Fifth, the algorithm must avoid creating a beast as long as possible, and in particular must not create a beast if entailment is found in the initialization phase. Our contribution is to present an algorithm that surmounts these difficulties.

The idea is to "unify" all corresponding arguments (formals and actuals linked together by equality constraints) with a modified version of the unification algorithm. Unification is done through "local" glasses. That is, where standard unification would modify a variable, the modification is done only if the variable is local. If the variable is global, the modification is done to the beast, which is a "shadow copy" of the global that is easily accessible from the global through a link. We do not assume anything about the representation of this link. There is only one condition it must satisfy: It must be unique for each function invocation, so that more than one invocation may be active at any moment.[4]

To save space and time, the beast contains pointers to terms that exist only once. There are two possibilities: pointers to global terms and pointers to routines for local terms. The beast contains a subterm t only if the corresponding subterms exist in more than one term. In this case t is the unification of these terms.

For example, assume the formal term is $f(U, U)$ where U is bound to $g(V, a)$. If the calling term is $f(X_1, X_2)$, then a beast is created which is just a pointer to the routine for the formal subterm $g(V)$. Both X_1 and X_2 can access the beast through their suspension list. If X_1 gets instantiated, say, $X_1 = g(s_1, a)$, then the beast contains the representation of the subterm $g(U, a)$ where U is a pointer to the subterm s_1. If then X_2 gets instantiated, say $X_2 = g(s_2, a)$, then the beast contains the representation of the subterm $g(s, a)$ where s is the unifier of s_1 and s_2. For another, visualized example, *cf.* the figure on page 22.

---

[4]If one has *deep guards*[12, 13], then a variable that is local with respect to one function invocation may be global with respect to another, and vice versa. The condition accounts for this case as well.

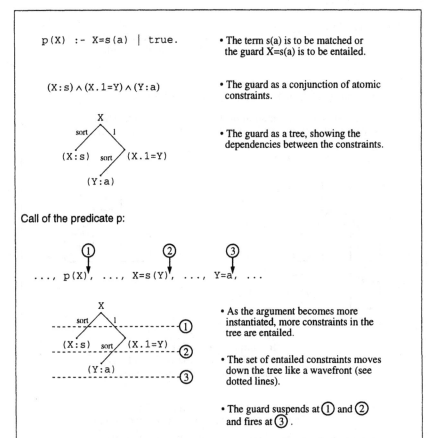

FIGURE 1.2. Descending the Wavefront

The definition: `p(X,Y)  :- X=Y | true.`

The call: `p(s, t)`   \ *s* and *t* are linked by an equality
constraint in the guard.

- Let terms *s*=a(b(C),D) and *t*=a(E,f), where {a,b,f} are
function symbols and {C,D,E} are unbound variables.

- The beast is a representation of the unifier of *s* and *t*. This unifier
is inaccessible from *s* and *t* except in the frame of the unification.

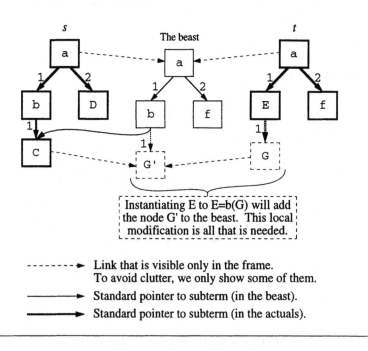

Instantiating E to E=b(G) will add
the node G' to the beast. This local
modification is all that is needed.

- - - - - - - - ▶ Link that is visible only in the frame.
To avoid clutter, we only show some of them.

——————▶ Standard pointer to subterm (in the beast).

━━━━━▶ Standard pointer to subterm (in the actuals).

FIGURE 1.3. Constructing the Beast

1.4   Precise Definition of the Algorithm

This section presents a concise and precise description of the algorithm. We use pseudocode to avoid committing ourselves to any particular representation of terms, although the reader may easily introduce representations such as hash tables or linked lists where appropriate. We recommend using the examples in section 1.5 as a guide when tracing through the pseudocode. We assume familiarity with concepts from Prolog implementation [1, 24]. We assume that all terms are dereferenced where necessary, and that trailing is done if the algorithm is embedded in a system that does backtracking. The algorithm itself has no need of trailing. The algorithm is presented in two parts: first, the routines related to the initialization phase (see figures 1.4 to 1.9) and second, the routines related to the incremental phase (adding feature, sort, or equality constraints during execution, see figures 1.10 to 1.12). Finally, a last section presents the "beast" unification routines (see figures 1.13 to 1.16) which are important primitives.

1.4.1   DEFINITIONS AND NOTATIONS

Assume that each function invocation has a unique identifier, F, that is different from all other invocations of the same or other functions. One way to implement F is as the *frame pointer*, that is, a pointer to the invocation's frame. We borrow this idea from the AKL implementation [12]. The frame contains the information necessary for the execution of an invocation of the function. It contains one field $F.S_x$ for each equality set S_x. The field $F.S_x$ contains one of three values: NULL, a global variable, or a beast. The frame contains the *count* field $F.count$, which counts the number of delayed static constraints. When this field reaches zero, the algorithm returns entailment.

To distinguish whether a term is local or global with respect to a particular function invocation, we store in each term the value of the frame pointer in which the variable is local. Then the test of locality or globality is just a comparison between the current frame pointer and the value of the frame pointer stored in the term.

Assume that X, Y, Z are global variables (*i.e.*, actual data), and that U, V are local variables represented as compiled code. We use $U.f$ to denote the term accessed through the f feature of U and $U.sort$ to denote the sort field of U. The resemblance of this notation to field selection in records is intentional. The actual implementation may be a record, a linked list, or a hash table that is indexed by f or sort.

We use $X.F$ to denote the collection of all information that is relevant for resumption when X is modified. There are four kinds of objects in $X.F$. These are represented as pairs (α, β) where α's possible values are known at compile time, and the type of β depends on α. Here are the objects:

- $(beast, W)$

  The beast W is the unifier of all known (actual and formal) terms in the equality set of which X is a member. If only a single such term is encountered, then no beast is created. W's root is local (*i.e.*, its frame pointer is F). W's arguments may be global (which is the case for a particular feature if only one member Z of the equality set has this feature and Z is global) or subroutines (if only one member U of the equality set has this feature and U is part of the function definition). $X.F$ may have zero or one *beast* objects.

- $(count, S_x)$

  The identifier S_x is unique for each statically known equality set of which X is a member. $X.F$ may have one *count* object per static equality set of which it is a member. The *count* object is used to detect when an equality constraint from the set S_x is satisfied. When unifying two globals X and Y, if both contain a $(count, S_x)$ object with the same S_x, then $F.count$ is decremented by one. All S_x are given unique fields $F.S_x$ in the frame.

- $(sort, U.sort)$

  The presence of this object in $X.F$ means that U.sort is a routine that checks whether the sort of X entails the corresponding sort in the formal argument. $X.F$ may have from zero *sort* objects up to a number equal to the number of dynamic equality constraints.

- $(f, U.f)$

  The presence of this object in $X.F$ means that f is a feature existing in the formal argument U corresponding to X, but not in X, and that $U.f$ is a routine corresponding to the formal subterm. Due to dynamic equality constraints, $X.F$ may have more than one $(f, U.f)$ object for a given f, up to a maximum equal to the number of atomic feature constraints containing f in the formal arguments.

  For example, consider X in the actual parameter $f(Z, X, X, Y)$ with formal parameter $f(U : t(f \Rightarrow A), U, V : t(f \Rightarrow B), V)$. To entail, X must have a feature f whose value entails both A and B. These two conditions are represented by the two objects $(f, U.f)$ and $(f, V.f)$, both of which are in $X.F$. The subroutines $U.f$ and $V.f$ represent the terms A and B.

1.4.2 INVARIANTS

These invariants are true just after the initialization phase and just after each step of the incremental phase. Understanding them makes the algorithm clearer.

- *Entailment Invariant*

  The number of constraints in the formal arguments that are delayed, *i.e.*, the size of the wavefront, is exactly the value in $F.count$. If $F.count$ is equal to zero, then the result of the algorithm is *entail*.

- *Disentailment Invariant*

  In each (statically or dynamically known) equality set of global variables $\{X_1, ..., X_n\}$, $n > 1$, there is one local term W (the "beast") that is pointed to by the entry $(beast, W)$ in $X_i.F$ for all X_i. Each $X_i.F$ has exactly one $(beast, W)$ object.

- *Count Invariant*

  The number of global variables X with the same $(count, S_x)$ object in $X.F$, if greater than zero, is equal to the number of delayed equalities in S_x minus one.

1.4.3 STRUCTURE OF THE ALGORITHM

The initialization phase consists of the function call. It is executed once. The incremental phase consists of three routines which are executed whenever one of the three atomic constraints is added to the actual arguments. Therefore there are four entry points to the algorithm:

- The initial call (see figures 1.4 through 1.9). This calls $match(X, U)$ to match the actual arguments with the formal arguments.

- Adding a sort constraint with $add\_sort(X)$ (see figure 1.10). This routine is executed after the sort constraint $X : s$ is added, *i.e.*, after X's sort is intersected with s.

- Adding a feature constraint with $add\_feature(f, X)$ (see figure 1.11). This routine is executed after a feature constraint $X.f = Y$ is added, *i.e.*, after the feature f is added to X.

- Adding an equality constraint with $add\_equality(X, Y)$ (see figure 1.12). This routine is executed after the equality constraint $X = Y$ is added, *i.e.*, after X and Y are unified.

Each of these four routines returns with one of three possible results: *entail*, *disentail*, or *suspend*. If the result is *suspend*, then further calls of the three incremental routines are allowed. If the result is *entail* or *disentail* then the frame F is no longer valid. All data structures $X.F$ may be discarded immediately and their space recovered, or the system may choose to wait until garbage collection recovers the space.

1.4.4 COMPILATION INTO STATIC CODE

The second argument U of $match(X, U)$ is always a statically-known formal argument, and therefore all calls to $match$ may be unfolded at compile time and converted into abstract machine instructions [10, 11]. This technique, partially evaluating a routine to obtain abstract machine instructions, has been applied before to unification [14, 24]. We make two important remarks regarding the partial evaluation. First, the three conditions *(U is the first element of S_x)*, *(U is not in any S_x)*, and *(U is in some S_x)* (see *match_sort*, *match_features*, and *match_equality* in figures 1.6, 1.7, and 1.8) are completely expanded at compile time, so they do not require any run-time checks. Second, the routines referred to by $U.f$ and $U.sort$ are just parts of the unfolded match routine.

The abstract machine instructions may be determined by inspection of $match(X, U)$. For example, each static equality constraint is compiled with one instruction that implements $match\_equality(X, U)$. This instruction must occur statically at each variable occurrence in S_x. All the "beast"-ly complexity occurs inside the instruction; viewed from the outside its compilation is simple.

1.4.5 THE INITIALIZATION PHASE

Figure 1.4 gives the pseudocode for a function call. The frame F is created with the following fields:

- A *count* field (initialized to zero).

- A field for each static equality set S_x (initialized to NULL).

- Other fields for head and body variables. These are ignored in this paper.

The function call uses the routine $match(X, U)$ which matches the global X with the local U (see figures 1.5 through 1.9). This routine is called once for each argument of the function. The routine is conveniently split into three parts:

- $match\_features(X, U)$ (see figure 1.6) matches all features of X against the features of U.

- $match\_sort(X, U)$ (see figure 1.7) matches the sort of X against the sort of U.

- $match\_equality(X, U)$ (see figure 1.8) tests the equality constraint of X relative to the equality set S_x of which U is a part (if there is such an equality constraint).

The routine $match(X, U)$ attempts to do as little work as possible. If X immediately entails or disentails U then there is no overhead: no data structures are created in memory and $F.count$ is not touched. As long as only satisfied equality constraints are encountered *match* avoids creating *beast* and *count* objects. A beast is created if one of two conditions holds:

- A static equality constraint is encountered that is not satisfied (see *match_equality* in figure 1.8). In this case a *count* object is created as well. For example, when testing $f(s(X), s(Y))$ against $f(U, U)$ a check must be done to see whether X and Y are compatible.

- A dynamic equality constraint is encountered for which the compatibility of the corresponding formal arguments must be tested (see *dynamic_add_beast* in figure 1.9). For example, when testing $f(X, X)$ against $f(s(U), s(V))$ a check must be done to see whether U and V are compatible.

Satisfied equality constraints do not touch the beast and non-satisfied equality constraints are unified with the beast.

1.4.6 The Incremental Phase

Information is added to the actual arguments of a function call in three ways, one for each kind of atomic constraint. The routines $add\_sort(X)$, $add\_feature(f, X)$, $add\_equality(X, Y)$ are called respectively after the sort constraint $X : s$, the feature constraint $X.f = Z$, and the equality constraint $X = Y$ have been added. The first two cases (see figures 1.10 and 1.11) are relatively straightforward.

The third case, adding an equality constraint, is done as follows (see figure 1.12). We assume the end of the dereference chain to be X. The value of $Y.F$ used in this routine ignores the dereference link added by the unification of X and Y. For correct disentailment checking, a beast is created combining all the information of X's beast (if it exists), Y's beast (if it exists), and all the $(f, U.f)$ and $(sort, U.sort)$ objects in $X.F$ and $Y.F$. For correct entailment checking, all the feature and sort objects of $Y.F$ must be moved to $X.F$, and the $(count, S_y)$ objects of $Y.F$ must be merged into those of $X.F$, decrementing $F.count$ when appropriate.

1.4.7 Beast Unification

The routines related to beast unification (see figures 1.13 through 1.16) are important building blocks for both phases of the algorithm. The routine $beast\_unify(W, Q)$ unifies W and Q through "local" or "frame F" glasses. That is, it modifies only variables that are local relative to F. Any attempt to modify a variable X that is not local to frame F will instead modify (or add, if it does not yet exist) a *beast* object in $X.F$. In the figures, we assume that X is global, Q is global or local, W is always local, and U is either a local term known at compile time or a frame field. The *beast_unify* routine uses the two routines *beast_unify_part*$(W, Q, sort)$ (see figure 1.14) to unify the sorts of W and Q and *beast_unify_part*(W, Q, f) (see figure 1.15) to unify the feature f of Q with the feature f of W if it exists. The last routine *add_beast*(W, X) (see figure 1.16) adds the beast W to the global variable X. In analogous fashion to *match*(X, U), all beast unification routines whose arguments are known statically (for example, the call *beast_unify*(S, U) in figure 1.8) may be compiled into WAM-like unification code.

1.5   Example Executions

In this section we present three examples which spotlight different aspects of the pseudocode definition of the algorithm.

The first example shows the common case of a function call that entails immediately. Consider the actual argument:

$$f(a(b), X, X)$$

with the formal argument:

$$f(a(b), U, U)$$

The execution trace starts with the call of the initial phase (see figure 1.4). The frame field $F.count$ is set to zero, which is the initial size of the wavefront. There are five constraints in the formal argument, namely $(U_1 : a)$, $(U_1.1 = V)$, $(V : b)$, $(U_2 = U_3)$, and $(U_2 : \top)$, where the three subterms are referred to by U_1, U_2, and U_3. There is a single equality set $S_x = \{U_2, U_3\}$, and a frame field $F.S_x$ corresponding to S_x. The final result is that $F.count$ remains equal to zero and $F.S_x = X$. The algorithm terminates with entailment. No memory operations were done except for the assignment to $F.S_x$.

The second example illustrates the working of *match_equality* (see figure 1.8). Consider the actual argument:

$$f(X, X, Y, X)$$

with the formal argument:

$$f(U, U, U, U)$$

There are three static equality constraints, corresponding to the equality set $S_x = \{U_1, U_2, U_3, U_4\}$, where the four subterm occurrences are denoted by U_1, U_2, U_3, and U_4. Matching the first subterm results in $F.S_x = X$. Matching the second subterm results in no operation being done. Matching the third subterm increments $F.count$, adds a $(count, S_x)$ object to $Y.F$ and $F.S_x.F$ (which is $X.F$), a $(beast, W)$ object to both $X.F$ and $Y.F$, and does the assignment $F.S_x \leftarrow W$. The beast W is a local term with sort $\top$. Matching the fourth subterm results in a few conditional tests, but nothing is modified. Note that nothing is done in the disentailment part because both $F.S_x$ and $X.F$ contain the same beast, namely W. The final result is that $F.S_x$ is equal to the beast W, that both $X.F$ and $Y.F$ contain two objects, namely $(count, S_x)$ and $(beast, W)$, and that $F.count$ is equal to one. A single static equality constraint remains to be checked.

The third example illustrates the creation of a beast with *beast_unify* (see figure 1.13). Consider the actual argument:[5]

$$f(X : s(X1 : t(X2)), Y : s(Y1))$$

with the formal argument:

$$f(U : s(V), U)$$

There are four constraints in the formal argument, namely $(U_1 : s)$, $(U_1.1 = V)$, $(V : \top)$, and $(U_1 = U_2)$, and a single equality set $S_x = \{U_1, U_2\}$. During the function's execution, a beast S is created in *match_equal*, and it is unified with the three terms $X : s(X1 : t(X2))$, $Y : s(Y1)$ and $U : s(V)$, through the calls *beast_unify*$(S, F.S_x)$ (where $F.S_x = X$), *beast_unify*(S, X) (where the X in figure 1.8 actually contains the value of Y), and *beast_unify*(S, U). The resulting beast S is put in $F.S_x$. The final result is that $X.F$ and $Y.F$ each contain two objects, $(count, S_x)$ and $(beast, S)$, and that $X1.F$ and $Y1.F$ each contain one object, $(beast, S1)$, where the beast $S = s(S1 : t(X2))$. Note that a subterm of the beast is local if it occurs more than once in an actual argument, that is, both S and $S1$ are local since they correspond to respectively X and Y, and $X1$ and $Y1$, but $X2$ is global since it occurs only once in an actual argument. The final value of $F.count$ is one since the only delayed constraint is $(U_1 = U_2)$.

1.6 Proof of Correctness

The above presentation of our algorithm is conceptually close to the specification of a constraint normalization procedure. Each state after any of its main execution steps represents a constraint. If $X.F$ contains the object $(beast, W)$, then this represents, with respect to the frame F, that the global variable X and the newly introduced local variable W are bound together; *i.e.*, it represents the equality constraint $W = X$. Clearly, the fields $X.f$ and X.sort together with their values represent respectively feature and sort constraints.

Because of space limitations in this paper we cannot make the correspondence between the algorithm and the constraint normalization procedure

---

[5]The notation X:s(t) gives the name X to the term s(t).

more explicit. For a precise description of the latter, we refer to [3, 4]. Let us just mention here that there exists a general implementation strategy called *relative simplification* [2] for testing whether the constraint γ entails or disentails the constraint φ. It consists of simplifying φ to φ' relative to γ. We have:

- φ' is the *True* constraint iff γ entails φ, and

- φ' is the *False* constraint iff γ disentails φ.

Roughly speaking, in the first case, entailed constraints are redundant and, therefore can be removed from φ until φ' is the empty conjunction, which denotes *True*. In the second case, carefully selected constraints from γ are copied over to φ and normalized together with the ones from φ until a clash is reached.

In [3], we find a version of the relative simplification scheme whose invariant ("the global parameters are not modified") is put to the extreme in that a global variable X is never bound, neither to a sort nor to another global variable. The idea is to simulate the binding of X to the global variable Y by introducing a new local variable W and binding it to X and to Y. This theoretical idea is implemented in our algorithm by the creation of the beast. As an example, take γ corresponding to the term $f(g(X), g(Y))$ and φ corresponding to $f(U, U)$; then one would add the constraint $(W = X) \wedge (W = Y)$ to φ.

In terms of our algorithm (and as stated by the Entailment Invariant), $F.count$ contains the number of constraints in φ that are delayed. This number is zero if and only if the number of non-redundant constraints in φ is zero, which is true if and only if the simplified constraint φ' is the empty conjunction. With the above result, this is the case if and only if the actual parameter entails the formal one.

Clearly, if our algorithm detects a clash, the actual and the formal parameters are non-unifiable. In order to prove the completeness of the algorithm, we use the completeness result of the general relative simplification scheme and the fact that the beast is a representation of the conjunction of the constraints relevant for deriving *False* (as stated by the Disentailment Invariant). Thus, our algorithm detects a clash if and only if the simplified constraint φ' is the *False* constraint. With the above result, this is the case if and only if the actual parameter disentails the formal one.

1.7   Conclusions and Further Work

In this article we have presented a truly incremental algorithm that determines entailment and disentailment of constraints over various kinds of trees in almost-linear time. We have shown the reader where the beast is, and left him to find the beauty by himself.

We are currently building a compiler for the LIFE language that implements this algorithm at the heart of its abstract machine. We have no performance results yet, but with true incrementality, we have a formal criterion that shows the superiority of our algorithm in comparison with other existing ones.

In the medium term, we intend to investigate the extension of the algorithm for deep guards and the use of global analysis techniques to increase its efficiency, in particular to minimize the number of beast manipulations.

Acknowledgements: The authors gratefully acknowledge the interaction with the other members of PRL's Paradise project, and especially the discussions with Bruno Dumant and Richard Meyer and the contributions of Gerard Ellis and Seth Goldstein during their internships in Paradise at PRL. We thank Hassan Aït-Kaci for helping us with his deep TEXnical knowledge.

1.8 Appendix: Pseudocode of the Beauty and the Beast Algorithm

---

define *the_function:*
    allocate a new frame F
    for all *equality sets S_x: $F.S_x$ ← NULL*
    F.count ← 0

    for all *actual-formal argument pairs (X, U):*
        match(X, U)
    endfor

    return *(if F.count=0 then entail else suspend)*

Figure 1.4. The initialization phase:
    The function call

---

define *match(X, U):*
    match_sort(X, U)
    match_features(X, U)
    match_equality(X, U)

Figure 1.5. The initialization phase:
    Matching an actual argument with a formal argument

```
define match_features(X, U):
    for all features f of U:
        if X.f exists then
            match(X.f, U.f)
        else
            if (f, V.f) in X.F then /* with same feature f */
                dynamic_add_beast(X, U, V, f)
            endif
            if (U is the first element of an Sₓ) or
               (U is not in any Sₓ) then /* known statically */
                increment F.count
                add (f, U.f) to X.F
            endif
        endif
    endfor
```

Figure 1.6. The initialization phase:
            Matching the feature constraints

```
define match_sort(X, U):
    if glb(X.sort, U.sort) = ⊥ then return disentail
    if not (X.sort ≤ U.sort) then
        if (sort, V.sort) in X.F then
            dynamic_add_beast(X, U, V, sort)
        endif
        if (U is the first element of an Sₓ) or
           (U is not in any Sₓ) then /* known statically */
            increment F.count
            add (sort, U.sort) to X.F
        endif
    endif
```

Figure 1.7. The initialization phase:
            Matching a sort constraint

define *match_equality(X, U):*
    if *(U is in some S_x)* **then** /* *known statically* */
        if $F.S_x = NULL$ **then** /* *for entailment* */
            $F.S_x \leftarrow X$
        else if $F.S_x \neq X$ **then**
            if not *((count,S_x) in X.F)* **then**
                increment F.count
                add (count,S_x) to X.F
            endif
            if $F.S_x$ *is global* **then** /* *for disentailment* */
                /* *This is only done once per S_x* */
                add (count,S_x) to $F.S_x.F$
                if *(beast, W) in X.F* **then**
                    $S \leftarrow W$
                else
                    $S \leftarrow$ *(new local term with sort $\top$)*
                endif
                beast_unify(S, $F.S_x$)
                beast_unify(S, X)
                beast_unify(S, U)
                $F.S_x \leftarrow S$
            else /* $F.S_x$ *is local* */
                if not *((beast, W) in X.F and $F.S_x = W$)* **then**
                    beast_unify($F.S_x$, X)
                endif
            endif
        endif
    endif

Figure 1.8. The initialization phase:
            Matching a static equality constraint

define *dynamic_add_beast(X, U, V, kind):* /* *kind $\in$ { sort, f }* */
    if *(beast, W) in X.F* **then**
        $S \leftarrow W$
    else
        $S \leftarrow$ *(new local term with sort $\top$)*
        beast_unify(S, X)
        beast_unify_part(S, V, kind)
    endif
    beast_unify_part(S, U, kind)

Figure 1.9. Add a beast to X if it has two objects of the same
            kind (*i.e.*, linked by a dynamic equality constraint)

```
define add_sort(X):
    /* For disentailment */
    if (beast, W) in X.F then
        beast_unify_part(W, X, sort)
    endif

    /* For entailment */
    for all (sort, U.sort) in X.F:
        if glb(X.sort, U.sort) = ⊥ then return disentail
        if X.sort ≤ U.sort then
            decrement F.count
            remove (sort, U.sort) from X.F
        endif
    endfor
    return (if F.count=0 then entail else suspend)
```

Figure 1.10. The incremental phase: Adding a sort constraint

```
define add_feature(f, X):
    /* For disentailment */
    if (beast, W) in X.F then
        beast_unify_part(W, X, f)
    endif

    /* For entailment */
    for all (f, U.f) in X.F: /* with same feature f */
        decrement F.count
        remove (f, U.f) from X.F
        match(X.f, U.f)
    endfor
    return (if F.count=0 then entail else suspend)
```

Figure 1.11. The incremental phase: Adding a feature constraint

```
/* Assume X is at the end of the dereference chain. */
define add_equality(X, Y):
     /* For disentailment */
     S ← if (beast, W) in X.F then  W else
          if (beast, W) in Y.F then  W else
          (new local term with sort ⊤)
     if not ((beast,_) in Y.F) then
               for all (f, U.f) in Y.F: beast_unify_part(S, U, f)
               for all (sort, U.sort) in Y.F: beast_unify_part(S, U, sort)
     endif
     if not ((beast,_) in X.F) then
               for all (f, U.f) in X.F: beast_unify_part(S, U, f)
               for all (sort, U.sort) in X.F: beast_unify_part(S, U, sort)
     endif
     add_beast(S, X)
     if (beast, W') in Y.F then
               add_beast(W', X)
     endif

     /* For entailment */
     move all (f, U.f) from Y.F to X.F
     move all (sort, U.sort) from Y.F to X.F
     /* Merge Y.F's count objects into X.F: */
     for all (count, S_y) in Y.F:
               if (count, S_y) in X.F then
                         decrement F.count
               else
                         add (count, S_y) to X.F
               endif
     endfor
     return (if F.count=0 then entail else suspend)
```

Figure 1.12. The incremental phase: Adding an equality con-
          straint

```
define beast_unify(W, Q):
    if (W ≠ Q) then
        if Q is global then
            add_beast(W, Q)
        else
            Q.deref ← W
        endif
        beast_unify_part(W, Q, sort)
        for all features f of Q:
            beast_unify_part(W, Q, f)
        endfor
    endif
```

Figure 1.13. Unification through local glasses

```
define beast_unify_part(W, Q, sort):
    W.sort ← glb(W.sort, Q.sort)
    if W.sort = ⊥ then return disentail
```

Figure 1.14. Sort unification through local glasses

```
define beast_unify_part(W, Q, f):
    if W.f exists then
        if W.f is global then
            /* That is, W.f is part of an actual argument. */
            /* Make a local copy of W.f and keep its */
            /* subterms global. */
            W' ← (new local term with sort W.f.sort)
            for all features g of W.f:
                W'.g ← W.f.g
            add_beast(W', W.f)
            W.f ← W'
        endif
        /* Now W.f is local */
        beast_unify(W.f, Q.f)
    else
        W.f ← Q.f
    endif
```

Figure 1.15. Feature unification through local glasses

define *add_beast(W, X):*
    if *(beast, W') in X.F* **then**
        /* There are two beasts: we must unify them! */
        beast_unify(W, W')
    else
        add (beast, W) to X.F
    endif

Figure 1.16. Add beast W to global variable X

1.9 REFERENCES

[1] Hassan Aït-Kaci. *Warren's Abstract Machine, A Tutorial Reconstruction*. MIT Press, Cambridge, MA, 1991.

[2] H. Aït-Kaci, A. Podelski, and G. Smolka. A feature-based constraint system for logic programming with entailment. In *5th FGCS*, pages 1012–1022, June 1992.

[3] H. Aït-Kaci and A. Podelski. *Functions as Passive Constraints in LIFE*. PRL Research Report 13. Digital Equipment Corporation, Paris Research Laboratory. Rueil-Malmaison, France, June 1991 (Revised, November 1992).

[4] H. Aït-Kaci and A. Podelski. Entailment and disentailment of order-sorted feature constraints. In *Proceedings of the Fourth International Conference on Logic Programming and Automated Reasoning*, Andrei Voronkov, ed., 1993 (to appear).

[5] Hassan Aït-Kaci, Richard Meyer, and Peter Van Roy. *Wild LIFE: A User Manual* (draft). Technical Note. Digital Equipment Corporation, Paris Research Laboratory. Rueil-Malmaison, France, April 1993.

[6] M. Carlsson, J. Widén, J. Andersson, S. Andersson, K. Boortz, H. Nilsson, and T. Sjöland. *SICStus Prolog User's Manual*. SICS, Box 1263, 164 28 Kista, Sweden, 1991.

[7] A. Colmerauer, H. Kanoui, and M. V. Caneghem. Prolog, theoretical principles and current trends. *Technology and Science of Informatics*, 2(4):255–292, 1983.

[8] A. Colmerauer. Equations and inequations on finite and infinite trees. In *2nd FGCS*, pages 85–99, 1984.

[9] M. Dincbas, P. Van Hentenryck, H. Simonis, A. Aggoun, T. Graf, and F. Berthier. The Constraint Logic Programming Language CHIP. In *FGCS'88*, pages 693–702, Tokyo, 1988.

[10] Gerard Ellis and Peter Van Roy. *Compilation of Matching in LIFE* (draft). Digital Equipment Corporation, Paris Research Laboratory.

Rueil-Malmaison, France, May 1992.

[11] Seth Copen Goldstein and Peter Van Roy. *Constraints, Control, and Other Ideas Concerning LIFE* (draft). Digital Equipment Corporation, Paris Research Laboratory. Rueil-Malmaison, France, January 1993.

[12] S. Haridi and S. Janson. Kernel Andorra Prolog and its computation model. In *7th ICLP*, pages 31–48, MIT Press, Cambridge, June 1990.

[13] M. Henz, G. Smolka, and J. Würtz. Oz - a programming language for multi-agent systems. In *13th IJCAI*, Chambéry, France, Aug. 1993.

[14] Peter Kursawe. How to invent a Prolog machine. In *3rd ICLP*, pages 134–148. Springer-Verlag Lecture Notes on Computer Science Vol. 225, July 1986.

[15] M. J. Maher. Logic semantics for a class of committed-choice programs. In *Fourth ICLP*, pages 858–876. MIT Press, 1987.

[16] Lee Naish. *MU-Prolog 3.1db Reference Manual*. Computer Science Department, University of Melbourne, Melbourne, Australia, May 1984.

[17] Andreas Podelski and Peter Van Roy. The Beauty and the Beast algorithm: Quasi-linear incremental tests of entailment and disentailment. To appear in *Proceedings of the International Symposium on Logic Programming (ILPS)*, Ithaca, New York, November 1994. MIT Press.

[18] Andreas Podelski and Gert Smolka. Situated Simplification. Submitted for publication.

[19] Vitor Santos Costa, David H. D. Warren, and Rong Yang. Andorra-I: A parallel Prolog system that transparently exploits both and- and or-parallelism. In *Proceedings of the 3rd ACM SIGPLAN Conference on Principles and Practice of Parallel Programming*, pages 83–93, August 1991.

[20] V. Saraswat and M. Rinard. Semantic foundations of concurrent constraint programming. In *18th POPL*, pages 333–351, Jan. 1991.

[21] Ehud Shapiro. The Family of Concurrent Logic Programming Languages. In *ACM Computing Surveys* 21 (3), pages 412-510, Sept. 1989.

[22] Gert Smolka. Residuation and guarded rules for constraint logic programming. PRL Research Report 12, Digital Equipment Corporation, Paris Research Laboratory, Rueil-Malmaison, France, June 1991.

[23] G. Smolka and R. Treinen. Records for logic programming. In *Proceedings of the Joint International Conference and Symposium on Logic Programming*, Washington, USA, pages 240–254, 1992.

[24] Peter Van Roy and Alvin M. Despain. High-performance logic programming with the Aquarius Prolog compiler. In *IEEE Computer* 25 (1), pages 54-68, Jan. 1992.

2

A Generalized Semantics for Concurrent Constraint Languages and their Abstract Interpretation

Christian Codognet[1]
Philippe Codognet[2]

ABSTRACT We present a framework for abstract interpretation of concurrent constraint languages. Abstract interpretation is based on the notion of abstraction between constraint systems, which are used to define both concrete and abstract domains. For two constraint systems $(\mathcal{D}, \vdash)$ and $(\mathcal{D}', \vdash')$, and a concrete program P over constraint system $(\mathcal{D}, \vdash)$, we define a corresponding abstract program P' over $(\mathcal{D}', \vdash')$ such that the execution of P' in $(\mathcal{D}', \vdash')$ performs the abstract interpretation of P. Our framework is based on a denotational semantics of concurrent constraint languages, where each agent is seen as a closure operator over the lattice defined by the constraint system. From a practical point of view, we show how such analysis can be implemented by means of a reexecution algorithm, extending thus a previous framework for abstract interpretation of concurrent logic languages. We also show how suspension analysis can be performed within this framework.

2.1 Introduction

Our work is intented to propose an abstract interpretation framework for the family of Concurrent Constraint (cc) languages proposed by [17, 18]. cc languages extend Constraint Logic Programming (CLP) [11, 23, 7] with concurrency features that have emerged from the domain of Concurrent Logic Programming. The key idea underlying the family of cc languages is to use constraints to extend the synchronization and control mechanisms of concurrent logic languages. Briefly, multiple agents (processes) run concurrently and interact by means of a shared *store*, i.e. a global set

---

[1]LIENS / University of Paris XIII, 45 rue d'Ulm, 75005 Paris, France, e-mail: `Christian.Codognet@ens.fr`

[2]INRIA Rocquencourt, B. P. 105, 78153 Le Chesnay, France, e-mail: `Philippe.Codognet@inria.fr`

of constraints. Each agent can either add a new constraint to the store (*Tell* operation) or check wether or not the store entails a given constraint (*Ask* operation). Synchronization is achieved through a *blocking ask*: an asking agent may block and suspend if one cannot state if the asked constraint is entailed nor its negation is entailed. Thus nothing prevents the constraint to be entailed, but the store does not yet contain enough information. The agent is suspended until other concurrently running agents add (*Tell*) new constraints to the store to make it strong enough to decide.

The denotational semantics of cc languages [19] consists in interpreting the basic operations in cc languages and the agents as *closure operators* over the underlying constraint system. A constraint system is a pair $(D, \vdash)$ where D is the constraint domain and $\vdash$ an entailment relation over D satisfying some simple conditions, and can be seen as a first-order generalization of Scott's *information sytems* [21].

Abstract interpretation is defined for cc languages in a way similar to what was done for CLP programs in [3] [4], in introducing a notion of abstraction (i.e. approximation) between constraint systems. If $(\mathcal{D}', \vdash')$ abstracts $(\mathcal{D}, \vdash)$, then for each program P computing on $(\mathcal{D}, \vdash)$, P can be syntactically transformed into a program P' computing on $(\mathcal{D}', \vdash')$ such that the computation of P' is an abstraction of that of P, and thus the static analysis of P is obtained in executing P'. This idea of performing abstract interpretation via the derivation of an explicit abstract program was first proposed in [8] for the special case of the so-called mode analysis of Prolog programs with a simple finite abstract domain. A tabulation mechanism was used in order to ensure the finiteness of the computation. By moving to the CLP (as in [4]) or cc framework (as in this paper), much power is gained, as any abstract domain can indeed be defined or rephrased as a constraint system. This approach has also been followed by [10]. Moreover in a constraint framework, one defines a general semantics $CLP(X)$ or $cc(X)$ over a generic constraint system X which can be used both for the concrete and abstract computations. This is obviously not the case for frameworks developped for Prolog.

In this paper, we define a denotational semantics for cc programs inspired by [19] but different in several features. Closure operators are defined directly as functions over stores instead of defining them via the set of their fixpoints. This will make it possible to derive a practical algorithm close to that of [2]. Also this leads us to the notion of reexecution in abstract interpretation of Prolog programs [1] [14]. Therefore abstract interpretation of cc languages can be done by only slightly modifying a reexecution-based algorithm for Prolog.

Remark that those practical considerations, made possible by the denotational semantics we propose, are not investigated in other frameworks of abstract interpretation for cc languages [9] [5]. The main contribution of [5] is the definition of a confluent (w.r.t. scheduling) operational semantics, close to the original proposal of [2] for languages with monotonic guards.

It is however not so clear how to derive an efficient algorithm from that operational semantics. On the other hand, confluency is naturally enjoyed by our semantics, thanks to the semantic equation defining the conjunction operator. [9] defines a denotational semantics in terms of input-output relations on stores which is very close to those of [19, 12] but unfortunately does not lead to a practical analysis algorithm.

The rest of this paper is organized as follows. Section 2 presents constraint systems. The syntax of cc programs is given in Section 3, while Section 4 is concerned with their semantics. Section 5 proposes a notion of abstraction between constraint systems, and defines abstract programs. An application to suspension analysis of cc programs is presented in section 6. Finally Section 7 adresses practical issues and a short conclusion ends the paper.

2.2   Constraint Systems

The simplest way to define constraints is to consider them as first-order formulas interpreted in some non-Herbrand structure, [11] in order to take into account the peculiar semantics of the constraint system. However a more general formalization was recently proposed by [20], which can be seen as a first-order generalization of Scott's *information sytems* [21]. The emphasis is put on the definition of an *entailment* relation (noted $\vdash$) between constraints, which suffices to define the overall constraint system.

Definition 1 *A constraint system is a pair* $(\mathcal{D}, \vdash)$ *satisfying the following conditions:*

1. $\mathcal{D}$ *is a set of first-order formulas (over a vocabulary containing an equality predicate "$=$") closed under conjunction and existential quantification.*

2. $\vdash$ *is an entailment relation between a finite set of formulas and a single formula satisfying the following inference rules:*

$$\Gamma, d \vdash d \ \textbf{(Struct)} \qquad \frac{\Gamma_1 \vdash d \quad \Gamma_2, d \vdash e}{\Gamma_1, \Gamma_2 \vdash e} \ \textbf{(Cut)}$$

$$\frac{\Gamma, d, e \vdash f}{\Gamma, d \wedge e \vdash f} \ (\wedge \vdash) \qquad \frac{\Gamma \vdash d \quad \Gamma \vdash e}{\Gamma \vdash d \wedge e} \ (\vdash \wedge)$$

$$\frac{\Gamma, d \vdash e}{\Gamma, \exists X. d \vdash e} \ (\exists \vdash) \qquad \frac{\Gamma \vdash d[t/X]}{\Gamma \vdash \exists X. d} \ (\vdash \exists)$$

   In $(\exists \vdash)$, X *is assumed not free in* Γ, e.

3. $\vdash$ *is* generic: *that is* $\Gamma[t/X] \vdash d[t/X]$ *whenever* $\Gamma \vdash d$, *for any term* t.

Constraint systems can nevertheless be built very simply in a straight-forward way from any first-order theory, i.e. any set of first-order formulas [20]. Consider a theory T and take for $\mathcal{D}$ the closure of the subset of formulas in the vocabulary of T under existential quantification and conjunction. Then one defines the entailment relation $\vdash_T$ as follows. $\Gamma \vdash_T d$ iff Γ entails d in the logic, *with the extra non-logical axioms of T*. Then $(\mathcal{D}, \vdash_T)$ can be easily verified to be a constraint system.

Observe that this definition of constraint systems thus naturally encompasses the traditional view of constraints as interpreted formulas.

Definition 2 *For a constraint system $(\mathcal{D}, \vdash)$ and a set V of variables, we will note D_V the set of stores of constraints of $\mathcal{D}$ on V, i.e. sets of elements of $\mathcal{D}$ using only variables of V.*

Observe that, for a given finite set V of variables (those of a given program, as will be seen later), D_V can be given a structure of complete ω-algebraic lattice with lub (noted $\sqcup$) defined as closure (by $\vdash$) of union and glb defined as intersection.

2.3   Syntax of cc programs

We will give an "algebraic" syntax for cc programs over a constraint system $(D, \vdash)$ defined by Table 2.2 below. This syntax is slightly different from the usual clausal syntax of concurrent logic languages (inherited from logic programming), but it better put the emphasis the basic operators of the language and it will therefore make it possible to simply derive the semantic equations from the syntax.

Programs are just sequences of definitions, associating an atomic formula with an *agent*. An agent is either a primitive constraint, a simple conditional (ask) agent, a conjunction (parallel composition), disjunction (backtracking search), existential quantification (local hiding), or atomic formula (procedure call), where $\overline{X}$ denotes a vector of variables.

Observe that the disjunction operator represents angelic non-determinism as in [12, 24] and not demonic non-determinism (indeterminism) as in [9, 5].

2.4   Semantics of cc languages

cc languages can been given simple denotational semantics, as proposed by [19]: agents are given denotations as closure operators over the underlying constraint system. A closure operator f over a lattice $(L, \sqsubseteq)$ is a unary function that is monotone (i.e., $f(x) \sqsubseteq f(y)$ whenever $x \sqsubseteq y$), idempotent (i.e., $f(f(x)) = f(x)$) and extensive (i.e., $x \sqsubseteq f(x)$). The operator corresponding to an agent is merely the operator that maps each input to the

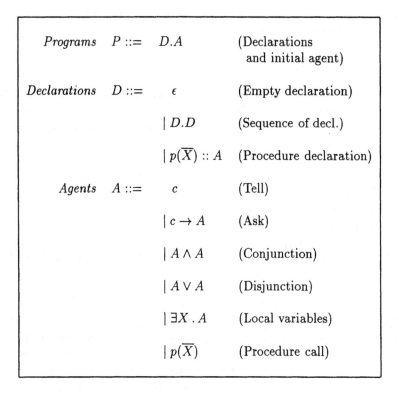

TABLE 2.1. Syntax

limit of all execution sequences of the agent on that input. It is not hard to show that, because of the monotonic nature of ask and tell operations, the operators thus generated are closure operators. More complex operators such as the cardinality operator or constructive disjunction can also be defined as closure operators [24].

The most important property of closure operators is that they can be completely characterized by the set of their fixed points — for, each input is mapped by such an operator to its least fixed point above that input. Indeed, a number of computationally important operations on closure operator have rather simple definitions in terms of sets of fixed points. For example, the parallel composition of two closure operators f and g corresponds logically to their conjunction, and yields a closure operator whose fixed points are precisely the intersection of the fixed points of f and g.

However we will not in this paper define denotations of operators by the set of their fixpoints as in [19], but rather give direct functional definitions. This will make it possible to derive an implementation from these semantics, as shown in section 6.

For the sake of simplicity, we will first consider *determinate* languages, that is, without the disjunction operator, and then extend it to non-determinate languages.

2.4.1 DETERMINATE CC LANGUAGES

Let $(\mathcal{D}, \vdash)$ be a constraint system, and P a cc program over $\mathcal{D}$. Let $\mathcal{V}$ be the union of the set of variables appearing in P and $\{\alpha_1, ..., \alpha_{\rho(p)}\}$ where $\rho(p)$ is the arity of a predicate p of maximal arity in P. Those last variables will be used for defining parameter passing, and we will note $\overline{\alpha}_i$ the vector of variables $(\alpha_1, ..., \alpha_i)$.

The denotation of an agent A is noted $[\![A]\!]$, and has type $Env \to D_V \to D_V$, where Env is a domain of environments (that of mappings from procedure names to agents). The denotation of a declaration K is noted $[\![K]\!]_{dec}$, and has type $Env \to Env$, while that of a program P (including the initial agent) is noted $[\![P]\!]_{prog}$ and has type D_V.

The semantic equations are then derived from the syntax of Table 2.1, as shown in Table 2.2 below.

(1) defines an eventual Tell, as usually. (2) presents an Ask operator as defined in [17]: if the constraint c is entailed the computation reduces to that of agent A, if $\neg c$ is entailed then the computation succeeds immediately, otherwise it suspends. Defining this behavior as a function from stores to stores, these two last cases coincides on the identity function. (3) describes an "ideal" And-parallel conjunction, we will return to that point in section 6. In (4), the existential quntification has been extended to finite stores in an obvious way, and hiding works as follows: A is first executed in a store were X is hidden, and X is again hidden in the resulting store. In (5) and (7), the variables $\overline{\alpha}_{\rho(p)}$ are used for parameter passing. They are equated with the call variables $\overline{X}$ in (5) (and obviously hidden outside the call), and equated with the variables $\overline{Y}$ of the procedure declaration in (7) (themselves also hidden).

2.4.2 NON-DETERMINATE CC LANGUAGES

For introducing disjunction, we have to consider sets of stores instead of stores as inputs and outputs of agents. 2^{D_V} can be given a structure of complete lattice by considering the Smyth order on 2^{D_V} as in the standard powerdomain constructions [16], see [12] for a complete and straightforward treatment. The type of the denotation $[\![A]\!]$ of an agent A is thus $Env \to 2^{D_V} \to 2^{D_V}$.

The disjunction operator is then simply treated as follows:

$$[\![A_1 \vee A_2]\!]\, e = [\![A_1]\!]\, e \,\cup\, [\![A_2]\!]\, e \qquad (10)$$

$$[\![c]\!]\, e = \lambda s\,.\, s \sqcup c \tag{1}$$

$$[\![c \rightarrow A]\!]\, e = \lambda s\,.\, \text{if } s \vdash c \text{ then } [\![A]\!]\, e\, s \text{ else } s \tag{2}$$

$$[\![A_1 \wedge A_2]\!]\, e = \lambda s\,.\, \mu c\,.\, ([\![A_1]\!]\, e\, c) \sqcup ([\![A_2]\!]\, e\, c) \sqcup s \tag{3}$$

$$[\![\exists X.A]\!]\, e = \lambda s\,.\, s \sqcup \exists X.[\![A]\!]\, e\, (\exists X\,.s) \tag{4}$$

$$[\![p(\overline{X})]\!]\, e = \lambda s\,.\, (\exists\, \overline{\alpha}_{\rho(p)}.[\![e\, p]\!]\, e\, (\overline{X} = \overline{\alpha}_{\rho(p)} \sqcup s)) \tag{5}$$

$$[\![\epsilon]\!]_{dec}\, e = e \tag{6}$$

$$[\![p(\overline{Y}) :: A]\!]_{dec}\, e = e[p \mapsto \exists \overline{Y}.(\overline{Y} = \overline{\alpha}_{\rho(p)} \wedge [\![A]\!]\, e)] \tag{7}$$

$$[\![D_1.D_2]\!]_{dec}\, e = [\![D_1]\!]_{dec}\, e \cup [\![D_2]\!]_{dec}\, e \tag{8}$$

$$[\![D.A]\!]_{prog} = [\![A]\!]\, ([\![D]\!]_{dec}\, [\,]) \, \emptyset \tag{9}$$

TABLE 2.2. Semantics

2.5 Abstraction

We can now introduce the notion of abstraction between constraint systems and that of abstract programs that will make it possible to perform abstract interpretation of cc programs. As the semantics defined above is parametric w.r.t. the constraint system, it works for both concrete and abstract programs.

Definition 3 *A constraint system* $(\mathcal{D}',\vdash')$ *abstracts a constraint system* $(\mathcal{D},\vdash)$ *w.r.t. a concretization function* γ *from D' to 2^D iff*

(i) γ *is monotone*

(ii) $\forall c \in D, \exists c' \in D'\,.\, c \in \gamma(c')$

(iii) $\forall c_1', c_2' \in D', \forall c_1, c_2 \in D\,.$
$\quad c_1 \in \gamma(c_1'), c_2 \in \gamma(c_2') \text{ implies } c_1 \wedge c_2 \in \gamma(c_1' \wedge c_2',)$

(iv) $\forall S' \in D', \forall c' \in D'\,.$
$\quad S' \vdash' c' \text{ implies } \forall S \in \gamma(S'), \forall c \in \gamma(c')\,.\, S \vdash c$

Definition 4 *Consider two constraint systems* $(\mathcal{D},\vdash)$ *and* $(\mathcal{D}',\vdash')$ *such that* $(\mathcal{D}',\vdash')$ *abstracts* $(\mathcal{D},\vdash)$ *with a concretization function* γ, *and a program P over $(\mathcal{D},\vdash)$. An abstract program P' over $(\mathcal{D}',\vdash')$ corresponding* *to P is a program formed by replacing all constraints c_i in P by constraints c_i' such that $c_i \in \gamma(c_i')$*

It is indeed easy to see that the computation of an abstract program P' abstracts the computation of P in the sense that the output constraints of P are contained in the concretization of the output constraints of P'.

Theorem 1 *Let $(\mathcal{D}', \vdash')$ be a constraint sytem abstracting another constraint system $(\mathcal{D}, \vdash)$, P be a program over $(\mathcal{D}, \vdash)$ and P' a corresponding abstract program over $(\mathcal{D}', \vdash')$. Then: $\forall s \in [\![P]\!]_{prog}, \exists s' \in [\![P']\!]_{prog}$ such that $\exists \sigma \in \gamma(s') / s \vdash \sigma$*

Proof: The only points where the computations differ are when constraints appear: Ask and Tell operations. For Tell, inclusion is ensured (as in [4]) by point *(iii)* of the definition of abstractions. For Ask, the abstract computation may suspend while the concrete one proceeds (as in [2]), and also in this case output of the abstract computation will be entailed (by monotonicity) by the concrete one.

Our notion of abstract domains as constraint systems makes it possible for dealing with several layers of abstraction, as originally proposed in [4]: a concrete constraint system can be approximated by an abstract one which is itself approximated by a third one, and so on. Such a construction can be particularly useful, as demonstrated by the termination analysis of Prolog programs described in [15]: from the original Prolog progam, one first constructs an abstract $CLP(\mathcal{R})$ program and then an abstract $CLP(Boole)$ program to perform the definiteness analysis of the $CLP(\mathcal{R})$ program. Observe that neither the framework of [9] nor that of [5] offers such a possibility.

2.6   Application to suspension analysis

Suspension analysis for concurrent logic languages has been first investigated in [2] under the name of deadlock analysis, and also developped in [6, 5]. The purpose of this analysis is to prove statically that the execution of a concurrent program will lead to a final state where all processes are terminated, i.e. none of them is suspended forever.

One of the main disadvantages of denotational frameworks w.r.t. operational ones is that the only observable of a computation is the final store, whereas an operational framework can observe both the final store and the final state of agents (e.g. terminated or suspended). It is therefore not surprizing that suspension analysis of concurrent logic or constraint languages has only be tackled in operational frameworks such as [2, 5]. We will present in the following a simple program transformation which makes it possible to perform suspension analysis in our denotational framework.

The program transformation consists in introducing for each Ask agent $c \to A$ defined in the program a new variable X whose groundness will represent the termination of this Ask agent, in the spirit of the (meta)algorithms of [22]. Roughly speaking, $c \to A$ will be replaced by $(X = Y) \wedge (c \to (A \wedge X = [])) \wedge (\neg c \to X = [])$. Hence X will be grounded if the store is strong enough to entail c or $\neg c$ and will remain unbound otherwise, i.e. if the Ask operation suspends. One also needs, because of the hiding of local variables and absence of global variables in cc languages, to introduce one extra parameter for each agent in order to collect the list of those extra variables. Therefore the groundness analysis of the transformed program will indeed perform the suspension analysis of the original program.

Observe that our transformation requires an underlying constraint system that includes lists, e.g. the **Herbrand** constraint system of Concurrent Logic Languages [22].

2.7   Practical issues

It is possible to derive a generic (fixpoint) algorithm that computes the functions defined by the previous semantic equations, in a way similar to that of [13] for Prolog. The main difference lies in the treatment of a conjunctive goal, as we have to compute a local fixpoint in our semantics for taking into account concurrent execution of agents. However, observe that the following property holds:

Lemma 1 *For two agents A_1 and A_2.*

$$\llbracket A_1 \wedge A_2 \rrbracket \, e \, s = \mu c \, . \, \llbracket A_2 \rrbracket \, e \, (\llbracket A_1 \rrbracket \, e \, (c \sqcup s))$$

Proof: this is obvious by the monotonicity and extensivity of A_1 and A_2.

Hence we have here a local fixpoint computation identical to that of the simpler algorithm of [2] for Concurrent Logic Languages, which critically relied on the monotonicity of guards (obviously satisfied by the Ask operator).

Moreover, such a local fixpoint computation is identical, *mutatis mutandis*, to the idea of reexecution which has been introduced in abstract interpretation frameworks (by [1] and developped by [14]) in order to improve precision. Therefore abstract interpretation of cc languages can be done by only slightly modifying a reexecution-based algorithm for Prolog.

2.8   Conclusion

We have presented a framework for abstract interpretation of concurrent constraint languages which is based on their denotational semantics and the notion of abstraction between constraint systems. It is both quite general and rather simple and appears as both a generalization and simplification of [2] and [4]. Moreover a practical implementation is possible by reusing and only slightly modifying a reexecution-based framework for Prolog. We have also sketched how to perform suspension analysis within this framework by reducing it to groundness analysis. What remains to be done is to investigate particular abstract domains to perform this analysis and others such as garbage-collection, scheduling of agents and removal of redundant Ask/Tell operations.

2.9 REFERENCES

[1] M. Bruynooghe. A practical framework for the abstract interpretation of logic programs. *Journal of Logic Programming*, 10(2):91-124, 1991.

[2] C. Codognet, P. Codognet and M-M. Corsini. Abstract Interpretation for Concurrent Logic Languages. In *proc. North American Conference on Logic Programming* , Austin, Texas, MIT Press 1990.

[3] P. Codognet and G. Filé. Computations, Abstractions and Constraints. Research Report 91-13, Università di Padova, 1991.

[4] P. Codognet and G. Filé. Computation, abstractions and Constraints in Logic Programs. In *proc. IEEE International Conference on Computer Languages*, IEEE Press 1992.

[5] M. Codish, M. Falaschi, K. Marriott and W. Winsborough. Efficient Analysis of Concurrent Constraint Logic Programs. In *proc. ICALP 93*, Springer Verlag 1993.

[6] M. Codish, M. Falaschi and K. Marriott. Suspension Analyses for Concurrent Logic Programs. In *proc. ICLP 91*, Paris, France, MIT Press 1991.

[7] A. Colmerauer. An introduction to PrologIII. *Communications of the ACM*, 28 (4), April 1990, pp 412-418.

[8] S. Debray and D.S. Warren. Automatic mode inference for Prolog programs. *Journal of Logic Programming, vol. 5 (3)*, 1988.

[9] M. Falaschi, M. Gabbrielli, K. Marriott and C. Palamidessi Compositional Analysis for Concurrent Constraint Programming. In *proc. LICS 93*, IEEE Press 1993.

[10] R. Giacobazzi, S. K. Debray and G. Levi. A Generalized Semantics for Constraint Logic Programs. In *proc. Fifth Generation Computer Sytems 92*, Tokyo, ICOT, 1992.

[11] J. Jaffar and J-L. Lassez. Constraint Logic Programming. Research Report, University of Melbourne, June 1986. Short version in *proc. 14th ACM conference on Principles Of Programming Languages, POPL'87*, ACM Press 1987.

[12] R. Jagadeesan, V. Saraswat and V. Shanbhogue. Angelic non-determinism in concurrent constraint programming. Technical Report, Xerox PARC, 1991.

[13] B. Le Charlier K. Musumbu and P. Van Hentenryck. A generic abstract interpretation algorithm and its complexity analysis. In *8th International Conference on Logic Programming*, Paris, MIT Press 1991.

[14] B. Le Charlier and P. Van Hentenryck. Reexecution in Abstract Interpretation of Prolog. In *proc. Joint International Conference and Symposium on Logic Programming*, Washington, MIT Press 1992.

[15] F. Mesnard. Termination analysis for Prolog programs (in French). Ph.D. dissertation, University of Paris-6, France, 1993.

[16] G. Plotkin. Domains. University of Edinburgh, 1983.

[17] V. A. Saraswat. *Concurrent Constraint Programming Languages*. Research Report CMU-CS-89-108, Carnegie Mellon University, 1989. Also (revised version) MIT Press 93.

[18] V.A. Saraswat and M. Rinard. Concurrent Constraint Programming. In *Proceedings of Seventeenth ACM Symposium on Principles of Programming Languages*, San Francisco, CA, January 1990.

[19] V.A. Saraswat, M. Rinard, and P. Panangaden. Semantic Foundations of Concurrent Constraint Programming. In *Proceedings of Ninth ACM Symposium on Principles of Programming Languages*, Orlando, FL, January 1991.

[20] V. Saraswat. The Category of Constraint Systems is Cartesian-Closed. In *proc. LICS'92, Logic In Computer Science*, IEEE Press 1992.

[21] D. S. Scott Domains for denotational semantics. In *proc. ICALP'82, International Colloquium on Automata, Languages and Programming*, Springer Verlag 1982.

[22] E. Shapiro. The Family of Concurrent Logic Languages. ACM Computing Surveys, September 1989.

[23] P. Van Hentenryck. *Constraint Satisfaction in Logic Programming*. MIT Press 1989.

[24] P. Van Hentenryck, V. Saraswat and Y. Deville. Constraint processing in cc(FD). Research Report, Brown University, 1991.

3

High-Level Constraints over Finite Domains

M. Anton Ertl[1]
Andreas Krall

ABSTRACT Constraint logic programming languages that employ consistency techniques have been used to solve many combinatorial search problems. In solving such problems, the built-in constraints often do not suffice. Unfortunately, new constraints defined with lookahead and forward declarations are often inefficient. In this paper, we present an efficient high-level constraint mechanism. High-level constraints are ordinary predicates with an additional constraint declaration. They offer fine-grained control over the tradeoff between pruning power and execution time and achieve huge speedups over lookahead declarations.

3.1 Introduction

Many real-world problems, e.g. resource allocation and scheduling, can be solved using consistency techniques integrated with logic programming [17]. This integration consists of adding domain variables and constraints to Prolog. Domain variables are logic variables, that have an associated finite set of values, the (finite) domain. The domain explicitly represents the values that the variable can be instantiated with. Constraints are predicates that remove inconsistent values from the domains of their arguments.

For example, given the variables X with the domain $\{1, 2, \ldots 6\}$ and Y with the domain $\{4, 5, \ldots 9\}$, the constraint X #> Y[2] immediately reduces (prunes) the domains to $\{5, 6\}$ and $\{4, 5\}$ respectively. A constraint is usually activated again later, when the domain of an argument changes. In the example above, if Y is instantiated with 5 (i.e., its domain is reduced to $\{5\}$), the constraint is woken and instantiates X with 6.

For a network of constraints this behaviour results in local propagation over the domains. I.e., if the domain of a variable changes, the constraints on

---

[1]Institut für Computersprachen, Technische Universität Wien, Argentinierstraße 8, 1040 Wien, Austria; {anton,andi}@mips.complang.tuwien.ac.at

[2]In our constraint logic programming system, Aristo, #>, #>= etc. are the constraint versions of Prolog's >, >= etc. Declaratively, #> means the same as >.

that variable are woken up. The constraints remove inconsistent values from the domains of their variables, waking up other constraints. This process continues until there are no more changes. To find solutions to the problem represented by the constraint network, this propagation is combined with a generator, e.g., a labeling predicate that instantiates each variable to some value of its domain.

There is one problem with this approach: the built-in constraints often do not suffice. They can be combined effectively in conjunctions, but not in disjunctions. Of course the usual Prolog approach to disjunctions can be used, i.e., creating a choicepoint. However, each choicepoint multiplies the work to be done, so this approach is often unacceptable. Even for conjunctions of constraints, there is sometimes a need for better pruning, which cannot be met by the local propagation mechanism alone.

To alleviate this problem, Van Hentenryck introduced facilities for defining new constraints in the constraint logic programming language: forward- and lookahead-declarations. These mechanisms work by checking the consistency for every possible combination of values from the domains of the variables. This method is very slow, making user-defined constraints useless in many cases, where the reduction in search space does not amortize the higher cost of constraint propagation.

In this paper we present a new, more efficient and more flexible method for defining high-level constraints. The **constraint** declaration is introduced in Section 3.2. Section 3.3 shows that it does not change the declarative semantics and discusses related issues. Section 3.4 presents examples. The relation to forward- and lookahead-declarations is discussed in Section 3.5. Section 3.6 discusses efficiency improvements and shows how the mechanisms of high-level constraints can be used to define built-in constraints. Our implementation is described in Section 3.7 and Section 3.8 presents a few empirical results.

3.2   High-Level Constraints

We call our mechanism high-level constraints, because they are written in the constraint logic programming language itself. In contrast, low-level constraints are written in the implementation language of the system, e.g. C.

Syntactically, high-level constraints look just like ordinary predicates (they also have the same meaning, see Section 3.3.1), except that we have to add a constraint-declaration:

> :- constraint C=*Head* trigger *Goal*$_1$ satisfied *Goal*$_2$.

The predicate that is declared as constraint (the constraint predicate) is given by *Head*. *Goal*$_1$ specifies when the constraint is woken up; *Goal*$_2$

specifies when the constraint is satisfied[3]. Using metalogical goals for these purposes offers maximum flexibility. C is used in $Goal_1$ to reference the constraint.

How does a high-level constraint work? Whenever the constraint is woken, the constraint predicate is executed and all solutions of the predicate are collected. For each variable occuring in the arguments of the constraint, the union of its domains over all intermediate solutions is computed; then the domain of the variable is reduced to this union. This reduction of the domains is the entire effect of the constraint. Choicepoints and bindings made during the execution of the constraint have no effect outside. After this reduction, the satisfaction goal $Goal_2$ is executed. If it succeeds, the constraint is satisfied and need not be woken up any more. If it fails, the constraint is not yet satisfied and is just put back to sleep until it is woken up again. If the constraint goal does not have any solutions, the constraint fails.

The constraint is not executed in the usual environment: Constraints outside the high-level constraint (outer constraints) are not woken up in the high-level constraint. In other words, the constraint works as if outer constraints did not exist. During the collection of solutions, floundering[4] constraints are ignored and the domains are used as they are.

The mechanism is illustrated by an example: the max(X,Y,Z) constraint holds if Z is the maximum of X and Y. It can be defined as follows:

```
:- constraint C=max(X,Y,Z)
     trigger trigger_minmax(X,C), trigger_minmax(Y,C),
             trigger_minmax(Z,C)
     satisfied one_var([X,Y,Z]).
max(X,Y,Z) :- X#>=Y, X=Z.
max(X,Y,Z) :- X#<Y,  Y=Z.
```

When max(X,Y,Z) is woken up and the variables have the domains

$$X \in \{2,3,5\}, \quad Y \in \{0,\ldots,4\}, \quad Z \in \{2,4,6,8\}$$

max(X,Y,Z) produces two intermediate solutions:

$$X = Z = 2, \quad Y \in \{0,\ldots,2\}$$

and

$$X \in \{2,3\}, \quad Y = Z \in \{2,4\}$$

The unions are:

$$X \in \{2,3\}, \quad Y \in \{0,1,2,4\}, \quad Z \in \{2,4\}$$

---

[3] A constraint is satisfied, if it need not be woken up again.

[4] A constraint flounders if the computation ends before the constraint is satisfied. This can be avoided by sufficiently instantiating the variables.

The effect of the activation of the constraint is to reduce the domains of the variables to these unions.

The `satisfied` goal in the example is `one_var(T)`, which succeeds if `T` contains at most one variable. This is a built-in, since it is frequently used (see Section 3.3.2).

Triggers work similar to Prolog II's `freeze/2`. They always succeed, and have the effect that the constraint is woken, when the variable's domain changes in a certain way.[5]

`trigger_minmax(V,C)` specifies that the constraint `C` is woken whenever the minimum or the maximum of the domain of `V` changes. It can be constructed from built-ins:

```
trigger_minmax(V,C) :- trigger_min(V,C), trigger_max(V,C).
```

We have four built-ins for specifying trigger conditions, corresponding to the wakeup mechanisms in our constraint logic programming system:

`trigger_ground(V,C)` Wake `C` up when `V` is instantiated (to an integer).

`trigger_min(V,C)` Wake `C` up whenever the minimum of the values in the domain changes, i.e., when the minimal value is removed from the domain.

`trigger_max(V,C)` Analogous to `trigger_min(V,C)`.

`trigger_size(V,C)` Wake `C` up whenever a value is removed from the domain.

The user can combine constraint declarations with coroutining declarations (e.g. NU-Prologs when-declarations). This can be used for delaying the first wakeup of the constraint until its arguments are instantiated sufficiently for achieving substantial pruning.

3.3   Properties and Restrictions

3.3.1   DECLARATIVE SEMANTICS

The declarative semantics of a program with constraint declarations are exactly the same as without constraint declarations, if the following condition is met: The `satisfied` goal must not succeed unless all combinations of values of the domain variables are consistent with respect to the constraint (see Section 3.3.2).

---

[5] Note that a conjunction of triggers means that the constraint is woken if any of the trigger conditions is satisfied. The trigger syntax has been criticized as inelegant, but we did not find a more elegant syntax that offers the same (or better) expressive power and does not cause a big implementation effort.

High-level constraints are based on two mechanisms: triggering/activation and summarizing solutions. The triggering mechanism just changes the order of execution, which has no influence on the declarative semantics. A constraint may be activated several times, but only the last time is important for the declarative semantics, since any solution that passes that activation also passes the others.

To prove the equivalence of the declarative semantics of the summarizing process, we show that it does neither remove nor add any solutions. The summarizing process collects all solutions of the constraint predicate and processes them by taking the union, so the summary obviously contains all solutions. Due to the restriction on the satisfaction condition, the summary of a satisfied constraint contains only combinations of values that are consistent with respect to the constraint, i.e., it contains only solutions.

If the constraint is not yet satisfied, it flounders. We can think of a floundering constraint as qualified answer; it represents all consistent combinations of values of the variables. The floundering behaviour may be changed by the constraint declaration, but the answers represent the same solution set.

3.3.2   SATISFACTION

The **satisfied** goal must only succeed if all combinations of the values in the domains are consistent. This is obviously the case when the constraint predicate succeeds and all arguments are ground. This condition is a bit too restrictive. A constraint is already satisfied, when there is at most one domain variable left [17] and all inconsistent values are removed from its domain, i.e. if there are no unsatisfied constraints within the high-level constraint. For some constraints it can be determined even earlier that there are no inconsistent combinations of values. E.g., X#<Y is satisfied when the largest value in the domain of X is smaller than the smallest value in the domain of Y.

3.3.3   PRAGMATICS

Of course, maintaining the declarative semantics is not very useful if the program loops endlessly or flounders due to the change in procedural semantics. Fortunately, this is not a problem in practice: In typical applications, every domain variable is instantiated eventually. Therefore, every constraint is satisfied and there can be no floundering. Endless loops can usually be avoided by making liberal use of coroutining.

To ensure that there is no floundering, the **trigger** goal must specify enough wakeup conditions. As a minimum, the constraint should be woken when one of its arguments is instantiated (i.e., **trigger_ground**), otherwise it could miss a decisive instantiation and remain unsatisfied forever.

```
:- constraint C = element(X,L,E)
    trigger trigger_size(X,C), trigger_size(E,C),
            trigger_listground(L,C)
    satisfied one_var([X,E|L]).
element(X,L,E):- element(X,L,E,1).

:- element(_,L,_,_) when L.
element(X,[E|Ls],E,X).
element(X,[_|Ls],E,N):- N1 is N+1, element(X,Ls,E,N1).

:- trigger_listground(L,_) when L.
trigger_listground([],_).
trigger_listground([V|Vs],C):- trigger_ground(V,C),
                               trigger_listground(Vs,C).
```

FIGURE 3.1. The element/3 constraint

Using other **trigger** goals causes more frequent wakeup[6] and earlier pruning, influencing performance. Which is best depends on the constraint and
sometimes on the application.

3.4   Examples

The constraint **element(X,L,E)** holds if E is the Xth element of the list L.
It is instrumental in solving many combinatorial search problems, e.g. the
cutting stock problem of [17]. It can be defined as high-level constraint by
just adding a constraint declaration to a declaratively programmed predicate (see Figure 3.1).

The **when**-declarations are coroutining declarations that delay the execution of the predicate until the specified arguments are instantiated.

The constraint **atmost(Nb,L,Val)** holds if at most Nb elements of L are
equal to Val. This constraint is needed in solving a car-sequencing problem
[5]. We could add a constraint declaration to the predicate described in [18],
but this would result in up to $2^{|L|}$ solutions per activation of the constraint,
i.e., each activation could cost exponential time. Our implementation is
natural and efficient (see Figure 3.2):

occurt(Nb,Val,L)[7] holds if exactly Nb elements of L are equal to Val.

---

[6] The goal trigger_min/2 (trigger_max) must be used in conjunction with
trigger_ground/2 or trigger_max/2 (trigger_min/2) to enforce triggering upon
instantiation.

[7] A   general-purpose   occur/3   can   be   defined   by   occur(N,Val,L):-
occurt(Nt,Val,L), N#=Nt.

```
atmost(Nb,L,Val):- occurt(N,Val,L), N#=<Nb.

:- occurt(_,_,L) when L.
occurt(0,_,[]).
occurt(N+D,Val,[V|Vs]):-
      [D] in 0..1, occur1(D,V,Val), occurt(N,Val,Vs).

:- constraint C = occur1(D,V1,V2)
   trigger trigger_ground(D,C), trigger_ground(V1,C),
           trigger_ground(V2,C)
   satisfied one_var([D,V1,V2]).
occur1(1,V,V).
occur1(0,V1,V2):- V1 #/= V2.
```

FIGURE 3.2. The `atmost/3` constraint

`occurt/3` creates one `occur1/3` constraint for each element, which checks the equality of one element with `Val`. `occurt/3` adds up the number of equalities, and `atmost(Nb,L,Val)` checks with the `#=</2` that they are less than or equal to `Nb`.

As soon as `Nb` variables in `L` become equal to `Val`, the sum reaches `Nb`, and the `#=</2` instantiates all other variables in the sum to 0. This in turn wakes the `occur1/3` constraints up, which then remove `Val` from domains of the rest of the variables via `#/=`.

3.5 Forward- and Lookahead-Declarations

This section describes the relation of our high-level constraint mechanism to forward- and lookahead-declarations. Basically, our high-level constraints can be seen as a generalization of lookahead declarations.

As an example, we will look at the constraint `disjunctive/4`. This constraint is used in scheduling applications.

A constraint declared with a lookahead declaration checks the consistency of every combination of values from the domains by running every combination through the predicate. Of course, this method is very time-consuming. In the example, if the variables `Si` and `Sj` have, e.g., 100 values in their domains, the constraint below would check 10 000 value combinations. Forward declarations can be mechanically transformed into high-level constraints with the same behaviour. E.g., the constraint

```
:- lookahead disjunctive(domain, ground, domain, ground).
disjunctive(Si,Di,Sj,Dj) :- Sj #>= Si+Di.
disjunctive(Si,Di,Sj,Dj) :- Si #>= Sj+Dj.
```

is equivalent to

```
:- disjunctive(Si,Di,Sj,Dj) when Di and Dj.
:- constraint C=disjunctive(Si,Di,Sj,Dj)
       trigger trigger_size(Si,C), trigger_size(Sj,C)
       satisfied one_var([Si,Sj]).
disjunctive(Si,Di,Sj,Dj) :- labeling([Si,Sj]),
                            disjunctive1(Si,Di,Sj,Dj).
```

```
disjunctive1(Si,Di,Sj,Dj) :- Sj #>= Si+Di.
disjunctive1(Si,Di,Sj,Dj) :- Si #>= Sj+Dj.
```

labeling/1 generates all combinations of values of the domain variables in its argument.

Forward declarations can be transformed in the same way, only the **when**-declaration is different; it allows only one variable:

```
:- disjunctive(Si,Di,Sj,Dj) when Di and Dj and (Si or Sj).
```

The high-level constraint version of the constraint is a bit slower than the lookahead declaration version, since the lookahead mechanism is more specialized. However, it is easy to make the constraint more efficient without losing pruning power: One variable can be left uninstantiated. This reduces the search process enormously, in the **disjunctive/4** example to less than 200 tries. This method works for all constraint predicates, unless they use built-ins that create a run-time error when presented with a variable.

Depending on the constraint, it may also be profitable to perform labeling after stating the subconstraints or to use domain-splitting instead of labeling, exploiting the pruning capabilities of the subconstraints.

We can do away with the labeling completely, if, for all alternatives, local propagation on the respective constraint networks is a satisfaction-complete[8] solver. This is the case for the **disjunctive/4** constraint[9], so searching is reduced to 2 tries.

For many constraints, it is also possible to use more restrictive triggering, resulting in fewer wakeups. E.g., in the case of **disjunctive/4**, **trigger_minmax/2** can be used without losing pruning power.

All these improvements and specialization of the satisfaction goal (Section 3.3.2) lead to the following **disjunctive/4**:

---

[8] In the CLP framework [8], a constraint solver is satisfaction-complete, if it can always decide whether a constraints network is satisfiable or not. Applied to finite domains this means that a satisfaction-complete solver always removes all values from the domains that are not consistent with the network of constraints. Partial lookahead constraints, forward-checking constraints and conjunctions of constraints are usually not satisfaction-complete.

[9] While the constraint #>=/2 is not necessarily satisfaction-complete when applied to general linear terms, it is satisfaction-complete for simple cases like V1 #>= V2+Const.

```
:- disjunctive(Si,Di,Sj,Dj) when Di and Dj.
:- constraint C=disjunctive(Si,Di,Sj,Dj)
     trigger trigger_minmax(Si,C), trigger_minmax(Sj,C)
     satisfied dommin(Si,Sil), dommax(Si,Siu),
               dommin(Sj,Sjl), dommax(Sj,Sju),
               (Siu+Di=<Sjl; Sju+Dj=<Sil).
disjunctive(Si,Di,Sj,Dj) :- Sj #>= Si+Di.
disjunctive(Si,Di,Sj,Dj) :- Si #>= Sj+Dj.
```

All the above improvements have the same pruning power as lookahead-declarations. For many applications it is also profitable to trade pruning power for time spent in the constraint by performing less labeling or fewer activations.

The implementation of our high-level constraint mechanism is quite similar to the implementation of forward- and lookahead-declarations, and takes about the same effort.

3.6 Refinements

3.6.1 OUTER CONSTRAINTS

As described in Section 3.2, constraints that were invoked outside the high-level constraint are not activated in the high-level constraint. The reason for this is not a theoretical difficulty, but a practical consideration: Suppose that there is a network of high-level constraints that internally perform a lot of labeling. The labeling of one variable in the constraint would wake up other constraints which would label other variables and so on. Eventually this would result in a complete labeling of the network, with the associated exponential run-time behaviour, but without the usual benefit of labeling, namely, a solution.

On the other hand, it would be nice to apply outer constraints during the execution of high-level constraints to achieve better pruning. The problematic behaviour arises when outer constraints create choicepoints. The solution is to execute only constraints that cannot create choicepoints, i.e. low-level constraints.

3.6.2 SINGLE SOLUTIONS

If a constraint predicate delivers only one solution (e.g., due to failure of all other alternatives), it no longer makes sense to apply the high-level constraint mechanism. The constraint predicate can be executed as normal predicate. It is then satisfied, unless it uses meta or extra-logical features. This avoids the overhead of solution collection and later wakeups. More importantly, it opens new avenues for pruning, since the subconstraints of such a high-level constraint are now visible outside.

3.6.3 BUILT-IN CONSTRAINTS

Our mechanism for defining high-level constraints can also be used by the language implementor for defining built-in constraints. E.g., #=</2[10] can be defined by:

```
:- builtin_constraint C = X#=<Y
      trigger trigger_min(X,C), trigger_ground(X,C),
              trigger_max(Y,C), trigger_ground(Y,C),
      satisfied dommax(X,MaxX), dommin(Y,MinY), MaxX=<MinY.
X #=< Y :- dommin(X, MinX), greater_equal_const(Y, MinX),
           dommax(Y, MaxY), less_equal_const(X, MaxY).
```

built-in predicate	Behaviour
dommin(X,MinX)	Unifies MinX with the smallest value in the domain of X
dommax(X,MaxX)	Unifies MaxX with the largest value in the domain of X
domlist(X,L)	Unifies L with the list of values in the domain of X
not·equal·const(X,Y)	Y must be an integer; remove Y from the domain of X
greater·equal·const(X,Y)	Y must be an integer; remove values <Y from the domain of X
less·equal·const(X,Y)	Y must be an integer; remove values >Y from the domain of X

TABLE 3.1. These built-in predicates can be used to build any constraint

dommin/2 and **dommax/2** are metalogical predicates for getting the minimum/maximum value in the domain of the variable. Integers are treated as domain variables with one value in the domain. **greater_equal_const/2** and **less_equal_const/2** are built-in predicates (i.e., not constraints) for updating the minimum/maximum of the variable's domain. A few such predicates (see Table 3.1) make it possible to define all constraints with the high-level constraint mechanism.

For such constraints the important feature of high-level constraints is the wakeup mechanism. Most of them have only one solution, so the solution collection mechanism is not necessary and would constitute unnecessary overhead. The constraint predicate can simply be executed. Note that, since the constraint predicate uses metalogical goals, the constraint is not satisfied after executing the predicate once, even though it has only one solution. Instead, it is satisfied only when the **satisfied** goal becomes true. Declaring the constraint as **builtin_constraint** (instead of **constraint**) indicates that this different treatment should be applied.

The benefits of using high-level constraints for defining built-ins are lower development costs. E.g., the low-level version of #=</2 constraint defined above takes 45 lines of C code in the Aristo system. In addition, if all low-level constraints are eliminated, the mechanism for handling them becomes

---

[10]This version cannot work with linear terms, only with plain variables. The general version requires more code.

unnecessary. The cost is of course lower performance. However, by using optimizing compiler technology [16, 10] this cost can be eliminated.

3.7 Implementation

When a high-level constraint is called, the system creates a *frozen constraint*, a data structure similar to a suspension [1] that contains the constraint goal and the **satisfied** goal. Then the **trigger** goal is called; the variable C, used as the second argument to the trigger built-ins, contains the frozen constraint. A trigger built-in inserts the frozen constraint into the list of constraints that are woken up when the specified attribute of the variable changes. E.g., **trigger_min(V,C)** inserts the frozen constraint C into the min-list of V.

What happens when the constraint is woken up depends on its type. For a constraint declared with **constraint**, room sufficient for the domains of the variables in the arguments of the constraint is reserved. In this space the resulting domains are constructed. They are initialized to empty. Then a procedure similar to **findall/3** is performed: If there is no solution, the constraint fails and backtracking is performed. If there is a solution, the values in the domains of the variables in the arguments are added to the appropriate result domains. Then backtracking is initiated. If there is another solution, then the process is repeated. Finally, the constraint goal will fail. If there was only one solution, the constraint is marked as satisfied and the constraint goal is meta-called (Section 3.6.2). Otherwise, the variables in the arguments of the constraint are reduced to the result domains; and the **satisfied** goal is called. If it succeeds, the constraint is marked as satisfied, otherwise as frozen (i.e., it might be woken up again).

The processing of a **builtin_constraint** is much simpler: The constraint goal is simply meta-called. Then the **satisfied** goal is called and processed as described above.

The restriction of not executing outer high-level constraints is implemented as follows: The system counts the depth of constraint processing; every frozen constraint has a field containing the depth where the constraint was called. A high-level constaint is only woken up, if the current level is the same as the level at the call of the constraint.

This implementation adds a few restrictions: The **trigger** and **satisfied** goals must not have any declarative meaning, i.e., they must not bind arguments of the constraint or add any constraints; they also must not create (permanent) choicepoints. The **trigger** goal must always succeed. These restrictions can be enforced at run-time by checking the last choicepoint and the entries on the trail.

3.8 Results

We implemented the high-level constraint mechanism described here. The times were measured using the Aristo system, a WAM-emulator based constraint logic programming system.

Solutions	low-level	forward	high-level	lookahead	high-level	choice
one	3.53ms	4.90ms	3.93ms	18.24ms	14.65ms	10.80ms
all	5.92ms	9.75ms	7.19ms	47.00ms	38.90ms	16.49ms

TABLE 3.2. Five houses timings

We compared four approaches: using a low-level constraint, our high-level constraint mechanism, forward checking, and using disjunctions as choices. We used the five houses puzzle [17] as benchmark. The solution involves a constraint **plusorminus/3**, which we implemented with all approaches. We have measured two high-level constraint versions: one with the same pruning power as forward checking, one with the same pruning power as lookahead. The times for finding the solution on a DecStation 5000/150 (50/100Mhz R4000, 46 SPECInt) are shown in Table 3.2. The *all* times include the time for proving that the puzzle has only one solution.

```
?- [A,B,C] in 1..N, max(A,B,C).
```

domain size N	hlc	lookahead
20	0.87ms	2360ms
50	1.12ms	36500ms
100	1.55ms	292000ms

TABLE 3.3. **max/3** timings (one activation)

We also compared the performance of one activation of the **max/3** of Section 3.2 with a full labeling (lookahead style) version of **max/3** (see Table 3.3, timings performed on a DecStation 5000/125 (25MHz R3000, 16 SPECInt)). Both versions have the same pruning power. As expected, the lookahead version becomes slower with the cube of the domain size. The high-level constraint version is between 2700 and 188000 times faster. Domain sizes in this range are not unusual for **max/3**. The significance of this example is not the enormous speedups; instead, it shows that lookahead declarations are often too slow in practice, while high-level constraints are usable.

3.9   Related Work

Section 3.5 compares our high-level constraints to forward- and lookahead-declarations [17].

The cardinality operator [18] can express disjunction and negation of constraints. It is based on constraint entailment (implication). In principle it can be applied to any domain (e.g. rationals). In contrast, our mechanism is restricted to finite domains, but it achieves better pruning. E.g., a cardinality operator version of `max/3` achieves no pruning for the example in Section 3.2, since it cannot show negative entailment of one of the two branches of `max/3`. The `atmost/3` example gives an idea how the cardinality operator can be emulated with high-level constraints.

Constraint simplification rules [6] replace or augment (combinations of) constraints with simpler constraints. They can simplify delayed user-defined predicates like `max/3`, but they achieve no pruning for the example in Section 3.2. Simplification rules are practical for stating more global relations and are complementary to high-level constraints.

Echidna [14] allows disjunctions of inequalities over real domains. The method employed for disjunctions can be seen as a specialization of our method for summarizing alternative intermediate solutions.

Generalised propagation [11] extends the propagation mechanism from finite domains to arbitrary domains. A propagation step for a goal results in an approximation of the solution set that is as close as can be represented in the domain. [11] does not say much about how to compute these approximations and when to perform propagation steps (when to wake up constraints). For finite domains, lookahead declarations are a specialization of generalized propagation. High-level constraints are a bit more general, as they can also express partial lookahead, i.e., an approximation that is not as close as possible.

[19] presents many ideas, among them constructive disjunction of constraints, which is further explored in [9]. As described in the latter paper, constructive disjunction is a combination of our summarizing process (called *global lookahead reduction* in [9]) with a specialization of the cardinality operator. All of these cardinality operator features are covered by our single solution refinement (see Section 3.6.2), except positive reduction which causes just early satisfaction of the constraint, but does not add to the pruning power. Surprisingly for papers that closely related, the discussion in [9] is quite disjoint with that in the present paper. E.g., there is no discussion of wakeup conditions.

The Nicolog system [15] uses a functional intermediate representation (the projection language) for constraint networks. Among other things, new constraints can be defined in this language. However, this language manipulates domains explicitly and is therefore lower-level than the logic programming approach used for high-level constraints defined with **constraint** declarations. On the other hand, it is higher-level than building constraints with `builtin_constraint` and the built-in predicates for manipulating domains.

[19] presents a powerful built-in constraint, similar to Nicologs projection language, which is described in more detail in [4]. The same comments apply as for Nicolog.

There is an even lower level than `builtin_constraint`, which relies on domain variables and a constraint wakeup mechanism: [2] implements a finite domain constraint solver with coroutining and backtrackable assignment. Metastructures [13] support user-enhanced unification for building constraint solvers [7] or coroutining.

Coroutining delays the execution of goals until they are sufficiently instantiated [3, 12]. Like constraint declarations, coroutining declarations do not change the declarative meaning of a program. The implementation of high-level constraints is closely related to the implementation of coroutining. However, they are different mechanisms for different purposes.

3.10   Further Work

[11] inspires the idea that a high-level constraint might not only reduce the domains, but might also add constraints that are satisfied (entailed) for all intermediate solutions. Since checking the entailment of every possible constraint is too much overhead, only a few constraints that are likely to be entailed should be checked. These constraints could be specified by the programmer or determined in a training run.

Specifying trigger and satisfaction conditions is too much work and error-prone. It may be possible to generate good conditions automatically, leaving only fine-tuning to the programmer.

Another interesting topic is negative high-level constraints. Currently, we can use DeMorgan's Law to push the negation down and then use negative versions of the built-in constraints. Apart from automating this transformation, there's also the negative forward checking inference rule [17].

3.11   Conclusion

We have presented a mechanism for defining high-level constraints over finite domains. It is achieved by mechanisms for waking constraints and for collecting and summarizing the solutions of a constraint predicate. Syntactically, high-level constraints are normal predicates with an additional constraint declaration.

High-level constraints allow a very fine-grained control over the choice between pruning power and execution time cost. The declarative meaning of the program is the same with and without constraint declarations. Our mechanism subsumes the domain- and forward-declaration mechanism of [17] and is as easy to implement. As free bonus, the builtin constraints can be. defined with this mechanism.

Acknowledgements: We are grateful to Franz Puntigam, Ulrich Neumerkel, Gregory Sidebottom, Konrad Schwarz, Thomas Graf, Bruno De Backer and Hendrick Lock for commenting on earlier versions of this paper, and to DMS Decision Management Systems GmbH for making Aristo available to us.

3.12   References

[1] Mats Carlsson. Freeze, indexing and other implementation issues in the WAM. In *Fourth International Conference on Logic Programming (ICLP-4)*, pages 40–58. MIT Press, 1987.

[2] Phillippe Codognet, François Fages, and Thierry Sola. A metalevel compiler of CLP(FD) and its combination with intelligent backtracking. In Frédéric Benhamou and Alain Colmerauer, editors, *Constraint Logic Programming: Selected Research*, pages 437–456. MIT Press, 1993.

[3] K. L. Clark, F. G. McCabe, and S. Gregory. IC-Prolog language features. In K. L. Clark and S.-A. Tärnlund, editors, *Logic Programming*, pages 253–266. Academic Press, London, 1982.

[4] Daniel Diaz and Phillippe Codognet. A minimal extension of the WAM for clp(fd). In *International Conference on Logic Programming (ICLP)*, pages 774–790, 1993.

[5] M. Dincbas, H. Simonis, and P. Van Hentenryck. Solving the Car Sequencing Problem in Constraint Logic Programming. In *European Conference on Artificial Intelligence (ECAI-88)*, München, 1988.

[6] Thom Frühwirth. Constraint simplification rules. Technical Report ECRC-92-18?, ECRC, 1992.

[7] Christian Holzbaur. *Implementation of Constraint Based Inference Mechanisms through Extended Unification*. PhD thesis, Technische Universität Wien, 1990.

[8] Joxan Jaffar and Jean-Louis Lassez. Constraint logic programming. In *Fourteenth Annual ACM Symposium on Principles of Programming Languages (POPL)*, pages 111–119, München, 1987.

[9] Jean Jourdan and Thierry Sola. The versatility of handling disjunctions as constraints. In *Programming Language Implementation and Logic Programming (PLILP)*, pages 60–74, 1993.

[10] Andreas Krall and Thomas Berger. Fast Prolog with a VAM$_{1p}$ based Prolog compiler. In *Programming Language Implementation and Logic Programming (PLILP '92)*, pages 245–259. Springer LNCS 631, 1992.

[11] Thierry Le Provost and Mark Wallace. Domain independent propagation. In *Proceedings of the International Conference on Fifth Generation Computer Systems*, pages 1004–1011, ICOT, Japan, 1992. Association for Computing Machinery.

[12] Lee Naish. *Negation and Control in Prolog*. Springer LNCS 238, 1986.

[13] Ulrich Neumerkel. Extensible unification by metastructures. In *Meta-90*, Leuven, 1990.

[14] Gregory Sidebottom and William S. Havens. Hierarchical arc consistency for disjoint real intervals in constraint logic programming. *Computational Intelligence*, 8(4):601–623, 1992.

[15] Greg Sidebottom. Compiling constraint logic programming using interval computations and branching constructs. Technical report, Simon Fraser University, 1993.

[16] Andrew Taylor. LIPS on a MIPS. In *Seventh International Conference on Logic Programming (ICLP-7)*, pages 174–185. MIT Press, 1990.

[17] Pascal Van Hentenryck. *Constraint Satisfaction in Logic Programming*. Logic Programming Series. MIT Press, Cambridge, Massachusetts, 1989.

[18] Pascal Van Hentenryck and Yves Deville. The cardinality operator: A new logical connective for constraint logic programming. In *Eighth International Conference on Logic Programming (ICLP-8)*, pages 745–759. MIT Press, 1991.

[19] Pascal Van Hentenryck, Vijay Saraswat, and Yves Deville. Constraint processing in cc(FD). Ftp from parcftp.xerox.com, file pub/ccp/ccfd/pldi-5.ps, 1991.

4

Integrating Constraints in an Object-Based Knowledge Representation System

Jérôme Gensel[1]

ABSTRACT Object-based knowledge representation systems benefit from the declarative power of the object formalism for modeling, organizing and storing large amounts of knowledge. They also offer powerful reasoning mechanisms (classification, inheritance, methods, etc.) which, applied on the current facts of a knowledge base, will deduce implicit or hypothetical facts and then increase the amount of knowledge.

Fully integrating constraints into an object-based representation model should not merely consist in constraining objects managed by the model (allowing the definition of horizontal links between them), but it should also lead to represent constraints with the help of objects (allowing to set, modify or delete them using the basic primitives of object manipulation provided by the model).

TROPES is an object-based knowledge representation system in which constraints are integrated as objects. We describe the main features of the system before detailing the different kinds of constraints available in TROPES. Constraint maintenance in TROPES is delegated to a constraint programming library through an interface we also present here. Constraint propagation serves as an inference mechanism for inferring missing values. Finally, we give some prospects of research offered by this constraint integration.

4.1 Introduction

Based on the principles (expressiveness, class specialization, inheritance, etc.) of the Object paradigm, object-based knowledge representation systems are built to describe, organize and store large amounts of knowledge. Moreover, by activating various reasoning mechanisms (like methods, instantiation, classification, etc.), they are able to produce new implicit or hypothetical facts from the knowledge they contain [14].

---

[1]INRIA Rhône-Alpes – Université Joseph Fourier, LIFIA/IMAG, 46 avenue Félix Viallet, 38031 Grenoble Cedex 1, France, e-mail: `Jerome.Gensel@imag.fr`

As defined in [12, 9], a constraint $C(x_1, \ldots, x_n)$ describes a relation that has to be maintained on a set $V = \{x_1, \ldots, x_n\}$ of variables (named the constrained variables), each x_i having an associate domain D_{x_i} of values. C can also be seen as a sub-set of the Cartesian product $D_{x_1} \otimes \ldots \otimes D_{x_n}$ which gives all the n-tuples $(v_1, \ldots, v_n)$, where $v_i \in D_{x_i}$, of compatible values for V.

In constraint programming languages, given a constraint satisfaction problem, defined by a set of constraints and the set of their constrained variables, a constraint solver is put in charge of applying satisfaction algorithms to generate, one, some or all the solutions, if they exist. This satisfaction process can be made easier by constraint propagation (which consists in eliminating from each domain, the values that can not appear in any solution) and/or by heuristics (which choose the next constraint to satisfy, the next variable to instantiate, the next value in a domain, etc.) [8].

Merging constraints and an object-based knowledge representation system must lead, not only to constrain objects, but also to represent constraints by objects. Constraints can then be manipulated like any other object of a knowledge base.

We describe here the integration of constraints, namely their expression and their maintenance, in an object-based knowledge representation system called TROPES.

While constraint expression is the matter of TROPES entities for knowledge representation, constraint maintenance is delegated to PECOS [7], a constraint programming library of the LE-LISP language [5], thanks to an interface between the two systems. Its role consists in translating any constraint involving TROPES attributes in an equivalent constraint posted on PECOS constrained variables, and, conversely, in transmitting to every constrained attributes the changes performed by PECOS on the corresponding constrained variables.

We present TROPES main principles before exposing the four kinds of constraints available. Then, the tasks performed by the interface with PECOS are stated. Finally, the contributions and the research perspectives stemming from this integration are listed.

4.2   Presentation of the TROPES System

TROPES [11] is a multiple-perspective knowledge representation system which is based on a class instance approach. In TROPES, a knowledge base is made of independent concepts. Each concept models a generic family of the real world and groups a set of instances. Different perspectives can be associated with a concept in order to capture the information particular to each of these views. In each perspective of a concept, classes are organized in a hierarchy and linked by the specialization link 'a-kind-of'. Each class, except the root of a hierarchy, has got only one superclass and thus inheritance is simple in TROPES. A class provides a description – called the class intention –, which can be seen as a record of the types of its attributes. The set of instances belonging to a class is called the class extension. An instance is attached to one and only one class in each perspective by the instantiation link 'is-a', but belongs to each class situated on a path from this class to the root (see Fig.4.1). The attribute values of an instance do satisfy the intentions of its belonging classes.

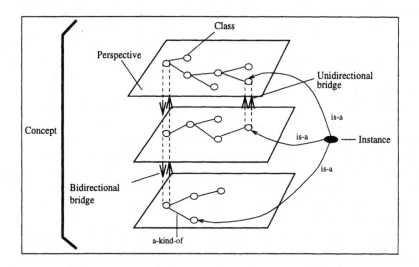

FIGURE 4.1. The main entities of the TROPES system

Each concept determines its proper set of attributes. Acting like a mask, each perspective makes use of only a subset of these attributes (those which are also visible under other perspectives and those which are visible only under this perspective). An attribute expresses either a property, or a 'part-of' relation link, or a relational link. It has a definition for the concept which states its general and constant features (type, method, etc.) and a definition for each class where it is redefined. In such a case, the type of the attribute is refined with the help of optional facets precising for the class:

1. Its new type (facet 'in')

2. The domain of its possible values (facet 'domain')

3. The domain of its impossible values (facet 'except')

4. Its cardinality, when the attribute has a value which is a list or a set of values (facet 'card')

Specialization between a class and one of its direct subclasses is obtained by addition, either of new attributes, or of constraints – specified by the facets presented above – on existing attributes. A subclass (resp. superclass) is said to be more specific (resp. general) than its superclass (resp. subclass). When the description of an attribute is not refined in a class, it is inherited from the superclass.

A bridge can be thrown over two classes (source and destination) of two different perspectives of a concept, in order to signify that a set relation holds between their extensions. A set equality corresponds to a bidirectional bridge, while a set inclusion is described by a unidirectional bridge. These bridges are mainly used during the classification process (described in [11]).

Instantiation is a TROPES mechanism which allows the creation of an instance, possibly incomplete, and its attachment to a class (by default, the root) in each perspective, under the consistency condition that every provided value satisfies the attribute type described in the class intention.

In TROPES, composite objects contain attributes for modeling a 'part-of' relation between them and their parts. In such objects, the values of these attributes are instances – called components – of other concepts. The components are dependent on the composite in both an existential (they were created for it) and exclusive (they cannot be the components of any other composite) way. Classifying an incomplete composite object can lead to the creation of the missing instances of components, according to their description [10].

A strategic knowledge to be applied in a problem solving process can also be described thanks to a task model available in TROPES. A task is a composite object whose instantiation and classification will produce a trace of its execution. This trace can then be used as an explanation of the reasoning process performed.

Finally, a reasoning maintenance system stores the justification and the descendants of any attribute and instance in order to ensure consistency when the knowledge base is modified.

The kernel of the TROPES system encompassing those features has been implemented in the LE-LISP language.

4.3   Constraints Expression in TROPES

4.3.1   MOTIVATIONS

Our motivations for integrating constraints stem from an acknowledgement of a need for expressing relations or properties about objects in TROPES.

Indeed, methods do not reveal themselves convenient when it is a matter of stating a relation between several attributes, mainly because methods are unidirectional while constraints are multi-directional. Only using methods to describe how to satisfy a relation compels the user to associate with each constrained attribute a method which is likely to compute its value from the other attribute values. In this case, the relation is not explicitly expressed but is implicitly represented by a diffuse set of methods. On the contrary, a constraint is a declarative statement which gathers a set of methods dedicated to the maintenance of the relation and which guarantees that the adequate method will be invoked when a change occurs in a constrained attribute. Moreover, using a constraint propagation, impossible values can be eliminated from the domains of constrained attributes. This permits to consider at any moment the effective domain of a constrained attribute and not only the one it has in the class intention. Finally, once a domain has been reduced to a singleton by the constraint propagation phase, it is considered that the possible value for the corresponding variable is unique and known.

In an object-based knowledge representation model, it has seemed to us natural to describe constraints also by objects. Then, the the chosen unit for describing a constraint is a TROPES. This class contains information about the parameters and the code function devoted to the constraint maintenance. The instantiation of such a constraint class corresponds to the effective setting-up of the constraint on the attributes given by the created constraint instance. Since constraints are TROPES objects, the user can define and manipulate them (definition, instantiation or setting-up, modification, deletion) without any change of formalism. On this account the integration performed here is a strong one.

The LE-LISP language, in which TROPES is implemented, has a constraint programming module, called PECOS, which has been used for constraint maintenance. It provides an efficient constraint propagation algorithm based on arc-consistency (or reduction of domain by deleting the impossible values) which is performed on the domain of each constrained variable as soon as the constraint is set and then at any time change occurs in the domain of a constrained variable (for example, when the variable is assigned a value). This library also offers a large range of predefined constraint functions, a module to extend this pool of constraints, functions of constrained variable manipulation and a non deterministic mode for generating the solutions. Using the predefined functions of PECOS allows the definition of arithmetic constraints ($=, \neq, <, >, \leq, \geq$) on expression made of arithmetic operators ($+, -, \times, \div$, etc.), numbers and TROPES attributes. But, more complex user-defined constraints, or conditional constraints can also be maintained. Although using PECOS spares us the definition of a constraint language, we had to resort to a linking interface for the coupling of the two systems.

Finally, in knowledge representation systems, relations are usually simply represented by attributes which model links between objects. Here again, those (inverse) links are spread out in each involved object. Moreover, typing and cardinality facets constitute the only expressible constraints about the nature and the number of the linked objects. It is much more difficult to express in a declarative way, constraints which are induced by the relation, i.e. which must be activated only when the link is established. Once again, classes reveal themselves suitable description units to capture the characteristics of a relation. Therefore, we propose to represent relations (distinct of the 'part-of' relation) in TROPES by classes which give not only a description of the belonging classes of the linked objects, but also the set of constraints induced by the relation. By this way, the semantics of a relation can be extended and automatically ensured by the constraint solver.

4.3.2   CONSTRAINTS AS UNARY PREDICATES

Typing facets can reveal themselves inadequate when it is a matter of stating a property any value provided for the attribute must satisfy (for instance, being an odd value). For this purpose, we have introduced a new facet 'cond' which indicates a unary predicate representing the property (see Fig.4.2).

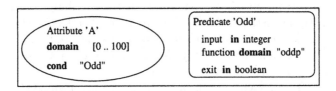

FIGURE 4.2. The value of attribute 'A' has to be an odd value, as it is mentioned by the facet 'cond'. In the predicate class 'Odd', the name of the boolean function to be executed is given. This execution will be activated by the instantiation of this predicate class.

A unary predicate is represented by a class of a concept "Predicates". This class describes the type of the unique argument (attribute 'input'), the code function to be executed in order to determine whether the property is satisfied or not (attribute 'function'), and, the boolean result of the execution (attribute 'exit').

In the presence of a facet 'cond', the checking of a candidate value for an attribute requires the instantiation of the corresponding predicate class. This instantiation activates the execution of the code function. The result is stored in the attribute 'exit'.

4.3.3   CONSTRAINTS AS OBJECTS

In TROPES, a predefined concept "Constraints" is devoted to the definition of constraint classes. A constraint class gives the type of each of its constrained variables, and the function devoted to the constraint maintenance which will effectively post the constraint. This function has only one parameter: the constraint instance (see Fig.4.3) whose attributes are the links between the constrained attributes and the constrained variables used by the constraint programming library PECOS. This function is then written using constraints functions of PECOS (see 4.4.1).

When an instance of constraint is created, if the values of the constrained attributes are all present, TROPES checks for the satisfaction of the relation (local consistency), otherwise it signals the inconsistency. If some attributes have no value, their domain is reduced in accordance with the constraint (arc-consistency). When a domain is reduced to a singleton, this value is propagated (value propagation) for reducing the other domains.

When a constrained attribute is assigned a value by the user for the first time, TROPES checks for its validity (i.e. it must belong to the constrained domain of the attribute, and not only to the domain defined in the class intention). Once it is accepted, this value is propagated: the domains of the other involved attributes are reduced. Whenever one of these domains becomes a singleton, then a value is inferred for the constrained attribute. Therefore, constraints provide a new inference mechanism for TROPES.

When the value of a constrained attribute is modified, its initial reduced domain (the one obtained by the reduction of the class intention domain by the set of constraints lying on the attribute) is restored. If the provided value is in the reduced domain, the status of the previous value is examined. If it was given by the user, its status is kept unchanged and the value is accepted after the modification has been propagated through the attribute descendants by the reasoning maintenance system. Otherwise (i.e. the previous value has been inferred by a constraint), its status must change (the value is now given by the user) as well as the direction of the constraint. In this latter case, one of the adjoining constrained attributes must be invalidated (i.e. its reduced domain is restored), then its new value is inferred. This choice is here made by the user, as we consider that, aware of the modification he or she has confirmed, he or she can may want to control farther the propagation. However, solution maintenance can be automatically performed [1] by an algorithm which generate every possible propagations in reaction to the modification of a constrained variable.

TROPES checks for the validity of the provided value and, if one (or more) of these constraints is no longer satisfied, the inconsistency is raised.

Constraints on Classes

A constraint on a class expresses a relation that holds between some attributes of the class. It can be seen as a property inherent to the class. As a consequence, every instance of this class must satisfy this constraint. For any TROPES class, the set of its constraints is given by a special attribute 'constraints' (see Fig.4.3).

```
Class 'Circle'
attributes = {center_x, center_y,
              radius, area, ...}
constraints = { (Pi-R2 area radius),
              ...}
```

```
Constraint 'Pi-R2'
x in real
y in real
constr-name    domain
               "tr-ct-pi-r2"
```

```
(defun tr-ct-pi-r2 (constr-inst)
  (ct-eq (tr-vcp 'x) (ct-fmul 3.159
        (ct-power (tr-pcv 'y) 2)
        )
  )
)
```

FIGURE 4.3. In the class 'Circle', the property: area = PI * radius * radius, is imposed by the constraint Pi-R2. The class 'Pi-R2' describes the type of each involved attribute and refers to a function 'tr-pi-r2', written by the user, which is in charge of setting effectively this constraint on each instance of the class. 'ct-eq', 'ct-mult' and 'ct-power' are PECOS predefined functions, while 'tr-pcv' gives the PECOS constrained variable associated with the TROPES constrained attribute.

Concerning TROPES bridges, a constraint lying on the destination class of a unidirectional bridge and involving attributes cwhich are ommon to the source class, must also be applied to the source class of the bridge, since every instance of the source class belongs to the destination class.

Down along the 'a-kind-of' link, the constraints of a class are inherited by its subclasses. If an inconsistency stands between an inherited and a defined constraint, it will be raised by the constraint maintenance system, at any instantiation.

The modification and the deletion of a particular instance of constraint posted on a class are not allowed. Indeed, the constraint being the property of the class, a particular instance of the class can not be released from this constraint separately. Therefore, all the instances of a constraint set on a class are hidden to the user. Only the deletion of the constraint in the set given by the attribute 'constraints' sets the class (i.e. all its instances) free from this deleted constraint.

Finally, since constraints are themselves classes, it is possible to define constraints on constraint classes (meta-constraints) but this characteristic has not yet been explored.

Constraints on Instances

In TROPES, a constraint can also be set dynamically upon attributes by simply instantiating the constraint class which corresponds to the relation which must be maintained. (see Fig.4.4).

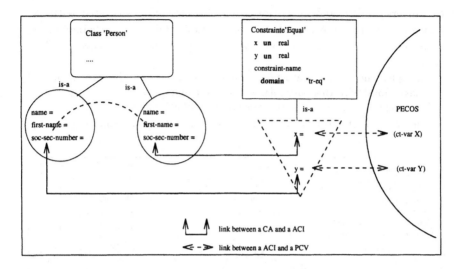

FIGURE 4.4. A unemployed cohabitee can benefit from the Social Security rights of its co-habitant. Then, for the administration, this two persons share the same Social Security number. This is described, in the knowledge base, by an equality constraint on this two particular instances of the class 'Person'. The link between a constrained attribute (CA) and its corresponding attribute in the constraint instance (ACI) and the link between the ACI and the PECOS constrained variable (PCV) are sketched.

As an accessible instance of constraint, a constraint on instances benefits from the other classical operations of manipulation (modification, deletion) provided by TROPES:

1. Modifying the value of an attribute in an instance of constraint comes down to either change the value of the constrained attribute corresponding to the parameter of the constraint, or to modify the value of a constant parameter.

2. Deleting an instance of constraint comes down to release the constrained instances from this link and to propagate the invalidity of any value previously inferred by the deleted constraint.

Constraints of Relations

Relational attributes in TROPES express the possible implication of any instance of a class in a particular relation with instances of another class (we restrict here our study to binary relations). These attributes convey a potentiality of the class: if they have no value, the instance is not (yet) in relation with others.

In TROPES, a relation is represented by a class which describes the two classes linked by the relation (providing in that way the definitions of the

two inverse links), and an optional set of constraints associated with the
relation (see Fig.4.5. Although the two relation attributes are defined in the
relation class, each of them is also visible (copied out) in its corresponding
class.

Example: The relation 'Father/Son' is established between the class 'Men' and
the class 'Boys' with this particular set of constraints:

The name of a son must be the same as his father's name.

The age of a son must be lower than fifteen years than his father's age.

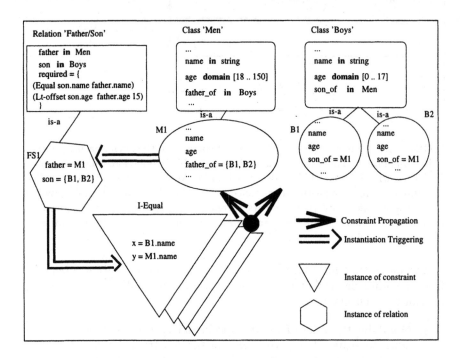

FIGURE 4.5. A relation class 'Father/Son' describes the relation given in the
example above. The instance 'FS1' symbolizes the relation that holds between
the instances 'M1' and 'B1' and between the instances 'M1' and 'B2'. The instantiated classes of constraints will control the domain of the constrained attributes
(namely, 'name' and 'age')

When one of the relational attributes is assigned a value for the first
time, the inverse link is updated and an instance of the relation class is
created. At its turn, this instantiation triggers off the instantiations of the
classes of constraints associated with the relation. Thus, constraints are
now fixed on attributes in the newly linked instances, placing them under
the control of the relation.

Similarly, the user can decide to instantiate a relation class. Then the
values of the new instance are transferred in the corresponding relational
attribute in each linked instance. If constraints are associated with the

relation, their classes are instantiated.

The modification of an instance of relation aims at extending, modifying or at reducing the set of the linked instances. When an instance is released from its relational link, the value of the relation attribute must be cancelled. Furthermore, the values inferred by any constraint of this relation are no longer valid and a lazy propagation must be activated to report the inconsistency.

The deletion of a relation instance releases the set of the linked instances. This changes must also be propagated.

4.4   Constraint Maintenance in TROPES

4.4.1   THE PECOS CONSTRAINT PROGRAMMING LIBRARY

The maintenance of the constraints described and set-up in TROPES is handled by PECOS. This LE-LISP library allows constraint programming with variables of any type over finite domains, with integer variables over enumerated domains, with integer or float variables over an interval, and with set variables whose domain is a set of sets of values.

PECOS offers basic operations for defining and manipulating variables on which constraints will be posted (declaration, assignment, value elimination from the domain, etc.). Once constrained variables are defined, predefined constraints (equality, comparison, arithmetic, cardinality, etc.) can be posted on them. Moreover, the user can define its own constraints thanks to a provided set of schemas based on a daemon mechanism. A schema mentions a condition (an event that modifies the domain of one of the constrained variables) and a propagation rule to be applied in reaction to this event in order to reduce the domain of the other adjoining constrained variables.

In PECOS, constraint propagation consists in:

1. Eliminating impossible values from the domains as soon as the constraint is posted. For example, let x in [0 10] and y in [0 5] be two integer variables. The constraint y $>$ x reduces the domains of both x in [0 4] and y in [1 5].

2. Propagating the modification of a domain to the other domains and, in case of assignment, propagating the value. In the example, if y is assigned the value 1 then x, by reduction of its domain to a singleton, is assigned the value 0.

PECOS proposes also a non deterministic programming mode, coupled with an integrated backtrack mechanism, which can be used notably to perform domain enumerations to get one, many or all of the solutions of the current constraint satisfaction problem.

Although PECOS manages constraints on LE-LISP objects and classes, this optional object-oriented constraint programming mode is not used by TROPES, but constraints on classes are treated in the same way (the constraint is uniformly applied to any instance of the class).

4.4.2   THE TROPES/PECOS INTERFACE

Although TROPES benefits from the PECOS constraint propagation power, an interface had to be built in order to link every constrained attribute in TROPES to an equivalent (i.e. with the same domain) constrained variable managed by PECOS. The role of this interface consists in:

1. managing a correspondence table which stores every link between a TROPES constrained attribute and a PECOS constrained variable. The interface controls the creation, update and deletion of PECOS constrained variables. Notably, it must be taken into account that the values of TROPES constrained attributes can be modified at any time during the lifetime of a knowledge base, whereas in PECOS, once a domain has been reduced to a singleton, any re-assignment is impossible.

2. offering constraint programming functions for defining and setting-up constraints on TROPES attributes (these functions use access functions to the correspondence table and PECOS predefined functions.

3. adapting the representation of complex domains of Tropes attributes to PECOS. For instance, when a domain is a union of intervals, a composite constrained variable is handled. It corresponds to a list of PECOS constrained variables (each having for domain one element of the union). Thus, a constraint posted on a composite variable is applied to each constrained variable. As soon as one of them has got an empty domain, which means that there is no value in the corresponding interval that satisfies the constraint, the union can be reduced and the constrained variable corresponding to the empty domain is removed from its composite variable.

4. analyzing and reacting to the error messages raised by PECOS. Non deterministic functions are then very useful to control fails and misfortunes and restore a valid state for the PECOS constrained variables (for instance, recovering their previous domain).

4.5   Contributions of this Integration

This integration allows now in TROPES the description of numerical relations in a declarative way and then improves the capabilities of representation of the model. Constraints establish horizontal links between attributes of one or many instances. Thanks to the constraint maintenance performed by PECOS, the consistency of any provided value for a constrained attribute is guaranteed. Moreover, constraints act as an inference mechanism since constraint propagation can deduce missing values.

However, if domains are reduced by arc-consistency, the network of constraints made of constraints on classes, constraint on instances and constraints of relations constitute a constraint network for which the search of solutions is not the main aim in TROPES. For this purpose, the enumerating functions of PECOS could be solicited for generating the solution(s) by enumerating them. This would lead, first to reduce yet more precisely the domains of constrained attributes, and then to the creation of sets of hypothetical instances (a set corresponding to a solution, i.e a set of instances whose constrained attribute values appear in a solution). At present, this integration only deals with consistency maintenance.

Finally, as a descriptive tool, constraints are used by two other main features of the model: composite objects and tasks. Thus, shared properties between a composite object and its components are expressed with constraints and, in the task model, equality constraints define the parameter passing between successive tasks [3].

4.6   Related Work

With regard to the integration of constraints in an object world as objects themselves, the principles presented above are more closely related to the ones advocated in the PROSE [1] or PECOS systems than to the representation of constraints chosen in the THINGLAB [2] or GARNET [13] systems.

In THINGLAB, constraints are relations between the parts of objects. A constraint is defined in a class of objects by a rule (a predicate to test whether the constraint is satisfied or not) and a set of methods (to be invoked to satisfy the constraint). Each time an object is created, the constraints of its belonging class are checked. For each unsatisfied constraint, the system tries to restore the relation by invoking the methods in the specified order. In TROPES, a constraint on classes is referred by the name of the class of constraint to instantiate and the attribute parameter to be constrained. The propagation methods are described by the PECOS constraint function.

TROPES also differs from the GARNET prototype-instance system where constraints are declared inside slots (or attributes) as formulas while relations are expressed by special slots (not classes) and serve two purposes: allowing inheritance of slot values (while it can be refined, if needed, by constraints in TROPES) and automatically creating inverse connections.

PROSE is above all an abstract model of constraints representation and manipulation designed for any object-oriented knowledge representation system though two implementations have been written using [4, 6]. This tool box proposes a general representation for constraints based on three classes: Variable, Constraint and Relation, and offers its own satisfaction and consistency maintenance algorithms. The setting-up of a constraint is also done by instantiating the Constraint class, the resulting instance links instances of the Variable class (objects representing the constrained variables) to an instance of the Relation class (which describes the predicate to satisfy and the inference rules for the values of the constrained variables). In TROPES, the Variable class does not exist because the constraint lies directly on the attributes, while a unique TROPES class of constraint groups the information which is distributed in PROSE in the Constraint and Variable classes. Consistency maintenance in TROPES is ensured by the Reasoning Maintenance System and by the TROPES/PECOS interface. Moreover, PROSE does not allow the declaration of constraints on a class which have to be satisfied by every instance.

As we said, PECOS offers oriented-object programming functions, allowing to constrain an object or a class of a LE-LISP object-oriented programming language. As a TROPES object (instance or class) does not correspond to an object of this language, a straight use of PECOS was not possible. Moreover, in PECOS, the setting-up of a constraint must be planned and performed from the definition of the class by specifying which attributes are susceptible to be constrained. In TROPES, the setting-up of constraints between instances does not impose this condition.

4.7   Future Work

A constraint management system is currently developed above the TROPES kernel.

Our conception work must now be carried out towards both the expression and the management of:

1. usual operators (union, intersection, composition, etc.) and properties ((anti) reflexivity, (anti) symmetry, transitivity, etc.) on relations, which are now considered as distinct entities in TROPES. These operators address the definition of a relation from existing relations whereas properties can be seen as meta-constraints on relations. This should lead to the integration of an algebraic query language similar to those used in database management systems.

2. control constraints on relations: Let R be a relation between two classes C and C', I and I' instances of respectively C and C'. One might impose that $\forall$ I, $\forall$ I', I R I', or impose a cardinality constraint on the number of I' $\in$ C' such that I R I' holds, etc.

3. constraints between instances of the same class (which is a particular case of a relation):

Let I and I' be two instances of a class C. One might impose that $\forall$ I, $\forall$ I', I $\neq$ I', I.attr Δ I'.attr, where Δ is an operator of comparison.

This kind of constraints introduces a notion of order between instances which is a useful feature in a temporal reasoning or in temporal constraints problems.

4. Constraints of evolution which oblige any new attribute value to satisfy a relation with regard to the previous value.

5. hierarchies of relations as it is suggested in [15]. Two semantics can be granted (see Example. 4.3.3)

The Father/Son relation can be seen as a sub-relation of the Father/Child relation (as a son is a child).

The Father/Son relation between the 'Men' class and the 'Boys' class can be seen as a sub-relation of the Father/Son relation considered on the unique class 'Human-Male' as the latter is a super class of both the 'Men' class and the 'Boys' class.

By specialization, the set of constraints associated with a relation should be inherited or reinforced in its sub-relations.

Finally, the interface TROPES/PECOS will have to exploit further the non deterministic programming mode. In particular, a domain enumeration can lead to an attempt of constraint resolution and, if it succeeds, to a hypothetical reasoning by creating the (hypothetical) instances containing the attribute values satisfying the network of constraints, in order to pursue and observe the parallel evolutions of a knowledge base.

4.8 Conclusion

TROPES is an object-based knowledge representation into which constraints are a declarative means for expressing relations both inside and between objects while constraint maintenance offers an inference mechanism based on a value propagation.

The constraint representation is devoted to TROPES classes, allowing the declaration, the setting-up, the modification and the deletion of a TROPES constraint by the classical object manipulation primitives of the model.

The constraint maintenance is delegated to PECOS, a constraint programming library, the trades off (the translation of the TROPES constraints in PECOS ones, the interpretation of the PECOS constraint satisfaction results) are directed by an interface linking the two systems.

This integration extends the range of expressible problems in offering a declarative way to maintain the consistency of new links between objects. It adds a new description level to the class entity in allowing the expression of properties about some attributes which must be satisfied by any instance of the class. Constraints can also be set upon an arbitrary set of instances, at any moment. Finally, composite objects and tasks, two other features of TROPES also benefit from the constraint maintenance.

Our research must now be directed towards both the concept of relation (operators, properties, query language, specialization), and the management of a hypothetical reasoning benefiting from the PECOS non deterministic primitives to explore different configurations (solution spaces) of a knowledge base.

4.9   REFERENCES

[1] P. Berlandier. *Étude de mécanismes d'interprétation de contraintes et de leur intégration dans un système à base de connaissances (in French)*. Phd-thesis, University of Nice Sophia Antipolis, France, 1992.

[2] A. Borning. The programming language aspects of THINGLAB, a constraint-oriented simulation laboratory. *ACM Transactions on Programming Languages and Systems*, 3(4):353–387, 1981.

[3] J. Gensel, P. Girard, and O. Schmeltzer. Integrating constraints, composite objects and tasks in a knowledge representation system. In IEEE Computer Society Press, editor, *Fifth IEEE International Conference on Tools with Artificial Intelligence*, pages 127–130, Cambridge (Boston), MA, USA, November 1993.

[4] ILOG S.A., Gentilly, France. SMECI *Version 1.3, User's Reference Manual*, 1988.

[5] ILOG S.A., Gentilly, France. LE-LISP *Version 15.24, User's Reference Manual*, 1991.

[6] ILOG S.A., Gentilly, France. LE-LISP *Version 16.01, User's Reference Manual*, 1992.

[7] ILOG S.A., Gentilly, France. PECOS *Version 1.1, User's Reference Manual*, 1992.

[8] V. Kumar. Algorithms for constraint satisfaction problems: A survey. *AI Magazine*, 13(1):32–44, 1992.

[9] A. K. Mackworth. Consistency in networks of relations. *Artificial Intelligence*, 8(1):99–118, 1977.

[10] O. Mariño. Classification d'objets composites dans un système de représentation de connaissances multi-points de vue (in french). In AFCET, editor, *Huitième Congrès Reconnaissance des Formes et Intelligence Artificielle RFIA '91*, pages 233–242, Lyon, France, November 1991.

[11] O. Mariño, F. Rechenmann, and P. Uvietta. Multiple perspectives and classification mechanisms in object-oriented representation. In L. C. Aiello, editor, *Ninth European Conference on Artificial Intelligence ECAI'90*, pages 425–430. Stockholm, Sweden, August 1990.

[12] U. Montanari. Networks of constraints: Fundamental properties and applications to picture processing. *Information Science*, 7:95–132, 1974.

[13] B. A. Myers, D. A. Giuse, and B. Vander Zanden. Declarative programming in a prototype-instance system: Object-oriented programming without writing methodswhout. *ACM Sigplan Notices*, 27(10):184–200, October 1992.

[14] F. Rechenmann, P. Fontanille P., and P. Uvietta. SHIRKA: *système de gestion de bases de connaissances centrées-objets, User's Reference Manual*. INRIA-IMAG, Grenoble, france, 1990.

[15] J. Rumbaugh. Relations as semantic constructs in an object-oriented language. In *OOPSLA '87*, pages 466–481. ACM, October 1987.

5

A CLP Approach for Examination Planning

Patrice Boizumault
Yan Delon
Laurent Péridy[1]

ABSTRACT In this chapter, we present an application of Constraint Logic Programming to the examination planning problem of our University. Each year, in June, 4000 students of various branches of instruction have to attend examination during a couple of weeks for academic reasons. The problem (for June 1993) consists of planning 308 different examinations on 33 half-days over 7 rooms of different capacities. A set of different and various constraints has to be satisfied. This problem has been identified by operations researchers as a scheduling problem with disjunctive and cumulative conjunctive constraints and classified as NP-complete (using a naive enumeration would lead to consider $(7 * 33)^{308}$ possibilities). The solution has been reached using the finite domains of CHIP. We have developed two versions of the application: one using Chipv3, and one using Chipv4 which owns special kinds of new constraints like the cumulative constraint. After having described the specific problem of our university, we will present the two developments and compare them. Finally, we will illustrate the huge capacity of prototyping and implementation of real-life applications in Constraint Logic Programming.

5.1 Introduction

Most educational institutions must schedule a set of examinations at the end of each session or year. In its simplest form, the problem can be defined as assigning a set of examinations to a fixed number of time periods so that no student is required to take more than one examination at any time. Over the last 30 years, various systems have been developed in different universities in order to solve this problem [31], [14], [7], [13], [29], [18]. All these proposals are related to a particular examinations planning, and are implemented by mixing various Operations Research (O.R.) technics

---

[1]Institut de Mathématiques Appliquées, Université Catholique de l'Ouest, 3 Place André Leroy, B. P. 808, 49008 ANGERS Cedex 01, France

(graph coloring, integer programming, heuristics for the knapsack problem, heuristics for the traveling salesman problem, ...) [16], [8]. In fact, classical O.R. approaches cannot be directly applied for this kind of problem. Dedicated algorithms must be conceived and implemented. From a software engineering point of view, the time spent in developing such programs is very important, and adding new constraints may lead to reconsider entirely the retained approach.

In this chapter, we show an application of Constraint Logic Programming to the examination planning problem of our University. Each year, in June, 4000 students of various branches of instruction have to attend examination during a couple of weeks (in fact during 33 half days). The problem (for June 1993) consists of planning 308 different examinations on 33 half-days using 7 rooms of different capacities. A set of various constraints has to be satisfied, and particularly several examinations can be assigned to a same room if they respect the capacity constraint. This problem has been identified by operations researchers as a scheduling problem with "disjunctive" and cumulative conjunctive constraints and classified as NP-complete (using a naive enumeration would lead to consider $(7 * 33)^{308}$ possibilities).

Our solution has been reached using the finite domains of CHIP [20], [12], [10]. We have developed two versions of the application: one using Chipv3, and one using Chipv4 which owns special kinds of new constraints like the cumulative constraint. First, we give a brief overview of O.R. approaches for solving the examination time-tabling problem. Then, after having described the specific problem of our university, we present our two developments and compare them. Finally, we illustrate the huge capacity of prototyping and implementation of real-life applications in Constraint Logic Programming [26], [27].

5.2   A Brief Overview of O.R. Approaches

In this section, we give an overview of O.R. approaches for solving the examination timetabling problem. First, we describe a solution to the simplified problem using graph coloring. Then we describe various applications that have been realised in different universities. Finally, we discuss the adequacy of O.R. for solving such problems.

5.2.1   SIMPLIFIED PROBLEM

In its simplest form, the problem can be defined as assigning a set of examinations to a fixed number of time periods so that no student is required to take more than one examination at any time. This problem is structurally similar to the vertex coloring problem studied extensively in the literature on graph theory [17]: each course is represented by a vertex, and an edge connects two vertices if the corresponding courses have at least one student in common and, hence, cannot be scheduled at the same time period. This problem (although NP Complete) is solved quite efficiently by Operations Research [17].

But practical examination timetabling problems differ from graph coloring problems [8] because they must take into account various kinds of constraints such:

- a limit on the number of students and/or examinations in any one period;

- room capacity constraints: (each examination is assigned to a particular room),

- consecutive examination constraints: (certain exams must occur in adjacent time periods),

- non consecutive conflict constraints: (no examinations in succession for any student),

- preassignments: (certain examinations are preassigned to specific periods),

- exclusions and time preferences: (certain examinations are excluded from particular periods)

- each student's examinations should be spread over the examination period.

These constraints are not required in all examination timetabling problems, and are specific to particular academic institutions. So, dedicated algorithms must be conceived in order to solve each type of examination timetabling problems.

5.2.2 VARIOUS APPLICATIONS

In this section, we give an overview of three systems that have been implemented in different universities. For more details, see [8] which gives a survey on examination timetabling problems.

In 1968, Wood devised an examination scheduling algorithm that was implemented at the University of Manchester (England). His primary concern [31] was that examinations had to be scheduled into a set of designated rooms. Moreover, he tried to minimize the number of conflicts (no consecutive examinations on the same day for any student). For this, Wood implemented a look-ahead algorithm, and assigned the selected room with the "closest fit", namely the least acceptable number of places. When his algorithm failed, Wood claimed that inspection of the conflict pattern related to the unscheduled courses "clearly" reveal the subjects which cause the difficulty. These subjects are preassigned manually and the algorithm is repeated.

In 1978, Carter developed an algorithm for final examination scheduling at the University of Waterloo (Canada). This system has been extended in 1985 for scheduling all area high school examinations. The basic algorithm uses graph coloring technics and integrates the ability to take into account preferred constraints as several courses must be preassigned to fixed time periods or no student should be required to sit for three or more consecutive exams.

In 1978, Desroches, Laporte and Rousseau presented the system HOREX, an appellation derived from the French "Horaire" for timetable. Their method consisted of the following general steps: first, they find p sets of non-conflicting examinations, where p is the number of period (graph coloring algorithm); then they combine these sets in order to have a minimum number of students having two examinations the same day (branch and bound code for integer linear programming); in order to maximize the number of examinations scheduled in the morning, they use a heuristic for the knapsack problem; the days are finally ordered using a traveling salesman problem heuristic in order to minimize the number of "successions" in which a student must take examinations on consecutive days.

5.2.3   ADEQUACY FOR EXAMINATION TIMETABLING PROBLEMS

As previously seen, an examination timetabling problem is very related to a particular academic institution. In each case, very specific constraints must be taken into account. Moreover, classical O.R. technics cannot be directly applied for this kind of problem. Dedicated algorithms must be conceived and implemented. From a software engineering point of view, the time spent in developing such programs is very important, and adding new constraints may lead to reconsider entirely the retained approach.

5.3   Problem Statement

Each year, in June, 4000 students of various branches of instruction have to attend examination during a couple of weeks for academic reasons (in fact during 33 half days). The problem for June 1993 consists of planning 308 different examinations on 33 half-days. For this, 7 rooms of various capacity can be used. Some rooms are not available every half-day, and moreover, several examinations can be assigned to a same room. This latter constraint differentiates our problem from that reviewed in section 2, for which each examination owned its proper room.

A set of different and various constraints has to be satisfied. We have classified these constraints in twelve categories according to their implementation in CHIP:

- C0, fixed date: the date of the examination is imposed.

- C1, 3 other universities depend on the university located in Angers. This creates some time constraints concerning the examination organization.

- C2, special orals: some examinations have to be planned very quickly because of the possibility of special orals. Notice that orals are managed independently by each department.

- C3, release date, due date: some examinations have to start after a release date and to finish before a due date.

- C4, examination incompatibilities: a student cannot attend several examinations at a time.

- C5, examination and half-day incompatibilities: some examinations cannot be planned on some particular half-days.

- C6, coupling: some examinations have to be planned on two consecutive half-days.

- C7, discoupling: some examinations have to be planned on different days: a time lag of k half-days must be left between two given examinations. Moreover, we know the precedence between the two examinations.

- C8, precedence constraints: an examination has to be planned obligatorily before another one.

- C9, time constraints concerning rooms: a four hours examination cannot take place in a room available only 3 hours.

- C10, room availability: several examinations can be assigned to the same room if they satisfy the capacity constraint.

- C11, priority is given to high capacity rooms. So examinations should preferably assigned to the rooms with the highest capacities.

Notice that the first eleven kinds of constraints are imperative ones, but the twelfth constraint can be considered as a preference one.

5.4   A Brief Overview of CHIP

CHIP (Constraint Handling In Prolog) is a Constraint Logic Programming language conceived at E.C.R.C. and now developed and distributed by Cosytec SA. CHIP owns three domains of constraints: finite domain terms, boolean terms and rational terms. In this chapter, we only use constraints over finite domains.

5.4.1   NUMERICAL CONSTRAINT HANDLING

Each constrained variable has a domain (set of scalar values) which must be declared a priori. CHIP provides three kinds of linear constraints: equality, disequalities, and inequality. Each one can be applied on linear terms built upon domain variables and constants.

5.4.2   SYMBOLIC CONSTRAINT HANDLING

CHIP also handles symbolic constraints. A very useful symbolic constraint is `element(N, List, Value)`. It specifies, as an internal system constraint, that the `Nth` element of the list `List` must have the value `Value`. `List` is a non empty list of natural numbers and `Value` is either a natural number, a domain variable or a free variable.

The most interesting use of the constraint `element/3` is when `N` or `Value` are domain variables. Therefore as soon as the domains of `N` or `Value` change, a new constraint is dynamically added and inconsistent values are removed from domains. CHIP provides also the `at_most/3` (`at_least/3`) constraints which enable to impose that at most (at least) `N` elements of a list `List` have the value `Value`.

5.4.3   THE CUMULATIVE CONSTRAINT

The cumulative constraint has been introduced in Chipv4 in order to solve scheduling and placement problems [1]. The `cumulative` constraint owns 8 arguments:

```
cumulative(LStarts, LDurations, LResources, ?, ?, High, ?, ?)
```

We have only mentioned the four parameters which have been used for solving our problem.

This constraint is usually presented taking a scheduling problem as example. Let us consider to schedule n tasks of known duration, and each task consuming a certain amount of an available resource. The cumulative constraint states that, at any instant t of the schedule, the summation of the amount of resource of the tasks that overlap t does not exceed the maximal amount of available resource.

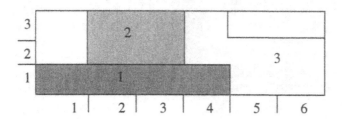

FIGURE 5.1. cumulative([1,2,4], [4,2,3], [1,2,2], 3)

- Let ListStarts = [S1, ...,Sn] be the list of the starting dates of each task ti, i in [1..n];

- Let ListDurations = [D1, ...,Dn] be the list of the duration of the tasks ti, i in [1..n];

- Let ListResources = [R1, ...,Rn] be the list of the amount of resource required by the tasks ti, i in [1..n];

- Let a = minimum(min(S1), ...,min(Sn)), and b = maximum(max(S1) + max(D1), ..., max(Sn) + max(Dn)); a is the smallest release date and b the largest due date of the schedule;

- Let High be the upper limit of the amount of available resource;

The following constraints are then enforced:

1. $\forall i \in [1..n], D_i > 0$,

2. $\forall i \in [1..n], R_i > 0$,

3. $\forall i \; a \leq i \leq b$,

$$max \sum_{j / S_j <= i < S_j + D_j} R_j = High$$

The last constraint specifies that, at any instant i of the schedule, the summation of the required amounts of resource of the tasks that are active (t_j) does not exceed $High$, the maximal quantity of available resource.

Let us consider three major uses of the cumulative constraint [1]:

1. Considering Figure 5.1, there are three tasks to schedule: the first task uses one unit of the resource during four consecutive periods; tasks 2 and 3 use two units during respectively two and three periods. At any time the total amount of resource used by the different tasks is always less then or equal to 3.

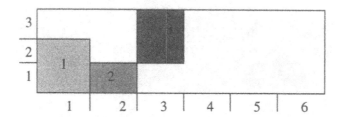

FIGURE 5.2. cumulative([1,2,2], [1,1,1], [2,1,2], 3)

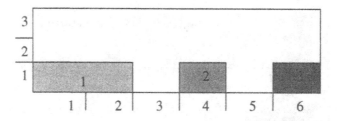

FIGURE 5.3. cumulative([1,4,6], [2,1,1], [1,1,1], 1)

2. For Figure 5.2, all the tasks duration are equal to one. This particular case corresponds to the bin packing problem [28]: m bins of fixed capacities and n objects of fixed size to put in these bins.

3. The third example (see Figure 5.3) forbids to have a cumulative amount of resource greater than 1. This corresponds in scheduling to the problem of two tasks that cannot be executed at the same time because their share the same resource, the so called disjunctive tasks.

5.5   Implementations in CHIP

Our problem fits directly with the finite domains of CHIP. In fact, every examination's date can be represented by a domain variable ranging over the 33 half-days. Each room can be identified by a scalar value ranging from 1 to 7. Morerover, we can naturally express all the constraints of our problem using the numerical and the symbolic constraints over finite domains of CHIP.

The usual development of an application over finite domains consists of modeling the data and the domain variables, thus imposing the constraints, and finally defining the labeling strategy [3]. We follow this pattern in our presentation. We describe the two implementations realised: one with

Chipv3 and one using the cumulative constraint of Chipv4.

5.5.1 MODELLING THE DATA

308 domain variables represent the 308 examinations to plan: L = [T1,...,T308]. The domain of each variable is determined by its release date and due date (data given by the university). The aim is to find, for each domain variable Tj, one half-day which satisfies all the constraints. Moreover, for each examination, we must assign it a room in respect to the capacity constraints.

How several examinations can be planned on the same half-day, it is important to know the cumulative number of students for each room and each half-day. So we use some Prolog terms which represent these informations (list of cumulative numbers for each room and each half-day, ...).

Finally, for each examination the number of students is known (data given by the academic services). The room calendar availability and the list of all the half-days duration are also given by the academic services.

5.5.2 IMPLEMENTING THE CONSTRAINTS

We have classified the various constraints in five categories according to their implementation:

- Constraints directly applied on the domains:

    1. C0 is translated by an equality constraint (40 constraints).

    2. C1, C2, C3 are translated by a restrictive definition of the domains (80 constraints).

- Incompatibility constraints:

    1. C4 is translated by a disequality constraint between two dvars (notice that there are 1930 such constraints).

    2. C5 is translated by a disequality constraint between a dvar and a constant (50 constraints).

- Precedence constraints:

    1. C6 Coupling: equality `Ti = Tj + 1`.

    2. C7 Discoupling: `Ti = Tj + k` (a lag of k half days must be left).

    3. C8 Classical precedence: `Ti + k <= Tj`. (There are 50 constraints of type C6, C7, C8)

- Time constraints: C9 For the `Ti` examination (duration: `DTi`), let `D=[D1,... ,D33]` be the list of the maximum durations of all the half-days. The conjunction: `element(Ti, D, Durat)`,

`DTi <= Durat` of constraints enables to impose time constraints concerning rooms availability. (There are 308 such constraints)

- The capacity constraints C10 et C11 are managed differently in Chipv3 and Chipv4.

5.5.3 IMPLEMENTATION WITH CHIPV3

The labeling stage consists of enumerating the various potential solutions. Obviously, the search space is a priori pruned by the active constraints. We developed various labeling strategies in order to have an efficient resolution of the problem. The constraint C10 concerning the room capacities is verified a posteriori after the labeling stage.

The labeling stage is implemented as follows:

```
labeling([], _).
labeling([T|Ts], Env) :-
      select_var(Var, [T|Ts], Rest, Env),
      select_value(Var, Env),
      select_room(Var, Room),
      verify_c10(Room, Env, NewEnv),
      labeling(Rest, NewEnv).
```

where `Env` mainly describe the list of cumulative number of students by half-day and by room.

- First approach: We select the domain variable Ti with the first-fail heuristic [19]. We instantiate the selected domain variable with the built-in predicate indomain/2. But, at the end of the labeling stage, we could have a set of examinations mutually incompatible and not enough half-days to plan them. This leads to inefficiency with a lot of useless backtracks.

- Second approach: We share out the examinations in order to have a uniform distribution of the cumulative numbers of students on all half-days. We keep the first-fail strategy but, with a user redefined predicate indomain/1, we assign the examinations to the half-days which have the smallest cumulative number of students (best-fit strategy). But, at the end of the labeling stage, some examinations with an important number of students have to be planned and it is not possible to find for them a room with a sufficient capacity.

- Retained approach: We replace the first-fail strategy by a new selection rule of the domain variable to instantiate. We sort the examinations in decreasing order of their number of students; for selecting the value, we keep the best-fit strategy.

Notice that when a Ti is instantiated (an half-day examination has been planned), we select the room which has the smallest capacity and which can accept the selected examination. Notice that this strategy doesn't respect the preference constraint C11.

5.5.4   IMPLEMENTATION WITH CHIPV4

With the cumulative constraint of Chipv4, we can impose the capacity constraint C10 before the labeling, and so get an a priori pruning of the search tree. Our problem can be modeled as a bin packing problem. In fact, we have m ($=7*33$) effective rooms of fixed capacity and n ($=308$) examinations to affect to these rooms. Each examination corresponds to a task of duration 1 consuming an amount of resource equal to its number of students.

We consider the list [S1, ..., S308] of the number of rooms, the list [D1, ..., D308] is of the form [1,..,1] and the list [R1, ..., R308] contains the number of students of each examination. Each Si is a domain variable whose domain is $1..7*33$.

The Si's are linked to the half day Ti and the room S by the fundamental relation $Si=7*(Ti-1)+S$. So, the constraint C10 can be stated as follows: cumulative([S1,...,S308], [1,....,1],[R1,...,R308],?,?,370,?,?) where 370 is the capacity of the largest room. The capacity constraints are now taken into account a priori.

This simple implementation would be sufficient if all the rooms would have the same capacity. But this was not the case. In order to solve this problem, we introduce virtual examinations in order to simulate an identical behavior of the rooms. For each room S, we introduce a virtual examination with an effective of 370 minus the capacity of S. With these extra examinations, we can now tackle uniformly the various rooms.

The labeling stage is now implemented as follows:

```
labeling([], _).
labeling([T|Ts], Env) :-
    select_var(Var, [T|Ts], Rest, Env),
    select_value(Var, Env),
    select_room(Var, Room, Env, NewEnv),
    labeling(Rest, NewEnv).
```

The main difference is that the capacity constraints are managed a priori thanks to the cumulative constraint.

We tried various labeling strategies. The first one corresponds to the standard first- fail strategy. The second one consists in sorting the examinations by their decreasing number of students, and then to affect each examination to the half day with the smallest cumulative number of students (best fit strategy). Then, we choose for the examination the largest available room in respect to the constraint C11.

5.6   Results

5.6.1   EFFICIENCY RESULTS

For June 93, we have about 2600 constraints, and we found a solution with 28 half days (which is less than the 33 half days imposed by the academic services). We can also prove that there is no solution under 28 half days in less than 10 seconds.

Then, we tested our various approaches on three kinds of datas : test1 are data for June 93, test2 (reps. test3) is June 93 where the number of students of each examination has been augmented by 5 (resp. 10). The computing times are given in seconds for the labeling stage on an IBM RS6000. Imposing the constraints takes 12s with Chipv3 and 18s with Chipv4. "no sol" indicates that we don't get any solution in 60 hours of computing time.

Results for the initial problem	test1	test2	test3
V3: First-Fail	41	no sol	no sol
V3: FF+Best Fit	28	no sol	no sol
V3: Decreasing+Best Fit	26	no sol	no sol
V4: First Fail	18	20	no sol
V4: Deacreasing+Best Fit	22	19	17

With Chipv3, the best fit heuristic give better results, but we don't get any solution with test2 and test3. With Chipv4, the cumulative constraint prunes a priori the search tree and gives better results. Moreover, we see that developing an "intelligent" labeling strategy is an important fact when using constraint logic programming over finite domains.

5.6.2   SOFTWARE ENGINEERING CONSIDERATIONS

We spent a couple of weeks to solve this real-life problem with Chipv3, The code (without the constraints which are stored in separate files) is about 200 lines. It necessitates 3 days to adapt the program to the requirements of the cumulative constraint. This proves the quality of software engineering development in Constraint Logic Programming Languages [2], [5], [26], [27], [9].

5.7   Adding Preference Constraints

The academic secretary has run the program and got the solutions as previously described. But, for important groups of students, the planning of their examinations was very near. They had by example two examinations planned on the same day. So the responsibles of each department decided to define the notion of "heavy examination", which corresponded to an important course. Then they asked not to plan two heavy examinations on two consecutive half days (this lead to 600 preference constraints).

This lead us to tackle with preference constraints of the form $Ti \geq Tj + 2$ or $Tj \geq Ti + 2$, which are called disjunctive constraints in the CLP community. First, we will describe the implementation of the disjunctions, and then discuss the problem of taking into account preference constraints.

5.8   Implementing Disjunctive Constraints

There are several ways to handle, with more or less efficiency, disjunctive constraints in CHIPv4 [5]. Let us consider two tasks Ti and Tj of duration Di and Dj which cannot be managed at the same time.

The first way is to introduce a choice point:

```
disjunctive(Ti,Di,Tj,Dj) :-
    Ti #>=Tj+Dj.
disjunctive(Ti,Di,Tj,Dj) :-
    Tj #>=Ti+Di.
```

This leads to a lot of inefficiency because the disjunction is not considered as a constraint. A lot of choice points are introduced and useless backtrackings occur. For our problem, such an implementation would lead to 2^{600} alternatives!

The second way if to use demons which implement conditional propagation:

```
disjunctive(T1, D1, T2, D2) :-
    if T1+D1 > T2 then T2+D2 <= T1,
    if T2+D2 > T1 then T1+D1 <= T2.
```

This implementation is more efficient, but is to weak to wake the constraints and prune the search tree.

The third way, is to use the cumulative constraint:

```
disjunctive(T1, D1, T2, D2) :-
    cumulative([T1,T2], [D1,D2], [1,1], 1).
```

We first tried to implement the preference constraints with the cumulative primitive, and we didn't get good results. In fact, the pruning realised was not enough efficient.

Finally, taking into account that the constraint was symmetrical ($|Ti - Tj| \geq 2$), we used the constraint **distance/4** of Chipv4 to implement the preference constraints. The constraint distance(X,Y,Op,K) states that $|X - Y|$ Op K, namely for us distance(Ti,Tj,>=,2). This led to very good results (a labeling in 25s for June 93 taking into account the 600 preference constraints). In fact, the **distance/4** constraint realise, in this case, a better pruning of the search tree.

There are other ways to tackle efficiently disjunctive constraints. In cc(FD) [21], the cardinality operator enables to impose that at least n and at most m constraints of the set of constraints must be verified. So, a disjunction may be specified as follow:

```
disjunctive(T1, D1, T2, D2) :-
    #(1, _, [T1>=T2+D2, T2>=T1+D1]).
```

Finally, another way to implement efficiently disjunctions is the notion of constructive disjunction proposed by P. Van Hentenryck [22], [23].

5.8.1 TAKING INTO ACCOUNT PREFERENCE CONSTRAINTS

In order to test the robustness of our approach, we run our software on one hundred benchmarks constituted by the datas of June 93 where the effective of each examination has been modified by +/- 10 percents.

On 100 tests, we got 55 answers in less than 20s of labeling time, taking into account the initial constraints plus the whole preference ones (3200 constraints). For the other 45 tests, we didn't get any answer in 5 mns of cpu time. In fact, for these tests experimentation shows that it would suffice to relax two or three constraints in order to solve efficiently the problem.

We have not yet in CHIP the ability to implement this treatment. Moreover, we cannot hierarchize the constraints as in HCLP(R) [6], because there are all at the same level. Proposals have been done for time-tabling problems: in [24] the system IHCS written in C enables to hierarchize constraints and implements an automatic relaxation using intelligent backtracking; in [11], X. Cousin proposes also a way to relax constraints and integrates this with CLEF, a CLP system written in Lisp [25].

We are currently developing a heuristic in order to manage such preference constraints. First, we impose the imperative constraints, and then we are trying to built sets of preference constraints which are inter-related, thus imposing then incrementally and finally exhibiting the problematic ones.

5.9   Extensions and Further Works

Our experience shows that the CLP programmer needs high level primitives to express its particular constraints (see cumulative/8 or distance/4). Such primitives must be efficiently implemented in order to reduce significantly the search space.

Our experience shows the importance of an intelligent labeling strategy. As quoted by E. Tsang, one important issue is the ordering in which the variables are labeled and the ordering in which the values are assigned to each variable. Decisions in these orderings could affect the efficiency of the search strategies significantly [30]. Another way to introduce more informations into the system is to add redundant constraints [20], [15], but this was not necessary and not adapted to our problem.

Our experience points out the importance of introducing the relaxation of constraints in CLP. Most real life problems (time tabling by example) induce imperative constraints and preference constraints. But with the CLP tools available today, we cannot efficiently tackle constraint hierarchization and constraint relaxation.

Finally our experience illustrates the huge capacity of prototyping and implementation of real-life applications in constraint logic programming. [2] We can solve problems with more than 3200 constraints. Moreover, The conciseness of the programs and the short development times lead us to develop rapidly alternative versions. Indeed, various heuristics have been developed, tested and validated in a very short development time.

Acknowledgements: We thank E. Pinson, M. Dincbas, M. Rueher for their fruitful comments. A preliminary version of this paper has been presented at 2nd International Conference on Practical Applications of Prolog [4].

5.10 REFERENCES

[1] A. Aggoun and N. Beldiceanu. Extending Chip in order to solve complex scheduling and placement problems. In *Journées francophones de la programmation en logique*, Lille, 1992.

[2] J. Bellone, A. Chamard, and C. Pradelles. Plane: An evolutive system for aircraft production written in Chip. In *First Int. Conference on Practical Applications of Prolog*, London, 1992.

[3] P. Boizumault, Y. Delon, and L. Péridy. Solving a real life exams problem using Constraint Logic Programming. In Manfred Meyer, editor, *Constraint Processing: Proceedings of the international workshop at CSAM'93*, DFKI Document D-94-13, German Research Center for Artificial Intelligence, Kaiserslautern, Germany, 1993.

[4] P. Boizumault, Y. Delon, and L. Péridy. Planning exams using Constraint Logic Programming. In *Second Int. Conference on Practical Applications of Prolog*, London, 1994.

[5] P. Baptiste, B. Legeard, and C. Varnier. Hoist scheduling problem: an approach based on Constraint Programming. In *IEEE International Conference on Robotics and Automation*, Nice, 1992.

---

[2] It is important to notice that the resolution of this real-life problem does not imply the systematic resolution of the general problem noticed in the introduction (scheduling problem with disjunctive and cumulative conjunctive constraints which is NP-Complete).

[6] A. Borning, M. Maher, A. Martingale, and M. Wilson. Constraint hierarchies and Logic Programming. In *Sixth Int. Logic Programming Conference*, Lisboa, 1989.

[7] A. M. Barham and J. B. Westwood. A simple heuristic to facilitate course time-tabling. *Journal of Operational Research Society*, 29, 1978.

[8] M. W. Carter. A survey of pratical applications of examination timetabling algorithms. *Operations Research*, 24(2), 1986.

[9] A. Chamard and A. Fischler. A workshop scheduler written in Chip. In *Second Int. Conference on Practical Applications of Prolog*, London, 1994.

[10] Cosytec SA, Orsay, France. *Chip user's guide*, 1993.

[11] X. Cousin. *Applications de la Programmation en Logique avec Contraintes au problème d'emploi du temps*. PhD thesis, Rennes University, France, 1993.

[12] M. Dincbas, P. Van Hentenryck, H. Simonis, A. Aggoun, T. Graf, and F. Berthier. The Constraint Logic Programming language Chip. In *International Conference on Fifth Generation Computer Systems*, Tokyo, 1988.

[13] S. Desroches and G. Laporte. Examination timetabling by computer. *Operations Research*, 1984.

[14] S. Desroches, G. Laporte, and J.M. Rousseau. Horex: a computer program for the construction of examination schedules. *INFOR 16*, 1978.

[15] M. Dincbas, H. Simonis, and P. Van Hentenryck. Solving large combinatorial problems in Logic Programming. *Journal of Logic Programming*, 8, 1990.

[16] D. de Werra. An introduction to time tabling. *European Journal of Operational Research*, 19, 1985.

[17] D. de Werra. Heuristics for graph coloring. *Computing Suppl.*, 7, 1990.

[18] R. Feldman and M. Golumbic. Optimization algorithms for student scheduling via constraint satisfiability. *The Computer Journal*, 33(4), 1990.

[19] R. Harralick and G. Elliot. Increasing tree search efficiency for Constraint Satisfaction Problems. *Artificial Intelligence*, 14, 1980.

[20] P. Van Hentenryck. *Constraint Satisfaction in Logic Programming*. MIT Press, 1989.

[21] P. Van Hentenryck. The cardinality operator : a new logical connective for Constraint Logic Programming. In *Eigth Int. Logic Programming Conference*, Paris, 1991.

[22] P. Van Hentenryck. Scheduling and packing in the constraint language cc(FD). Technical report, CS Department, Brown University, 1992.

[23] P. Van Hentenryck, V. Saraswat, and Y. Deville. Implementation and evaluation of the constraint language cc(FD). Technical report, CS Department, Brown University, 1992.

[24] F. Menez, P. Barahona, and P. Codognet. An incremental constraint solver applied to a time-tabling problem. In *thirteenth conference on expert systems*, Avignon France, 1993.

[25] J. P. Le Pape and D. Ranson. Clef or programming with constraints, logic, equations and functions. In *4th Int. Conference on Software Engineering and its Applications*, Toulouse, France, 1991.

[26] M. Rueher and B. Legeard. Which role for CLP in software engineering? an investigation on the basis of first applications. In *First International Conference on Practical Applications of Prolog*, London, 1992.

[27] M. Rueher. A first exploration of PrologIII's capabilities. *Software-Practice and Experience*, 23(2), 1993.

[28] Rayward Smit and Shing. Bin packing. *Bulletin of the IMA*, 19, 1983.

[29] A. Tripathy. School timetabling: a case in large binary integer linear programming. *Management Science*, 13(12), 1984.

[30] E. Tsang. *Foundations of Constraint Satisfaction*. Academic Press, 1993.

[31] D. C. Wood. A system for computing university examination timetables. *Computer Journal*, 11, 1968.

6

The Many Paths to Satisfaction

Eugene C. Freuder[1]

ABSTRACT Constraint satisfaction problems can be represented in may different ways. Here a single, simple problem is approached from a variety of perspectives.

6.1 Introduction

When I was asked to give a talk at the ECAI'94 Workshop on Constraint Processing, it occurred to me that the participants could arrive speaking many languages. I am not referring to languages like French and English, or even languages like Lisp and Prolog. Constraint satisfaction problems can be represented in the languages of many different research communities.

I felt that it might be helpful to put together a kind of Rosetta stone for constraint satisfaction, by representing a single simple problem in many different ways. The figures that follow are the result of that effort.

While obviously they have limited value on their own, it is hoped that collected here together they might:

- initiate exploration

- facilitate comparison

- encourage cross-fertilization.

I want to emphasize that this listing is *not*:

- exhaustive: it does not cover all approaches

- comprehensive: it does not cover alternatives within a given approach

- a survey: it merely provides a single pointer into each literature.

Constraint satisfaction problems involve finding *values* for problem *variables* subject to *constraints* that specify which combinations of values are

---

[1]Department of Computer Science, University of New Hampshire, Durham, NH 03824 USA, e-mail: ecf@cs.unh.edu

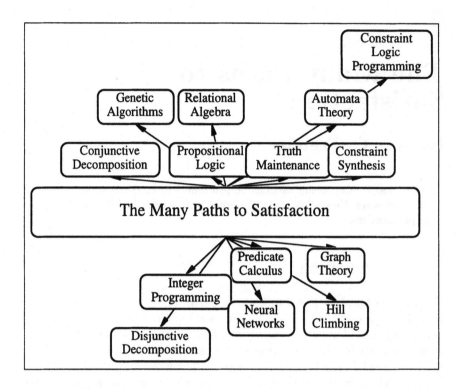

allowed. I use throughout a simple map coloring example in which the variables are countries, the values are colors and the constraints specify that the countries sharing a border cannot have the same color.

It is fascinating both how many applications there are for this simple problem solving paradigm, and how many approaches there are to solving these problems. The first step in finding a solution is problem representation. Once a problem is represented as, e.g. a problem in logic or graph theory, then the problem solving tools of that discipline can be brought to bear.

My focus here is on representation, and I represent the same, simple coloring problem in over a dozen different ways. After an intial introduction as a constraint network, we view our coloring problem as a problem in:

- Predicate Calculus (Figure 6.2)

- Propositional Logic (Figure 6.3)

- Truth Maintenance (Figure 6.4)

- Integer Programming (Figure 6.5)

- Automata Theory (Figure 6.6)

- Graph Theory (Figure 6.7)

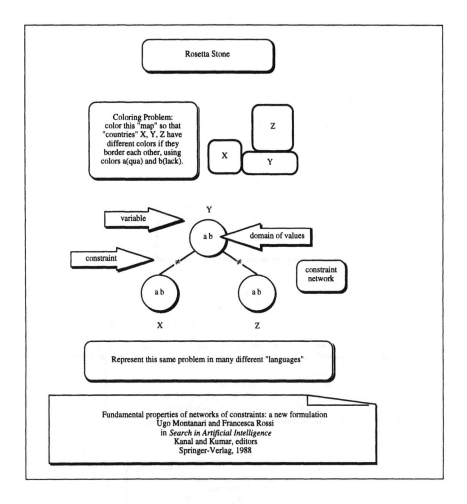

FIGURE 6.1. The Rosetta Stone for Constraint Satisfaction

- Hill Climbing (Figure 6.8)

- Neural Networks (Figure 6.9)

- Genetic Algorithms (Figure 6.10)

- Relational Algebra (Figure 6.11)

- Constraint Synthesis (Figure 6.12)

- Disjunctive Decomposition (Figure 6.13)

- Conjunctive Decomposition (Figure 6.14)

- Constraint Logic Programming (Figure 6.15)

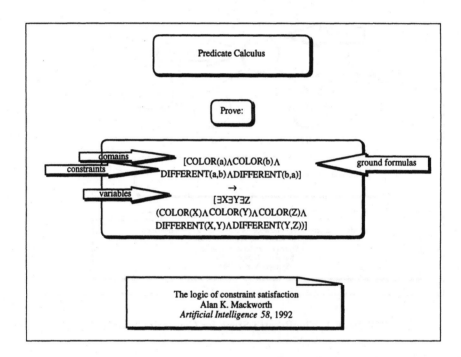

FIGURE 6.2. Predicate Calculus

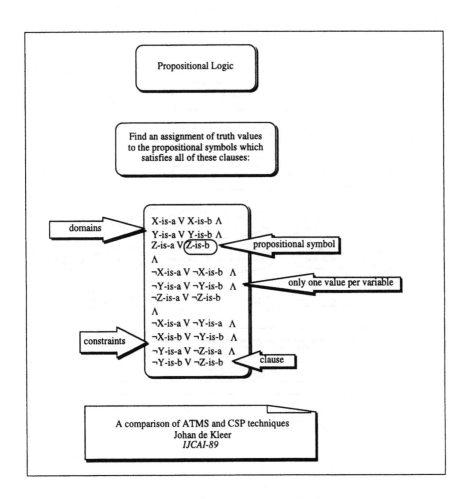

FIGURE 6.3. Propositional Logic

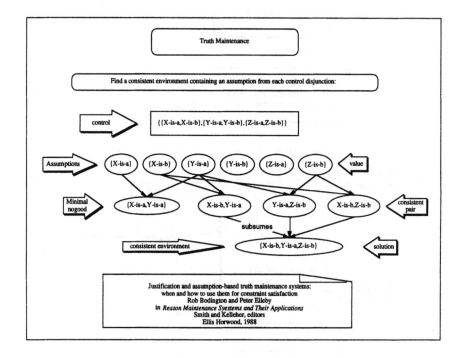

FIGURE 6.4. Truth Maintenance

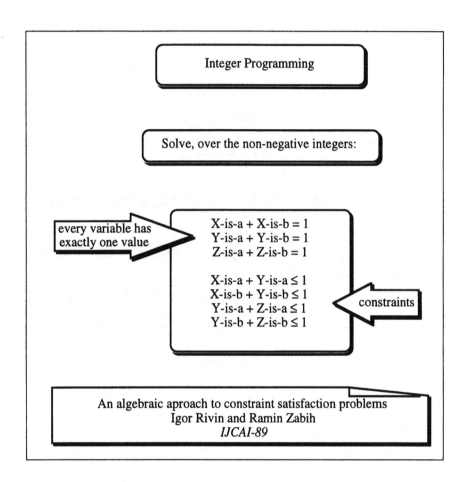

FIGURE 6.5. Integer Programming

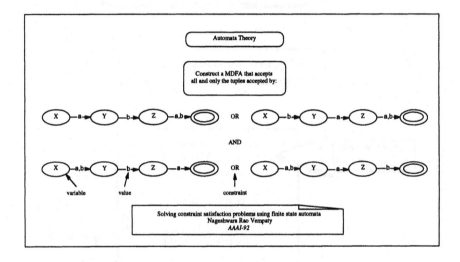

FIGURE 6.6. Automata Theory

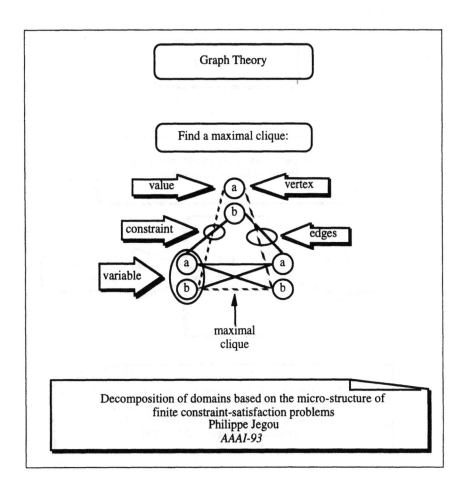

FIGURE 6.7. Graph Theory

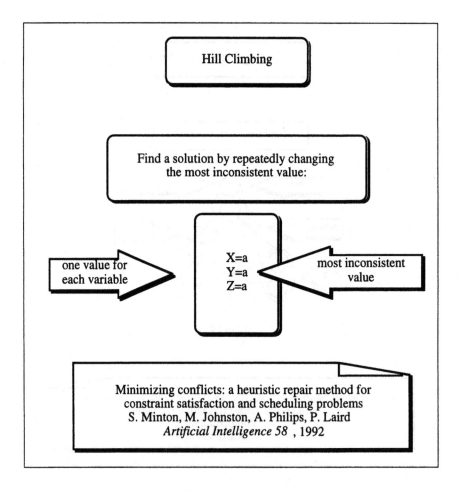

FIGURE 6.8. Hill Climbing

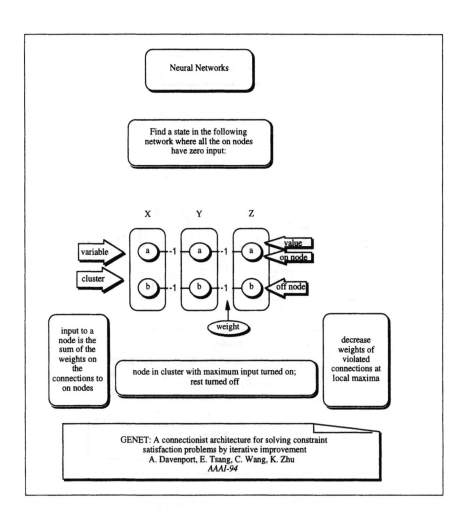

FIGURE 6.9. Neural Networks

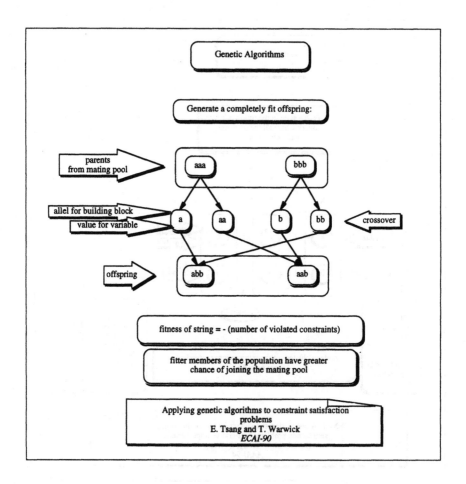

FIGURE 6.10. Genetic Algorithms

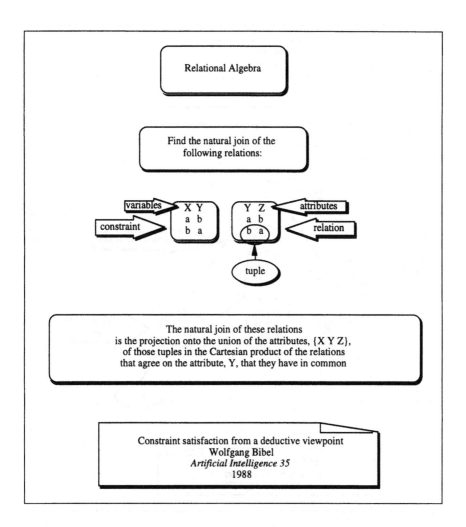

FIGURE 6.11. Relational Algebra

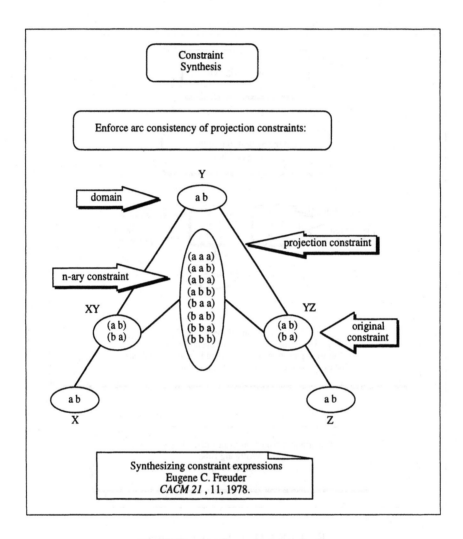

FIGURE 6.12. Constraint Synthesis

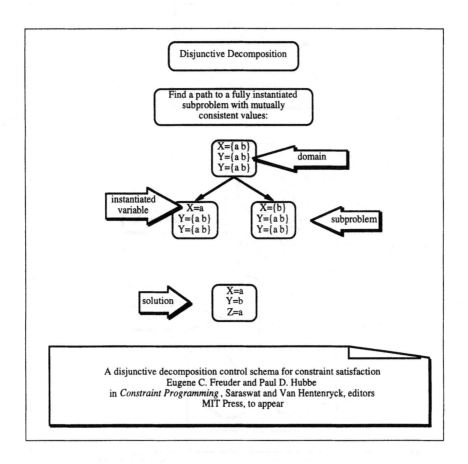

FIGURE 6.13. Disjunctive Decomposition

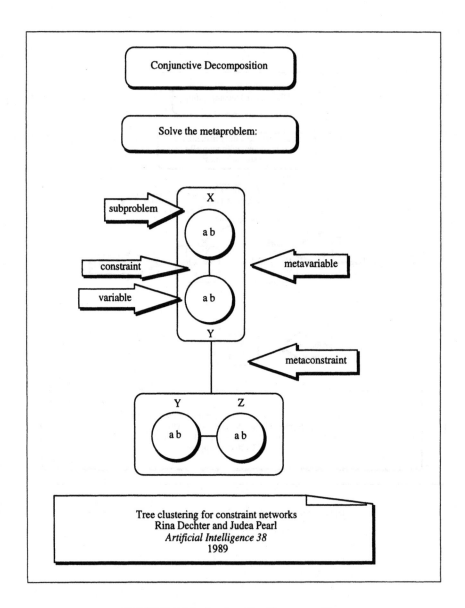

FIGURE 6.14. Conjunctive Decomposition

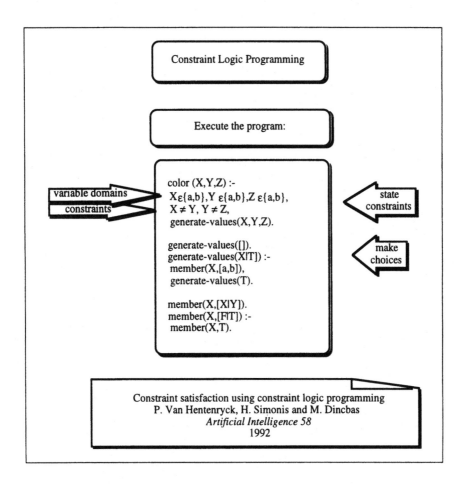

FIGURE 6.15. Constraint Logic Programming

Acknowledgements: This material is based on work supported by the National Science Foundation under Grant No. IRI-9207633.

7

Directed Arc Consistency Preprocessing

Richard J. Wallace[1]

ABSTRACT A constraint satisfaction problem (CSP) may be overconstrained and not admit a complete solution. Optimal solutions to such partial constraint satisfaction problems (PCSPs), in which a maximum number of constraints are satisfied, can be found using branch and bound variants of CSP algorithms. Earlier work has shown how information gained through local consistency checking during preprocessing can be used to enhance search through value ordering heuristics and local lower bound calculations that involve only neighboring variables. The present work describes a family of strategies based on *directed* arc consistency testing during preprocessing. With this approach inconsistency counts associated with each value (the number of domains that offer no support for that value) are obtained that are non-redundant, since they are unidirectional. They can, therefore, be used to obtain global lower bounds that involve the entire set of variables. By computing directed arc consistency in each direction, full arc- inconsistency counts can also be obtained, thus retaining the benefits of full arc consistency checking, while improving lower bound calculations. Retrospective and prospective algorithms that incorporate the results of directed arc consistency checking are described. Tests with random problems show improvements, sometimes marked, over the best branch and bound PCSP algorithms heretofore described.

7.1 Introduction

Constraint satisfaction problems (CSPs) involve assigning values to variables which satisy a set of constraints. A partial constraint satisfaction problem (PCSP) is one that is 'overconstrained', so there is no assignment that can satisfy all its constraints. In this case it may still be useful to have an assignment of values to variables that satisfies as many constraints as possible.

The need for good partial solutions to unsolvable CSPs has been noted in several areas of application, e. g., various kinds of scheduling problems

---

[1] Computer Science Department University of New Hampshire Durham, NH 03824 USA, e-mail: rjw@cs.unh.edu

([2]; [5]; [6]), interface management ([1]), and crop rotation ([3]). Indeed, such applications may be more common than those in which a complete solution can be obtained.

The focus of the present work is on complete methods, which, in contrast to heuristic methods, can provide solutions to a given problem that are *guaranteed to be optimal* . In this paper optimality refers to the number of satisfied constraints, so an optimal solution is one in which the number of satisfied constraints is maximal. In this case, therefore, complete algorithms solve the maximal constraint satisfaction problem or MAX-CSP. In recent years complete algorithms have been developed for MAX-CSPs that are based on branch and bound methods ([8]; [11]).

Complete algorithms are the procedures of choice if problems are small enough that all or most can be solved quickly through this approach. These methods are also needed for evaluation of the goodnes of results returned by heuristic methods, and they can be used to obtain accurate sample statistics for sets of problems, such as average number of constraint violations and average number of optimal solutions. With more efficient algorithms of this type, we can extend the range of problems in which all instances can be solved to optimality in a reasonable amount of time.

The best procedures for solving ordinary CSPs use techniques for establishing local consistency, before search begins as well as during the search process ([9] [10]). Unfortunately, one cannot establish local consistency for PCSPs in the same fashion, since values cannot be discarded simply because they are inconsistent. Nonetheless, preprocessing strategies have been devised that are based on the same local consistency tests as with CSPs, and that provide information that can enhance the efficiency of subsequent search ([8]). All of the preprocessing methods described in this paper evaluate arc consistency, i. e., consistency between values in pairs of variables that share a constraint.

A simple procedure of this sort is to make a single pass through the entire set of variables, testing each value for support among the values in related (i. e., constrained) variables; if none of the values of one of these latter variables can support the value tested, this lack of support is tallied. The resulting *inconsistency counts* (or arc consistency counts) can improve the efficiency of search in two ways ([8]):

(i) they can be incorporated into measures that give a minimum cost of using a particular value (in terms of number of violated constraints); values that are clearly too costly can be discarded without further testing,

(ii) they can be used to order values associated with a variable. Values having smaller counts are tried first, since they are more likely to be included in an optimal solution than values with larger counts.

These techniques are relatively cheap compared to hybrid methods that interleave local inconsistency testing with search (e. g., "look ahead by one" in [11]). The major computations are done during a preprocessing step and are polynomial in their time complexity. During search the information obtained during preprocessing can be looked up rather than calculated anew at each step.

One limitation of previous preprocessing techniques is that it is not possible to calculate 'global' lower bounds, i. e., costs based on information from values associated with every variable in the problem. This is because arc consistency counts for values associated with different variables may reflect the same constraint violation, so they cannot be summed. As a result, one must be satisfied with 'local' cost calculations, using single arc consistency counts.

This limitation can be overcome by checking for inconsistency in only one direction, i. e., testing values in variable u for support in variable v, but not testing values in v for support in u. A potential drawback is that the counts will be lower on average. However, that limitation can be overcome by tallying directional counts for both directions separately. Total inconsistency counts can then be obtained by adding directional counts for any value, and global lower bound calculations can be obtained from one or the other set of directional counts.

Directed arc consistency counts are tallied in terms of an initial variable ordering, so that they refer to variables that are before or after the current value in the search order. Moreover, by separating inconsistency tallies into forward and backward counts, one can choose the counts that are likely to give better values for lower bounds at different points in search. This gives rise to a variety of strategies for improving search efficiency, as shown below.

Section 2 presents some background for this work. Section 3 gives a description of the directed arc consistency algorithm, shows how inconsistency counts are incorporated into search algorithms, and describes strategies based on directed arc consistency. Section 4 presents experimental comparisons between these new methods and the best branch and bound algorithms studied in earlier work. Concluding remarks and suggestions for further work are given in Section 5.

7.2   Background: Basic Concepts

A constraint satisfaction problem (CSP) involves assigning values to *variables* that satisfy a set of *constraints* among subsets of these variables. The set of values that can be assigned to one variable is called the *domain* of that variable. In the present work all constraints are binary, i. e., they are based on the Cartesian product of the domains of two variables. A binary CSP is associated with a constraint graph, where nodes represent variables and arcs represent constraints.

CSP algorithms can be divided into two general types. *Retrospective* algorithms compare each value, x, that is assigned to a variable against the values already chosen for other variables, to determine whether x is consistent with past assignments. *Prospective* algorithms compare each assigned value against the domains of the unassigned (or future) variables to determine which of the values in these domains are consistent with the values already assigned. In this way domains can be successively restricted by successive assignments.

Branch and bound algorithms can be based on either retro- or prospective strategies. These algorithms associate each path through a search tree with a cost function that is non-decreasing in the length of the path. Search down a given path can stop when the cost of the partial assignment of values to variables is at least as great as the lowest cost yet found for a full assignment. The latter, therefore, sets an *upper bound* on the cost function. In addition to calculating the cost at a particular node, projected cost can be calculated to produce a higher, and therefore more effective, *lower bound.* The present algorithms use the number of violated constraints incurred by the partial assignment of values to variables as a cost function; this is called the *distance* of a partial solution from a complete solution. Maximal solutions are associated with minimum distances.

Variable ordering heuristics are based on problem parameters such as domain size and degree of a node in the constraint graph. For example, variables can be ordered by decreasing degree of a node. Another heuristic that has proven useful for PCSPs is to choose a variable with the largest number of constraints shared with those already instantiated; this is the maximum width of the node of that variable with respect to the variable ordering ([7]). This can be combined with a second heuristic that is used to break ties; the result is called a conjunctive width heuristic ([12]).

7.3 Directed Arc Consistency and DAC-Based Strategies

Directed arc consistency (DAC) involves pairwise tests between variables that share a constraint, in common with other arc consistency techniques (Figure 7.1). Unlike full arc consistency, checking is done in one direction only (as in [4]), who first proposed the idea of directed arc consistency). For example, if variables u and v share a constraint, and the direction is from u to v, then for each value a in u, each value b in v is checked to see if it is consistent with a. Values in u, on the other hand are not checked to see if they are consistent with b. If a is not consistent with any value in the domain of v, then the inconsistency count associated with a is incremented. In a DAC procedure, a variable ordering is first established together with a direction of checking (forward or backward) with respect to that ordering.

The major use of arc consistency counts (either full or directed) is to restrict search by calculating better lower bounds. As each value is considered for assignment to a variable, its associated count derived during preprocessing is added to the current distance. If this sum is at least as

```
Establish search order for variables
Set dac-count for each domain value to 0

For each variable v_i
    for each value a in domain d_i
        for each variable v_j later than v_i in the
        ordering such that v_i and v_j share
        a constraint
            if there is no value b in domain d_j
            such that (a, b) is in the constraint
            between v_i and v_j
                increment the dac-count for a
```

FIGURE 7.1. Directed arc consistency for PCSPs (in this case checking is in forward direction, i. e., each value is tested for support in domains of future variables).

great as the current upper bound, the value can be discarded without further testing (Figure 7.2). The sum of distance plus count (distance + ct_{jx} in Figure 7.2) is, therefore, a 'local' lower bound, i. e., a minimum cost that reflects inconsistencies with respect to neighboring variables only.

Unlike full AC counts, DAC counts allow a 'global' lower bound to be calculated. In this case the minimum count for each future variable (other than the current variable) can be summed and this sum added to the distance plus current count. (The sum of the minimum counts for future variables is the term, Σ min ct_{ky}, in Figure 7.2.) This cannot be done with full AC counts because AC counts associated with values in different domains may refer to the same constraint. The minimum counts are, therefore, not independent. Because DAC counts are independent, the sum of the counts can also be included in lower bound calculations during consistency checking (see Figure 7.2, Subroutine). (For forward DAC counts, the count for the current value can also be included.)

Another view of the basic DAC strategies is shown in the upper two lines of Figure 7.3. In this figure, curr-count under Search Test = ct_{jx} in Figure 7.2, while global lb = Σ min ct_{ky}; Consistency Test refers to the comparison with N in the subroutine of Figure 7.2, and under this heading, curr-count again = ct_{jx} (which can be incorporated into distance in the subroutine call of Figure 7.2), while global lb = dac-min-sum. In both forward- and backward- directed DAC, the global lower bound is based on DAC counts for values in domains of future variables. Hence, there can be no redundancy with the current distance, which is restricted to constraints among past variables, or with the current DAC count, because the latter 'looks' for support in the same direction (indicated by the direction of the arrow). The difference is that forward-directed DAC counts refer to

---

```
distance = 0, N = ∞

While upper bound N > 0
  If all values have been tried for first variable chosen
    exit
  else
    Choose future variable v_j as the current variable
      For each value x in domain d_j
        if (distance + ct_jx + Σ min ct_ky) ≥ N
            {k are future variables ≠ j}
          try next value
        else if all variables are now instantiated
          save solution and set N = distance
        else if test-constraints(v_j, x, distance, Σ min ct_ky)
          returns nil, try next value
        else add x to partial solution, set distance
        to value returned by test-constraints and
        exit for-loop      {choose next variable}
      If all values have been tested
        return v_j to set of future variables and
        continue with previous variable chosen

Subroutine:

test-constraints (current-variable, current-value,
          distance, dac-min-sum)

local: add-to-distance, initially 0

for each past variable, v_i, that shares a constraint with
current-variable
  if value assigned to v_i is inconsistent with current-value
    increment add-to-distance
    if (distance + add-to-distance + dac-min-sum) ≥ N
      return nil

return (distance + add-to-distance)
```

FIGURE 7.2. Backtracking branch and bound algorithm for PCSPs incorporating directed arc consistency counts (underlined parts).

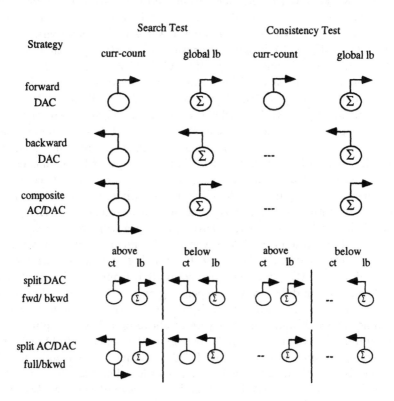

FIGURE 7.3. DAC-based strategies for retrospective algorithms. Components of each strategy, named in column 1, are represented by circles with arrows pointing in the direction of nonsupport (left refers to past variables, right to future variables). curr- count is the DAC count for the value currently considered for assignment. global lb is the global lower bound based on the sum of the minimum counts for each future domain (note summation signs in circles). above and below refer to the level of the 'split' in the variable order. Dashed lines indicate that a term cannot be used because of redundancy with inconsistencies found during consistency checking.

variables 'farther ahead' in the search order (arrow pointing right), while backward-directed counts refer to previous variables (arrow pointing left).

In their simplest form DAC counts based on forward or backward consistency checking have the disadvantage that the counts may be much less than full AC counts. In this case there is a tradeoff between the extra factor(s) allowed in lower bound calculations and the possible reduction in the count for the current value. Moreover, if the minimum counts are mostly 0, there may be no benefits from global lower bound calculations.

This tradeoff can be avoided altogether, using strategies that combine full AC and DAC counts (composite AC/DAC in Figure 7.3) or which use different combinations of backward and forward counts depending on the level of search (split DAC or split AC/DAC in Figure 7.3). In the composite strategy both forward and backward DAC counts are calculated during preprocessing. These are combined to make full AC counts for each value, while, in addition, partial sums of minimum counts are calculated from the forward DAC counts. With respect to Figure 7.2, this means that ct_{jx} is a full AC count, while the sum is based on forward DAC counts. In the schematic of Figure 7.3, the circle representing the count has arrows pointing in both directions. Note that, for this strategy, the global lower bound must be based on forward DAC counts (arrow pointing right), since backward DAC counts for future variables could be redundant with the forward component of the AC count. In 'splitting' strategies, both forward and backward DAC counts are also computed. Counts and partial sums are then set up in different ways depending on whether the level of search is above or below the level of the 'split'. (Cf. Figure 7.3: note that each coupling of search and consistency tests above or below the split can be superimposed on the related single strategy in the upper part of the figure.) For example, suppose that a split DAC technique is used and the split is after the fourth variable in the search order. Then the forward DAC strategy can used for variables 1-4, and the backward DAC strategy used for later variables.

The discussion so far has been primarily about retrospective algorithms. However, forward DAC counts can also be used with prospective algorithms that do a limited amount of inconsistency checking, such as forward checking.

In forward checking for PCSPs ([11]), a value a being considered for assignment to variable u is tested against values in the domain of each uninstantiated (future) variable v, if there is a constraint between u and v. If b, belonging to the domain of v, is inconsistent with a, then an inconsistency count associated with b is incremented. This forward-checking count (FC count) is a kind of backward DAC count which is only valid for the current instantiation of the set of past variables. If the sum of this count and the current distance is as great as the current upper bound, b can be discarded from the future domain, given a partial instantiation that includes value a in the domain of u. In addition, a global lower bound can be calculated, based on the sum of the minimum FC counts for future domains. (See Figure 7.4.)

Since FC counts are a special type of backward DAC count, they are independent of forward DAC counts. Moreover, since DAC counts refer to entire domains, they are not affected by value deletion during preclusion. This means that FC counts, forward DAC counts, sums of minimum FC counts and sums of minimum forward DAC counts can all be summed to form a lower bound. In this procedure, therefore, search efficiency, in terms of number of nodes visited, must always be at least as good as with ordinary forward checking.

Arc consistency counts (full AC or DAC) obtained during preprocessing can also be used to reorder domain values prior to search ([8]). The most straightforward heuristic is to order the values of each domain by increasing arc consistency count. Previous analysis has shown that this allows better solutions to be found earlier in search, which lowers the upper bound more rapidly ([12]). This method is independent of the lower bound calculations, so it can be used separately as well as in tandem with the latter.

7.4   Experiments

Algorithms were evaluated using random problems (generated according to a "random parameter model" (cf. [12], Exper. 1) modified to give a constant number of constraints) with mean domain size $= 4.5$ and with contraint graphs varying in density according to the formula, $(n - 1) + k(n/2)$, where n is the number of variables, $n - 1$ edges form a connected graph and $k \geq 1$. In these problems the average degree of a node in the constraint graph was, therefore, equal to $k + 2$. (In this model tightness is allowed to vary between the greatest possible limits and is independent for each constraint. Problems are built beginning with a randomly generated spanning tree, and then adding the required number of edges.)

For each problem type, 25 instances were tested. The main performance measure was number of constraint checks (ccks), i. e., tests that value x of variable u is consistent with value y of variable v. Since number of ccks was highly correlated with number of backtracks and run time, only the former are reported here. When preprocessing was done, these ccks were included in the total.

In the first experiment DAC-based strategies for retrospective algorithms were compared using simple backtrack search without variable ordering heuristics (lexical search order). The problems were small (number of variables, $n = 10$) because backtracking branch and bound with lexical ordering can require 10^8 ccks even for slightly larger problems and because in this case the entire range of problem densities could be examined.

In this experiment all DAC-based strategies improved the performance of backtracking. Selected results are shown in Figure 7.5. More generally,

```
distance = 0, N = ∞

While upper bound N > 0
  If all values have been tried for first variable chosen
    exit
  else
    Choose a future variable vᵢ as the current variable
      For each value x in domain dᵢ
        if (distance + fc-ctᵢₓ + Σ min fc-ctⱼᵧ
            + dac-ctᵢₓ + Σ min dac-ctⱼᵧ) ≥ N
            try next value
        else if all variables are now instantiated
          save solution and set N equal to distance
        else if preclude (vᵢ, x, distance)
              returns nil, try next value
        else add x to partial solution and exit for-loop
      If all values have been tested
        return vᵢ to the set of future variables,
        reset future domains and continue
        with previous variable chosen

Subroutine:

preclude (current-variable, current-value, distance)

for each future variable, vⱼ, that shares a
constraint with current-variable
  for each value y in domain dⱼ
    if y and current-value do not satisfy the constraint
    in question
      increment count fc-ctⱼᵧ
      if (distance + fc-ctⱼᵧ + dac-ctⱼᵧ) ≥ N,
        discard y

  if no values remain in dⱼ return nil
```

FIGURE 7.4. Directed arc consistency incorporated into forward checking. 'fc-ct' refers to count produced (during preclusion) by forward checking. Inclusions based on DAC counts are underlined.

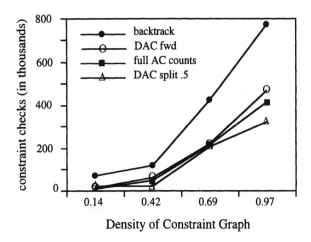

FIGURE 7.5. Enhancement of backtrack search with DAC counts obtained during preprocessing. 10- variable problems, lexical variable ordering, value ordering based on inconsistency counts. DAC fwd = forward DAC, full AC counts = full arc consistency counts, DAC split .5 = split DAC strategy using composite strategy above and backward strategy below split in middle of search order. Densities correspond to average degrees of 3, 5, 7 and 9 in constraint graph.

the composite strategy (not shown) gave the best results for the very sparse problems (.14 density, $k = 1$), and for other problems the split DAC strategy shown in Figure 7.5 was best. This strategy also outperformed one based on full AC counts as problem density increased. Splitting in the middle of the search order (.5) gave better results than splits at .3 or .7 of the way through, for all but the very sparse problems; in the latter case .7 was slightly better. In addition, the composite/backward splitting strategy was consistently better than the forward/backward.

For these problems, variable ordering heuristics afforded appreciable improvement over lexical ordering (e.g., between one and two orders of magnitude at density = .14, and by factors of 3-5 at density = .97, depending on the strategy). However, the relative performance of the different preprocessing strategies was unchanged. Except for problems with almost complete constraint graphs (density = .97), the (maximum) width/(minimum) domain size heuristic was the best. For problems with density = .97, (minimum) domain size was somewhat better.

Backmarking for PCSPs (described in [8]) outperformed backtracking by a factor of three to five. When this algorithm was used with the best DAC strategy and with the width/domain size variable ordering, average performance ranged from 300 ccks at density = .14 to 30,000 at density = .97.

Use of DAC counts with forward checking led to a marked improvement

TABLE 7.1. Mean constraint checks for backmarking and forward checking on 20-variable problems of varying density

algorithm	.06	.12	.18	density .23	.29	.41
backmark/AC	19,683	96,615	591,716	8,655,756		
backmark/DAC	24,337	104,974	580,505	4,470,242		
FC	22,169	43,784	142,922	926,734	2,010,804	
FC/AC-val	5,263	23,696	123,853	540,782	1,612,509	3,257,560
FC/DAC	6,536	12,328	67,879	304,050	781,884	1,914,404
FC/DAC/AC-val	6,762	10,597	66,469	292,687	771,143	1,906,045
FC-dy	39,176	169,870	940,160	1,215,249	910,956	2,044,428
FC-dy/AC-val	29,435	120,589	1,465,054	922,381	856,992	1,081,088
mn. distance	3.2	4.2	7.2	9.4	13.9	19.6

Backmark/AC uses full AC counts for value ordering and lower bound calculations. (It is the RPO algorithm described in [8]); backmark/DAC uses a split/composite heuristic with the splitting factor = .5; FC= forward checking, FC-dy is forward checking with dynamic search rearrangement based on domain size; /AC-val refers to value ordering based on full arc consistency counts; mn. distance is the mean optimal distance (minimum number of constraint violations) for each set of problems. Density is in terms of edges added to a spanning tree.

in the performance of this algorithm (Figure 7.6). In general, forward checking gave better results than the retrospective algorithms tested, especially for the two higher densities. FC-DAC with value ordering based on full AC counts gave only slightly better results than FC-DAC with DAC-based value ordering for these small problems.

Twenty-variable problems of the same type as the ten-variable problems, and with densities up to .41 ($k = 7$), were tested using the best retrospective and prospective algorithms. In each case the best variable ordering heuristics were also used: width/domain size for backmarking and (decreasing) degree of node for forward checking. Forward checking with dynamic search rearrangement based on domain size was also tested. (This was an important variant to test here, since DAC-based strategies do not allow dynamic rearrangement of the variable ordering during search.)

The main results were (see Table 7.4):

(i) At densities between .06 ($k = 1$) and .35 ($k = 6$), inclusive, forward checking using DAC-based strategies outperformed all other combinations of algorithms and heuristics. Even at a density of .41, DAC-based techniques were better than algorithms that did not use some form of information gained during preprocessing.

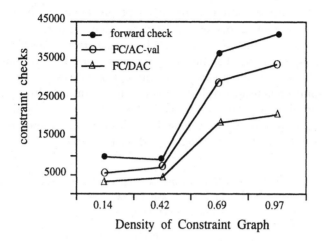

FIGURE 7.6. Influence of value ordering and DAC- based bounding strategies on performance of forward checking. Ten-variable problems, lexical ordering. FC/AC-val = forward checking with value ordering based on full AC counts, FC/DAC = forward checking with forward DAC counts for lower bound calculations and value ordering.

(ii) Forward checking with dynamic search rearrangement was the worst algorithm at densities up to about .30. At a density of .41 this algorithm was able to outperform forward checking with fixed order heuristics, but only if values were ordered by AC counts. Although the data are incomplete, it appears that, as density increases, there is a reversal in relative performance, so that dynamic ordering (based on domain size) is eventually superior to fixed ordering heuristics. (Improvement in relative performance of dynamic ordering with increasing density was observed in earlier work, using 20-variable problems generated with a different probability model; cf. [12]. The same results have since been found using forward checking with DAC-based strategies; interestingly, for these problems in which average tightness can be varied independently of density, the reversal occurred at a higher density for harder problems having tighter constraints than for easier problems with loose constraints. Also, in subsidiary experiments with 15- and 25-variable problems of the same type as in the present experiments, DAC-based procedures were better than dynamic search rearrangement to a density of at least 0.3.)

(iii) Except for very sparse problems, forward checking with fixed ordering was appreciably better than the best retrospective algorithm.

(iv) For these problems, value ordering by full AC counts in combination with DAC-based lower bound calculations resulted in only a modest improvement over ordering based on DAC counts.

Subsidiary experiments were run using problems with densities of .12

and .23, to compare strategies based on preprocessing with the effect of starting with a good upper bound (such as might be derived by heuristic methods or earlier runs of branch and bound). Forward checking with degree ordering was used. The initial bound was either the optimal distance for that problem or one greater than the optimal distance. In the former case, no solution is returned, but, presumably a solution with this distance was already obtained, and the present procedure serves to confirm that it is, indeed, an optimal solution. Results in this case are, therefore, the best that can be obtained by choosing a good initial bound.

TABLE 7.2. Mean constraint checks for forward checking and DAC-based forward checking on sparse problems of increasing size

	number of variables		
	20	30	40
FC	22,169	300,640	1.1×10^8
FC/AC-val	15,263	227,201	5,123,153
FC/DAC	6,536	126,671	2,904,476
FC/DAC/AC-val	6,762	112,863	1,356,062
mn. distance	3.2	4 .0	4.6

Forward checking uses variable ordering by decreasing degree. Other terms are defined in the notes to Table 1.1.

In these experiments, for an optimal initial bound, the average number of ccks was 18,749 for problems with density = .12 and 317,042 for problems with density = .23. With an initial bound one greater than optimal the corresponding means were 24,118 and 476,758. This procedure by itself does not, therefore, improve on DAC-based forward checking, even without considering the expense required to find the initial upper bound. In addition, comparison with the FC/AC-val combination shows that, unless the initial upper bound is optimal, the results are not appreciably better than using a good value ordering based on information gained during preprocessing. This suggests that, finding an upper bound through prior search will not be not be as efficient as the present preprocessing techniques, and for heuristic techniques to be viable in this capacity, they must find solutions with optimal distances in most cases.

Sparse problems with 30 and 40 variables were also tested (Table 7.4). DAC-based strategies again yielded better performance than ordinary forward checking or forward checking with value ordering based on AC counts. At 40 variables, the difference was appreciable: the mean for FC/DAC was two orders of magnitude better than that for forward checking alone. With the larger problems, use of full AC counts to order values also afforded significant improvement over ordering based on DAC counts, cutting the work on average by a factor of two.

For large sparse problems, the character of the distribution of performance across a set of problems becomes increasingly important. These distributions are strongly skewed: the majority of problems are relatively easy, so there is a marked peak at the left of the distribution, and there is a sprinkling of very hard problems that gives the distribution a long tail on the right. (In this connection, it may be noted that for PCSPs there is no restricted region of very hard problems, as there is with CSPs; there seem to be hard problems in every part of the parameter space, while average difficulty increases with increasing density or constraint tightness.) This is reflected in the medians of distributions, since this statistic is not as influenced by the size of extreme scores, so that for skewed distributions this will be appreciably less than the mean. Thus, for the 40-variable problems the medians were 1.1 million, 893 thousand, 446 thousand and 259 thousand for FC, FC/AC-val, FC/DAC and FC/DAC/AC-val, respectively. This shows that most of the difference in means, particularly for comparisons with forward checking without preprocessing, was due to a few very hard problems. At the same time, the ordering of these algorithms remained the same, and the difference between the extremes was still appreciable.

7.5   Conclusions and Future Directions

Strategies based on local consistency testing improve the search efficiency of branch and bound algorithms for solving MAX-CSPs with relatively little extra effort. Tightening lower bound estimates with DAC-counts results in a significant enhancement of performance of the best complete algorithm for this problem. Value ordering based either on DAC- or AC-counts also improves performance. Since these two strategies are largely independent, they are even more effective when they act in concert. With the best available implementation on a fast machine all but the hardest 40-variable problems from the sample tested could be done in seconds with these techniques.

Not surprisingly, there are many important open questions in regard to these techniques, among them the following:

(i) Most of the results reported here are based on a specific type of random problem. Subsidiary experiments, mentioned above, indicate that these results are not peculiar to the present problems. However, these tests were still based on random problems, using different methods of generation (described in [8]). Results are still needed for problems with more structure.

(ii) It is not yet clear what the largest problem size is for which these methods can return optimal solutions in all or most cases without excessive effort (say, $\leq 10^7$ constraint checks). Recent results suggest that, for 60-

variable problems comparable to those in Table 7.4, the mean number of constraint checks required to solve all problems is 10^8. In addition, the range of densities over which the required effort is not excessive narrows as problems get bigger, and may be $\leq .1$ for problems of 40 or more variables. At the same time, since performance distributions are so strongly skewed, most problems can be solved in fewer constraint checks than that given by the group mean. (In this connection, it should be noted that for these problems, determining whether a complete solution exists was much, much easier than finding a guaranteed optimal solution.)

(iii) The present work has been restricted to the simple case of problems in which violations of different constraints are treated equally. Obviously, the present methods can be extended to problems with weighted constraints (cf. [11]). The best DAC-based procedures should prove effective over at least a range of such problems, especially in conjunction with forward checking, since lower bounds obtained with these techniques must be as least as large as those obtained with forward checking alone.

Acknowledgements: This material is based on work supported by the National Science Foundation under Grant No. IRI-9207633.

7.6 REFERENCES

[1] A. Borning, R. Duisberg, B. Freeman-Benson, A. Kramer, and M. Woolf. Constraint hierarchies. In *Proceedings OOPSLA-87*, pages 48–60, 1987.

[2] R. Bakker, F. Dikker, F. Tempelman, and P. Wognum. Diagnosing and solving overdetermined constraint satisfaction problems. In *Proceedings IJCAI-93*, pages 276–281, 1993.

[3] R. Buick, N. Stone, R. Scheckler, and J. Roach. Crops: a whole-farm crop rotation planning system to implement sustainable agriculture. *AI Applications*, 6:29–50, 1992.

[4] R. Dechter and J. Pearl. Network-based heuristics for constraint satisfaction problems. *Artificial Intelligence*, 34:1–38, 1988.

[5] R. Feldman and M.C. Golumbic. Optimization algorithms for student scheduling via constraint satisfiability. *Computer Journal*, 33:356–364, 1990.

[6] M. Fox. *Constraint-directed Search: A Case Study of Job-Shop Scheduling.* Morgan Kaufmann, Los Altos, CA, 1987.

[7] E.C. Freuder. A sufficient condition for backtrack-free search. *Journal of the ACM*, 29:24–32, 1982.

[8] E.C. Freuder and R.J. Wallace. Partial constraint satisfaction. *Artificial Intelligence*, 58:21–70, 1992.

[9] R.M. Haralick and G.L. Elliott. Increasing tree search efficiency for constraint satisfaction problems. *Artificial Intelligence*, 14:263–313, 1980.

[10] D. Sabin and E.C. Freuder. Contradicting conventional wisdom in constraint satisfaction. In *Proceedings ECAI-94*, pages 125–129, 1994.

[11] L. Shapiro and R. Haralick. Structural descriptions and inexact matching. *IEEE Transactions on Pattern Analysis and Machine Intelligence*, 3:504–519, 1981.

[12] R.J. Wallace and E.C. Freuder. Conjunctive width heuristics for maximal constraint satisfaction. In *Proceedings AAAI-93*, pages 762–768, 1993.

8

In Search of Exceptionally Difficult Constraint Satisfaction Problems

Barbara M. Smith[1]

ABSTRACT It has been observed by several authors that for many NP problems, a sharp peak in the median cost to find a solution can be seen as an order parameter is varied; the peak occurs at the phase transition as problems change from being under-constrained and easy to solve to over-constrained and insoluble. More recently it has been observed that individual problems which are very difficult can be found at some distance from the peak in the median cost. This paper investigates these exceptionally difficult problems in the context of binary constraint satisfaction problems, and addresses the following questions: how can problems which are difficult to solve arise in a region where most problems are easy to solve? Are the problems which are difficult to solve inherently harder than similar problems, or does the difficulty depend on the solution method?

Experimental results show that some problems *are* inherently more difficult than other similar problems and that an important factor is the diversity in the set of solutions to the problem. Exceptionally difficult problems can also occur if the search space induced by the search algorithm is unusually large. The existence of occasional very difficult problems in a region where most problems can be expected to be easy has implications for the use of the phase transition to guide the solution strategy.

8.1 Introduction

Cheeseman, Kanefsky and Taylor [2] note that for many NP-complete or NP-hard problems, a phase transition can be seen as an order parameter is varied; the transition is from problems that are under-constrained, and so relatively easy to solve, to problems that are over-constrained, and so relatively easy to prove insoluble. They observed that the problems which are on average hardest to solve occur between these two types of relatively easy problem.

---

[1]Division of Artificial Intelligence, School of Computer Studies, University of Leeds, Leeds LS2 9JT, U.K.

Mitchell, Selman and Levesque [4] report similar experience for satisfiability problems, and Williams and Hogg [9, 10, 11] have developed approximations to the cost of finding the first solution and to the probability that a problem is soluble, both for specific classes of constraint satisfaction problem (graph colouring, k-SAT) and for the general case. Prosser [19] has carried out an extensive series of experiments to investigate the phase transition in binary CSPs; in [6, 7], the author investigates the extent to which it is possible to predict the location of the phase transition in binary CSPs.

It has been observed by Hogg and Williams [3] in graph colouring problems and by Gent and Walsh [2] in satisfiability problems, that although there is a well-defined peak in the *median* cost to find a solution in the region of the phase transition, this is often not where the hardest individual instances occur. Given a large sample of problems, outliers may occur, in the form of individual problems which are very hard to solve, at a value of the order parameter for which most problems are relatively easy to solve. Gent and Walsh, for instance, report that one particular satisfiability problem, generated by a method considered to produce easy problems, required over 350 million branches to solve, using a standard algorithm: this was more than the total number of branches required to solve 1000 problems of the same size, selected from the region where on average problems are hardest.

This paper considers this phenomenon for binary constraint satisfaction problems. It considers the following questions: how can problems which are difficult to solve arise in a region where most problems are easy to solve? Are the problems which are difficult to solve inherently harder than similar problems, or does the difficulty depend on the solution method?

8.2   The Experimental CSPs

In order to examine the phase transition and the occurrence of exceptionally difficult problems, a series of experiments was carried out using sets of randomly-generated binary constraint satisfaction problems. Each set of problems is characterised by four parameters: n, the number of variables; m, the number of values in each variable's domain; p_1, the probability that there is a constraint between a pair of variables, and p_2, the conditional probability that a pair of values is inconsistent for a pair of variables, given that there is a constraint between the variables.

Since the ultimate aim in considering sets of randomly-generated CSPs is to be able to make predictions about the behaviour of problems of a given size, with particular observed numbers of constraints and numbers of inconsistent pairs of values, it was decided to generate sets of problems in which p_1 and p_2 specify precisely, rather than on average, how many constraints and pairs of inconsistent values there should be. Hence, for each set of randomly-generated problems, the number of constrained pairs of variables is exactly $p_1 n(n-1)/2$, and for each pair of constrained variables, the number of inconsistent pairs of values is exactly $m^2 p_2$. This is done by randomly permuting a list of the possible variable pairs and choosing the first $p_1 n(n-1)/2$, and then for each constrained pair of variables, randomly permuting the m^2 possible pairs of values and choosing the first $m^2 p_2$. The phase transition from under-constrained to over-constrained problems occurs as p_2 varies, while n, m and p_1 are kept fixed.

In order to observe the phase transition as p_2 varies, it is necessary to choose an algorithm and to solve a set of problems. For these experiments, the forward checking algorithm was chosen, with a variable ordering heuristic using the fail-first principle: the first variable to be instantiated is the one which is most constrained, and thereafter, the next variable to be instantiated is one with fewest remaining values in its domain (see [8] for a description of this and other CSP search algorithms).

In the first experiments, samples of problems with $n=8$, $m=10$ and $p_1=1.0$, and p_2 varying, were generated. None of these problems are particularly difficult to solve; indeed it is perfectly practicable to find all solutions to a large sample of problems, even for quite small values of p_2, as will be seen. Furthermore, as every problem has the same constraint graph (the complete graph, K_8), there is less variation between them than in samples generated with $p_1 < 1$. Nevertheless, an examination of the median and the maximum cost for these problems does suggest how and where very difficult instances might arise in a set of larger or less well-behaved problems.

Figure 8.1 shows the median cost, measured by the number of consistency checks required to find one solution or prove that there is no solution, for each value of p_2. The maximum and minimum number of consistency checks are also shown. The values are based on samples of at least 500 problems over the phase transition, and 1000 problems where the highest values of the maximum are occurring ($0.39 \leq p_2 \leq 0.43$). The vertical lines in Figure 8.1 show the range of values of p_2 over which the phase transition occurs: this is referred to in [6, 7] as the *mushy region*. The boundaries of the mushy region are defined arbitrarily as the largest value of p_2 for which at least 99% of problems in the sample are soluble and the smallest value for which at least 99% are insoluble. For this particular set of problems, the overall maximum cost is observed just outside the mushy region, where almost all problems have solutions, and is due to a soluble problem.

In investigating the maximum cost, it is first of all obvious that the cost of finding the first solution (if there is one) is bounded by the cost of finding all solutions. Figure 8.2 is similar to Figure 8.1 but shows the cost of finding all solutions, or proving that there are none; the region to the right of the mushy region (for $p_2 > 0.55$) therefore shows identical data to Figure 8.1.

Figures 8.1 and 8.2 suggest that the greatest potential for outliers exists in the mushy region and in the region where all problems are soluble, i.e. where there is a wide gap between the median cost of finding one so-

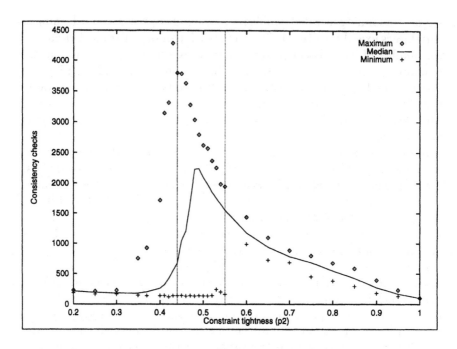

FIGURE 8.1. Cost of finding one solution or showing that there are none for CSPs with $n=8$, $m=10$, $p_1=1.0$

lution and the upper limit on this cost, i.e. the maximum cost of finding all solutions. We should not expect to find exceptionally difficult problems occurring in the insoluble region, since insoluble problems already require a complete search, which is relatively cheap at these values of p_2. This is consistent with the experimental data reported in [2] and [3].

8.3   Problems with No Solutions

¿From Figures 8.1 and 8.2 it can be conjectured that if an exceptional insoluble problem occurs at a low value of p_2, where almost all problems are soluble, it will be very expensive to prove insoluble, by comparison with the average cost of finding a single solution to a soluble problem at the same value of p_2. The best estimate of the cost of proving the problem insoluble is given by the median cost curve in Figure 8.2, which rises steeply as p_2 decreases. At the same time, the median cost of finding a single solution, in the region where almost all problems are soluble, is decreasing steeply with p_2. This argument also accounts for the fact that the maximum cost continues to increase, throughout the mushy region, as p_2 decreases, even when the median cost is falling rapidly from its peak; the maximum cost

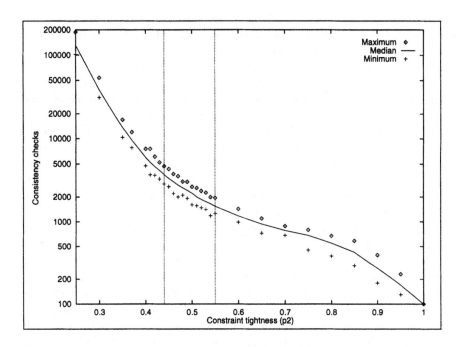

FIGURE 8.2. Median cost (to find all solutions or show that there are none) for CSPs with $n=8$, $m=10$, $p_1=1.0$

is usually, at these values of p_2, due to one of the (increasingly rare) insoluble problems, whereas the median is more representative of the soluble problems.

On the other hand, if a soluble problem occurs in the insoluble region (at $p_2 > 0.55$, for the data shown in Figures 8.1 and 8.2) it can be expected to be relatively easy to solve, since Figures 8.1 and 8.2 show that the average cost of performing a complete search at these values of p_2 is falling as p_2 increases, and performing a partial search, to find a single solution, cannot be more expensive. To summarise, an insoluble problem occurring in the soluble region will be exceptionally difficult to solve; a soluble problem occurring in the insoluble region will be relatively easy to solve, so that as already noted, outliers are unlikely to occur in the insoluble region.

8.4 Soluble Problems

Although some very difficult problems, particularly on the edge of the phase transition, are insoluble and can be explained as in the last section, this does not account, in general, for outliers occurring in the soluble region. We now need to consider how a soluble problem can be much harder to solve than other problems with the same values of n, m, p_1 and p_2. The cost of solving a problem is obviously algorithm-dependent: a problem is difficult to solve for a particular algorithm if its solution cost is much more, for that algorithm, than the cost of other similar problems.

When applied to a particular CSP, the algorithm will generate a search space; to find all solutions to the CSP it must explore the whole of this space, whereas if only one solution is required, it can terminate as soon as the first one is found. It is possible that some problems are found to be exceptionally difficult because they require the algorithm to search a much greater proportion of the total search space before finding a solution than do other similar problems. (This ignores, for the time being, the possibility of significant differences in the size of the search space for different problems with the same parameter values.)

Any depth-first search algorithm, no matter how inefficient, can solve a given CSP (if it is soluble) almost immediately, provided that it happens to make a correct choice of value for each variable that it considers. Hence, the algorithm only needs to search a large proportion of the search space if it makes unlucky choices, i.e. it chooses values for variables which do not lead to a consistent solution (*and* there are many unlucky choices to be made, i.e. many values for many variables will not lead to a consistent solution). Whether or not a given problem is exceptionally difficult for a given algorithm therefore partly depends on the decision rules for choosing the variable and value ordering.

This suggests that it would be useful to think of a problem as potentially exceptionally difficult (p.e.d.) if, for some variable and value ordering, a backtracking depth-first search algorithm will not find a solution until it has explored most of the search space. This definition may not be of much practical use, since we may only be able to recognise p.e.d. problems if they are *actually* exceptionally difficult for the algorithm being studied, or by finding all the solutions and examining them to see if it would be possible to make many wrong choices in the search for a solution. However, the definition makes clear that a problem that is actually easy in a particular case might still be p.e.d.; it might also be true that when an exceptionally difficult problem is found, all other similar problems, with the same values of n, m, p_1 and p_2, are also p.e.d.

Suppose we confine our attention to the first variable chosen for instantiation by the algorithm. The algorithm might always choose variable 1 to instantiate first, or (as in the experiments reported here) the most constrained variable, or have some other decision rule. It then considers each value for this variable in some order, exploring the subspace resulting from each instantiation in turn, until it reaches a correct choice, i.e. an instantiation of the first variable which is part of a complete solution. No matter how good the algorithm's variable- and value-ordering heuristics are, they are still heuristics and cannot guarantee to make a correct choice in every case. Unless every value for the first variable participates in a complete solution, there is a chance that the algorithm may make one or more wrong choices for the first variable before finding a solution. If the first value it considers is correct, and there are say 10 possible values, then we might expect that a complete solution will be found before the algorithm has explored 1/10 of the whole search space; on the other hand, if there is only one possible value for this variable and it happens to be the last value that the algorithm chooses, then we might expect that the algorithm must explore at least 9/10 of the search space before finding a solution. (This, of course, assumes a considerable degree of uniformity throughout the search space, but seems reasonable as a working approximation.) In the latter case, the problem is p.e.d.; in the former case, it might be, if the first value for the first variable is the only correct one.

A problem is therefore p.e.d. if the number of values which are correct, i.e. form part of a complete consistent solution, is very small for at least one variable. The more variables this is true of, and the fewer correct values each variable has, the more likely it is that the problem will actually be difficult to solve.

An obvious class of p.e.d. problems are those with only one solution, when each variable has just one correct value. There is then a chance (though very small) that the correct value will be the last one chosen by the algorithm for each variable; in that case, the algorithm will have explored the whole search space before finding the solution. Equally, there is a chance that the algorithm will make the correct choice first for each variable and find the solution immediately. Unless the algorithm has a value ordering heuristic which does better than random choice, it will have to search through half the search space, on average, before finding the solution (and this has been experimentally verified).

Problems which have more than one solution, but still very few, should be correspondingly easier to solve, provided that the solutions are uniformly distributed through the search space independently of one another. So we should expect to find the first of two solutions after exploring, on average, 1/3 of the total search space, the first of three solutions after exploring, on average, 1/4 of the search space, and so on. In fact, solutions tend to cluster together and are not uniformly distributed, so that it is on average very little easier to find one of three or four solutions than it is when there is only one solution. Even if solutions were uniformly distributed through the search space, if the number of solutions is very small, the number of possible values for each variable which are part of a complete solution must also be small, so that these problems must be p.e.d.

For sets of problems of the kind shown in Figure 8.1, it is only in the mushy region that problems with very few solutions occur. For other types of problem, this is not necessarily the case. [7] discusses the expectation and variance of the number of solutions, which can be calculated for CSPs generated as described above. For the problems shown in Figure 8.1, both the expectation and variance are small in the mushy region: at the point where approximately half the problems are insoluble, those problems which have solutions have very few of them. On the other hand, for problems which have sparse constraint graphs (e.g. $p_1 = 0.1$), at the point where half the problems are insoluble, the expected number of solutions is large and the variance is extremely high. As p_2 gets smaller, the expected number of solutions increases very rapidly, but so does the variance. It is conceivable that even at some distance from the mushy region occasional problems with few solutions may occur and thus sometimes be very difficult to solve, whereas most problems with the same values of n, m, p_1 and p_2 will have very many solutions, so that one can be found very quickly.

8.5   Problems with Many Solutions

So far, this paper has considered problems which are very difficult to solve either because they are insoluble, in a region where most problems are soluble, or because they have very few solutions. This section will show that even if problems have many solutions, it can sometimes be difficult to find one.

A set of larger problems, with $n = 20$, $m = 10$ and $p_1 = 0.5$ was generated, with p_2 varying from 0.33 to 0.41, so as to cover the phase transition and part of the soluble region: 500 problems were generated for each value of p_2.

For $p_2 \geq 0.36$, the maximum cost in each case is due to an insoluble problem; the maximum cost for a soluble problem occurs at $p_2 = 0.35$. However, at that value for p_2, the expected number of solutions[2] is 169. The obvious conjecture is that the maximum cost occurs for a problem with far fewer solutions than the average; this seems a reasonable supposition, given that there are 2 problems in the sample which are insoluble, and so it can be expected that some of the soluble problems have only a few solutions. However, re-solving this problem (problem Max) in order to find all solutions shows that it has 124 solutions, so that it is not exceptional in this respect. How can it happen that a problem with this many solutions is hard to solve, and can it be related to the discussion of p.e.d. problems in the last section?

Problem Max takes approximately 11 times as many consistency checks to solve (153,643) as the median cost at $p_2 = 0.35$. In turn, the median is approximately 15 times the minimum cost at this value (854 consistency checks). This raises the additional question of whether the problem giving the minimum cost (problem Min) is inherently easier than problem Max,

---

[2] given by the formula $m^n(1-p_2)^{n(n-1)p_1/2}$ i.e. the number of possible assignments of m values to n variables, multiplied by the probability that a randomly-chosen assignment is consistent. The relationship between the expected number of solutions and the peak in median cost is discussed in [6] and [7].

or whether it is also p.e.d., although actually easy in this case.

Figure 8.3 shows the distribution of cost to find the first solution for the 500 problems solved at $p_2 = 0.35$; the problems are shown in ascending order of cost. Problems Max and Min (appearing in the distribution as problems 1 and 500) are clearly both statistical outliers.

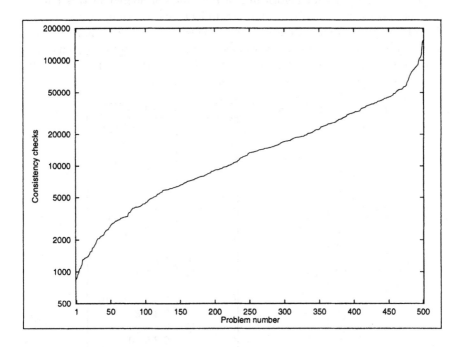

FIGURE 8.3. Cost of finding one solution or showing that there are none for 500 CSPs with $n=20$, $m=10$, $p_1=0.5$, $p_2 = 0.35$

Finding all solutions for both problems shows that the sizes of their search spaces are not very different; problem Max takes 188,077 consistency checks compared to 154,289 for problem Min. Hence, although the algorithm generates a larger search space for the more difficult problem, the difference does not account for the difference in the costs of finding the first solution. However, examining the solutions to problem Max shows clearly why it is so difficult to solve for this particular algorithm, even though it has 124 solutions: the algorithm selected variable 10 for this problem as the first variable to instantiate (because it was the most constrained variable), and then considered the values for this variable in numerical order. *Every* solution to this problem has the value 10 for variable 10, so that it was the last value considered.

Problem Min, on the other hand, has only 52 solutions, so on the basis of that information alone, it might be expected to be more difficult to solve than problem Max. However, examination of these solutions shows that there is no variable which has fewer than 3 correct values (i.e. values appearing in one of the 52 solutions). It is exceptionally easy to solve in this case because the value 1 happens to be a correct value for the first variable it considers (variable 11).

Table 8.1 shows the set of correct values for the two problems, and it is clear from this that, for algorithms of the kind considered in this paper, problem Max is potentially much more difficult to solve than problem Min. Even though it has more solutions, each one is very similar to many others, and they all have a great many variable assignments in common (6 variables have only one correct value). So in any search space, the solutions are likely to be encountered in clusters, rather than being uniformly spread.

Problem Max		Problem Min	
Variable	Correct values	Variable	Correct values
1	4	1	1 3 4 5 8
2	1 4	2	4 6 7 8
3	2 8	3	2 3 5 6 8 9
4	5 7	4	3 5 7 9 10
5	1 5	5	1 4 5 6 9 10
6	1 3 6	6	3 4 7 8 9
7	5	7	1 5 6 8 9 10
8	6	8	1 3 4 7 8 9 10
9	7 8	9	1 2 5 8 9 10
10	10	10	1 7 10
11	4 6 8	11	1 6 7 10
12	4 6	12	4 5 8 10
13	1	13	2 3 4 7 8 9 10
14	1 6	14	2 3 4 8
15	7 10	15	2 5 8
16	2 7	16	6 8 9 10
17	2 10	17	6 7 8 9
18	6 9	18	1 6 9
19	4 6 9	19	2 6 9 10
20	5	20	1 2 5 8

TABLE 8.1. Set of correct values for problems Max and Min

The solutions to problem Min, on the other hand, are much more diverse, as shown by the fact that the number of correct values is much higher. The solutions will be spread throughout the search space, so that a search algorithm is likely to find one of them quite quickly.

Hence, as well as being easier to solve for this particular algorithm (including its variable and value ordering rules), problem Min is likely to be much easier to solve than problem Max for any similar algorithm.

It is, of course, intuitively obvious that if solutions are clustered together they may be hard to find. However, it is surprising that randomly-generated problems with the same parameter values and not too dissimilar numbers of solutions, could be so different in the diversity of their solutions. As yet, it is not known whether there is any easily-measurable problem characteristic which could be used to distinguish problems with diverse solutions, like problem Min, from problems with more uniform solutions, like problem Max.

8.6 Differences in Search Space Size

It has so far been assumed that the search spaces induced by an algorithm for a set of problems with the same values of n, m, p_1 and p_2 with be approximately the same size, with Figure 8.2 indicating the degree of variation to be expected. If this is the case, then differences in the proportion of the search space that has to be explored before finding the first solution must account for the differences in difficulty and the occurrence of occasional very difficult problems, as already discussed.

However, a further set of experiments shows that this is not the full story. 1000 problems were generated with $n=20$, $m=10$, $p_1=0.3$ and $p_2=0.5$[3]. The constraint graphs were vetted to ensure that they were all connected graphs, so that the problems could not be decomposed into subproblems. Of the 1000 problems, 948 were soluble, showing that this value of p_2 lies on the edge of the mushy region.

Having chosen the first variable to instantiate, say $v1$, the algorithm used in the experiments considers the values of this variable in numerical order (1 to 10). If the variation in the cost of finding a solution depends almost entirely on what proportion of the search space has to be traversed before a solution is found (rather than on variation in the size of the search space), there should be a strong correlation between the cost and the value assigned to $v1$ in the solution. A problem in which the value 10 is assigned to $v1$ should take roughly 10 times as many consistency checks as a problem in which $v1 = 1$ in the first solution. (In fact, if $v1 = 10$, then this is the only possible value for this variable, so that the problem is p.e.d. in the terminology of the last section.)

Figure 8.4 shows the relationship between a composite value representing the values assigned to $v1$ and to the second variable in the solution, and the cost of finding the solution. It can be seen that there is indeed an approximate linear relationship between the two (allowing for the log scale on the vertical axis; for comparison, the dashed line shows an exact linear relationship, the coefficients of which were selected by eye). However, although the problems with $v1 = 10$ are difficult, many other problems in the set are equally difficult, and the five most difficult problems have $v1 < 10$. Moreover, a noteworthy feature of Figure 8.4 is that there is a very difficult problem for which $v1 = 1$. This strongly suggests that the search space for

---

[3]These values were chosen because Pat Prosser had found an exceptionally difficult problem instance at the same values (private communication).

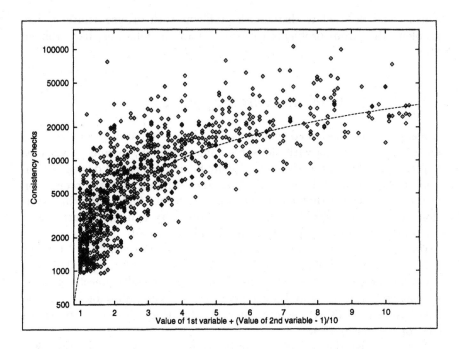

FIGURE 8.4. Relationship between the solution and the number of consistency checks for a set of 948 soluble problems with $n=20$, $m=10$, $p_1=0.3$, $p_2=0.5$

this problem (problem 568) must be much larger that that for most of the other problems. Re-solving problem 568 to find all solutions took 320,000 consistency checks. By comparison, the 52 insoluble problems, which also require a complete search, took between 12,000 and 97,000 consistency checks.

There is clearly, from these few examples, a much greater variation in search space size for this set of problems than for those shown in Figure 8.2. One possible explanation of this is that Figure 8.2 represents a set of problems with $p_1=1.0$, and therefore with the same constraint graph, whereas in Figure 8.4, with $p_1=0.3$, each problem has a different constraint graph. To investigate whether the search space size depends on the constraint graph, five individual problems were selected from the original set of 1000 and for each problem, 25 new problems with the same constraint graph were generated. All solutions were found for these 125 problems. One of the five problems selected was problem 568, already mentioned. Problems 351 and 139 are the easiest and the most difficult, respectively, of the insoluble problems. Problem 796 is the easiest problem for which $v1 = 10$; problem 564 is the easiest problem for which the first two variables both have value 1. Figure 8.5 shows the results for the five new problem sets, and clearly shows that the size of the search space does depend on the

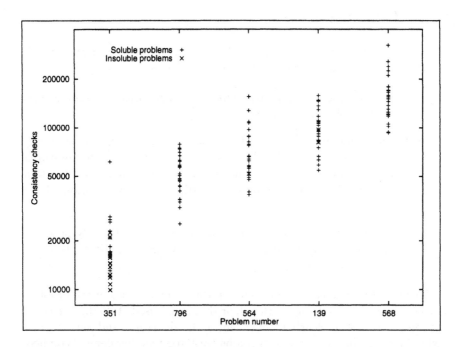

FIGURE 8.5. Cost of finding all solutions for five sets of 25 problems with $n=20$, $m=10$, $p_1=0.3$, $p_2=0.5$; problems in a set have the same constraint graph.

constraint graph. For instance, the easiest of the 568 problems is harder than the hardest of the 351 problems.

It is not necessarily true, however, that the constraint graph of problem 568 produces problems which are inherently more difficult than those derived from problem 351. Apart from the constraint graph, another factor that all the problems in a set have in common is the choice of first variable to instantiate. This choice is made by the algorithm solely on the basis of the information available from the constraints, whereas later variable choices can make use of information from the search so far (for instance, in choosing a variable with smallest remaining domain). Experience with different heuristics for selecting the first variable indicates that problems which are more difficult than average under one heuristic can become easier than average if the heuristic is changed. This suggests that the size of the search space may not depend just on the constraint graph but also on the interaction between the constraint graph and the selection of the first variable.

8.7   Conclusions

This paper has identified three possible reasons for the occurrence of exceptionally difficult constraint satisfaction problems:

- the problem is insoluble, when most problems with the same values of n, m, p_1 and p_2 can be solved.

- the problem either has very few solutions or, although it has many solutions, they are clustered together in a limited region of the search space, and, because of the variable and value ordering, the algorithm will not reach any of the solutions until it has traversed most of the search space.

- the search space induced by the algorithm is exceptionally large, so that, wherever the solutions occur, it will take a long time to reach the first one.

The first two reasons given depend on the characteristics of the problem rather than, or as well as, on the algorithm being used. Whether or not a problem is soluble is clearly independent of the algorithm, and the extent to which the solutions to a problem can be clustered together depends on how many solutions there are and on their diversity. Problems with the same values of n, m, p_1 and p_2 can be very different in the diversity of their solutions; hence some problems are inherently more difficult than other similar problems, independently of the number of solutions that they have. This requires further investigation, to see whether it is possible to predict the diversity of a problem's solutions before solving the problem.

The second reason also implies a mismatch between the variable and value ordering used by the algorithm and the problem being solved. It has been suggested that this may also be true for the third reason: although variations in the search space size are apparently due to differences in the constraint graphs, it has been proposed that a mismatch between the constraint graph and the algorithm's choice of first variable to instantiate is also a factor.

It is tempting to suggest that exceptionally difficult problems are likely to occur when the search space is exceptionally large and at the same time the diversity of the solutions is low. However, some preliminary work on sparse constraint graphs suggests that these two events are unlikely to occur in the same problem. It has been shown in [7] that for sparse constraint graphs, the location of the phase transition depends not just on n, m and p_1, but also on the constraint graph. That is, if a set of problems is generated as described earlier, but so that all problems in the set have the same constraint graph, then the phase transition for this set of problems may be significantly different from that of another problem set with the same parameter values but a different constraint graph. This is

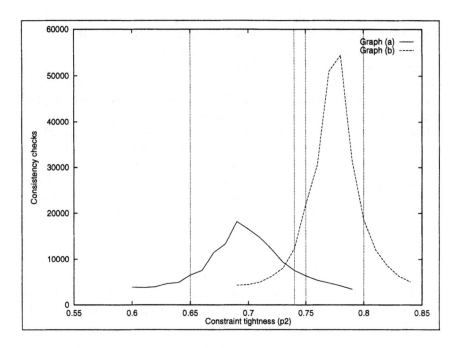

FIGURE 8.6. Phase transition for two sets of $\langle 30, 10, 0.1 \rangle$ CSPs with different constraint graphs

demonstrated in Figure 8.6, which shows the phase transition for two sets of $\langle 30, 10, 0.1 \rangle$ problems with different graphs (each point represents the median consistency checks to solve 300 problems). Graph (a) is from a set of randomly-generated graphs and has a very irregular degree distribution. Graph (b) was hand-generated and is as close to regular as possible (28 vertices have degree 3, 2 have degree 2, giving the required total of 44 constraints). Figure 8.6 shows also that the effort required to solve a problem or to show that it has no solution depends on the constraint graph, at least during the phase transition. Comparison with Figure 8.2 suggests that the size of the induced search space will be much greater for the regular graph than for the irregular graph for values of p_2 below the mushy region.

On the other hand, there are indications that the kind of clustering seen in the solutions to Problem Max is more likely to occur when the constraint graph is irregular; further work is therefore needed to establish whether the occurrences of exceptionally difficult problems can be explained by the reasons given above.

The ultimate aim in investigating phase transition phenomena is to be able to predict where an individual problem lies in relation to the phase transition, and hence to predict whether it is almost certain to be insoluble (in which case there is probably no point in making the attempt), almost certain to be easily soluble, or (in the mushy region) a hard problem which may or may not be soluble. The rare occurrence of exceptionally difficult problems in an otherwise easy region of the parameter space is an obstacle to this endeavour. Hence one reason for investigating these exceptionally difficult problems is to find out if it is possible to predict when they will occur, so as to have some idea in advance of how long it will take to solve a given problem. The fact that in randomly-generated CSPs with many solutions it may happen that every solution is very similar to many others is also somewhat surprising and may have implications for the design of algorithms. Exceptionally difficult problems also have their uses in improving existing search algorithms; they are cases where the algorithm being used fails spectacularly, and careful investigation of the individual problem and the reasons for the failure may indicate may indicate how to avoid a similar failure in future.

8.8 REFERENCES

[1] P. Cheeseman, B. Kanefsky, and W. Taylor. Where the *Really* Hard Problems are. In *Proceedings IJCAI-91*, volume 1, pages 331–337, 1991.

[2] I. P. Gent and T. Walsh. Easy Problems are Sometimes Hard. Research Paper 642, Department of A.I., University of Edinburgh, 1993.

[3] T. Hogg and C. P. Williams. The Hardest Constraint Problems: A Double Phase Transition. *Artificial Intelligence*, **69**, pages 359-377, 1994.

[4] D. Mitchell, B. Selman, and H. Levesque. Hard and Easy Distributions of SAT Problems. In *Proceedings AAAI-92*, pages 459–465, 1992.

[5] P. Prosser. Binary constraint satisfaction problems: some are harder than others. In A. Cohn, editor, *Proceedings of ECAI-94*, pages 95–99. Wiley, 1994.

[6] B. Smith. Phase Transition and the Mushy Region in Constraint Satisfaction Problems. In A.G.Cohn, editor, *Proceedings ECAI-94*, pages 100–104, Aug. 1994.

[7] B. M. Smith. Locating the Phase Transition in Constraint Satisfaction Problems. Research Report 94.16, School of Computer Studies, University of Leeds, May 1994.

[8] E. Tsang. *Foundations of Constraint Satisfaction*. Academic Press, 1993.

[9] C. Williams and T. Hogg. Using Deep Structure to Locate Hard Problems. In *Proceedings AAAI-92*, pages 472–477, 1992.

[10] C. Williams and T. Hogg. Extending Deep Structure. In *Proceedings of AAAI-93*, pages 152–158, 1993.

[11] C. Williams and T. Hogg. Exploiting the Deep Structure of Constraint Problems. *to appear in Artificial Intelligence*, 1994.

9

Using Bidirectionality to Speed Up Arc-Consistency Processing

Christian Bessière[1]
Jean-Charles Régin[2]

ABSTRACT In [2, 1], Bessière and Cordier said that the AC-6 arc-consistency algorithm is optimal in time on constraint networks where nothing is known about the constraint semantics. However, in constraint networks, it is always assumed that constraints are bidirectional. None of the previous algorithms achieving arc-consistency (AC-3 [8, 9], AC-4 [10], AC-6) use constraint bidirectionality. We propose here an improved version of AC-6 which uses this property. Then, we claim that our new algorithm is optimal in the number of constraint checks performed (i.e. given a variable, value, and arc ordering, it performs the minimum possible number of constraint checks according to these orders).

9.1 Introduction

In the last five years, the number of applications using constraint networks has dramatically increased. It appears that the more constraint networks are used, the simpler the constraint satisfaction techniques involved in the applications are. In fact, a great part of real-life applications using constraint networks are limited to a forward-checking search procedure [7], or use an arc-consistency filtering algorithm before or during the search. This is one of the reasons why arc-consistency remains a hot area in the CSP community [2, 1, 11, 12]. Improving the efficiency of arc-consistency algorithms improves in the same way the efficiency of all applications using arc-consistency as a filtering step.

Recently, Bessière and Cordier [2, 1] provided an algorithm, AC-6, which they claim to be optimal in time on constraint networks where nothing is known about the constraint semantics. However, in constraint networks, it

[1]LIRMM, UMR 9928 University of Montpellier II/CNRS, 161, rue Ada, 34392 Montpellier Cedex 5, France, e-mail: bessiere@lirmm.fr

[2]GDR 1093 CNRS, LIRMM, UMR 9928 University of Montpellier II/CNRS, 161, rue Ada, 34392 Montpellier Cedex 5, France, e-mail: regin@lirmm.fr

is always assumed that constraints are bidirectional (i.e. if the combination of values a for a variable i and b for a variable j is allowed by the constraint between i and j, then the combination b for j and a for i is allowed by the constraint between j and i), and none of the previous algorithms (AC-3 [8, 9], AC-4 [10], and AC-6) use this fact[3].

In this paper, we propose AC6++, an improved version of AC-6 which uses constraint bidirectionality. We claim that AC6++ is optimal in the number of constraint checks performed[4]. Moreover, AC6++ avoids the explosion of space complexity, keeping it at $O(ed)$, like AC-6 (where e is the number of constraints and d the size of the largest domain).

The rest of the paper is organized as follows. Section 9.2 gives some preliminary definitions on constraint networks and arc-consistency. Section 9.3 presents the algorithm AC6++. In section 9.4, an experimental comparison of AC-6 and AC6++ is given. Section 9.5 contains a conclusion.

9.2 Background

A *network of binary constraints* (CN) is defined as a set of n variables $\{i, j, ...\}$, a domain $D = \{D_i, D_j, ...\}$ where D_i is the finite set of possible values for variable i, and a set of binary constraints between variables. A *binary constraint* (or relation) R_{ij} between variables i and j is a subset of the Cartesian product $D_i \times D_j$ that specifies the allowed pairs of values for i and j. $R_{ij}(a, b)$ is true when the pair consisting of the element a of D_i and the element b of D_j is permitted; value false means the pair is not permitted. In all networks of interest here constraints are *bidirectional*, i.e. $R_{ij}(a, b) = R_{ji}(b, a)$. This is not a restriction.

A *directed graph* G can be associated to a constraint network, where nodes correspond to variables in the CN and two arcs (i, j) and (j, i) link nodes i and j every time there is a relation R_{ij} (and so R_{ji}) on variables i and j in the CN. In the following, the function Γ will be used, where for every node i, $\Gamma(i)$ is the set of nodes j such that $(i, j) \in arcs(G)$.

A solution of a constraint network is an instantiation of the variables such that all constraints are satisfied.

Having the constraint R_{ij}, value b in D_j is called a *support* for value a in D_i if the pair (a, b) is allowed by R_{ij}. A value a for a variable i is *viable* if for every variable j such that R_{ij} exists, a has a support in D_j. The domain D of a CN is *arc-consistent* for this CN if for every variable i in

---

[3]E.C. Freuder has just proposed an algorithm, AC-7, which uses that fact. AC6++ and AC-7 have been first presented in the same workshop ([4] and [6] respectively)

[4]An improved version of AC-6 (named AC6+), which uses constraint bidirectionality, was proposed in [3]. But it was not optimal in the number of constraint checks performed.

the CN, all values in D_i are viable. When a CN has a domain D, we call *maximal arc-consistent domain* of this CN domain $AC(D)$, defined as the union of all domains included in D and arc-consistent for this CN. $AC(D)$ is also arc-consistent and is the domain expected to be computed by an arc-consistency algorithm.

9.3 The new algorithm using bidirectionality

9.3.1 PREAMBLE

As we have seen in the definition above, and as Mohr and Henderson underlined in [10], arc-consistency is based on the notion of support. As long as a value a for a variable i (denoted by (i, a)) has supporting values on each of the other variables j linked to i in the constraint graph, a is considered a viable value for i. But once there is a variable on which no remaining value satisfies the relation with (i, a), then a must be eliminated from D_i.

AC-6, which assigns an ordering of the values in every D_i, checks one support (the first one) for each value (i, a) on each constraint R_{ij} to prove that (i, a) is currently viable. When (j, b) is found as the smallest support of (i, a) on R_{ij}, (i, a) is added to S_{jb}, the list of values currently having (j, b) as smallest support. If (j, b) is removed from D_j then AC-6 looks for the next support in D_j for each value (i, a) in S_{jb}. But AC-6 does not use the fact that $R_{ij}(a, b) = R_{ji}(b, a)$. When it looks for a support for (j, b) on R_{ji}, it does not use the fact that $R_{ij}(a, b)$ has perhaps already been checked for some (i, a) when looking for supports for values in D_i.

The purpose of AC6++ is to achieve arc-consistency after an optimal number of constraint checks, using constraint bidirectionality. It only performs a constraint check $R_{ij}(a, b)$ when none of the previously done constraint checks is sufficient to prove that (i, a) has a support in D_j, and moreover, when neither $R_{ij}(a, b)$ nor $R_{ji}(b, a)$ have been checked before. It is built to maintain true the properties below during the whole algorithm:

1. never checking $R_{ij}(a, b)$ if there exists b' still in D_j such that $R_{ij}(a, b')$ has already been successfully checked.

2. never checking $R_{ij}(a, b)$ if there exists b' still in D_j such that $R_{ji}(b', a)$ has already been successfully checked.

3. never checking $R_{ij}(a, b)$ if:

   (a) it has already been checked

   (b) $R_{ji}(b, a)$ has been checked before.

4. keeping an $O(ed)$ space complexity.

Properties (1), (2), and (3) define what we call the optimality of AC6++. So, optimality is defined according to a variable ordering, a value ordering, and an arc ordering. It does not imply the minimum number of constraint checks, but a minimal number according to the ordering used [14].

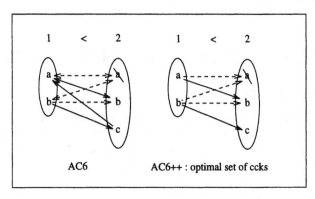

FIGURE 9.1. A sample CSP

Consider the simple problem of Fig. 9.1 for illustration purposes. There are two variables *1* and *2* with domains $\{a, b\}$ and $\{a, b, c\}$ respectively, linked by the constraint "inferior in the lexicographic order". An arrow from a value v for *1* to a value w for *2* indicates that the constraint check $R_{12}(v, w)$ has been performed. A double ended arrow indicates that both $R_{12}(v, w)$ and $R_{21}(w, v)$ have been checked. A solid arrow indicates a successful check; a dotted arrow indicates that the check was false. In this example, AC-6 needs 9 constraint checks where only 5 were necessary to achieve arc-consistency. AC6++ avoids useless constraint checks by enforcing properties (1), (2), and (3). Property (2) forbids $R_{21}(b, a)$ and $R_{21}(c, a)$. Property (3b) forbids $R_{21}(a, a)$ and $R_{21}(a, b)$ in addition. Both of these properties forbid $R_{21}(b, a)^5$. Properties (1) and (3a) were already enforced by AC-6 (but not by AC-3 or AC-4).

Every time a constraint check $R_{ji}(b, a)$ is performed, AC6++ needs to store this information to avoid future $R_{ij}(a, b)$ or $R_{ij}(a, b')$ checks forbidden by properties (3b) and (2). This storage must be done in a careful way to avoid falling into the trap of an $O(ed^2)$ space complexity. Then, there are two differences with the data structure of AC-6. First, S_{ia} sets are split into S_{ija} sets: each value (i, a) has a set of values supported by it per constraint instead of one for all the constraints. $b \in S_{ija}$ implies (i, a) is known as supporting (j, b) on R_{ji}, then (i, a) is compatible with (j, b). Hence, an $R_{ij}(a, b)$ is checked if and only if $S_{ija} = \emptyset$, otherwise we know (i, a) has a support on R_{ij} without any new constraint check. Property (2) holds. Property (3b) holds for successful constraint checks. Second, arrays *inf-*

---

[5] We can see that neither $R_{12}(a, c)$ nor $R_{21}(c, a)$ are checked by AC6++.

support are added. *inf-support*$[(i,j),a]$ represents the smallest value in D_j which may be compatible with (i,a). These arrays are needed to ensure property (3b) for negative constraint checks and property (3a)[6]. Property (1) is inherent in the principle of AC-6.

9.3.2   THE ALGORITHM

Here is the data structure of AC6++:

- A table M of Booleans keeps track of which values of the initial domain are in the current domain or not ($M(i,a)=$**true** $\Leftrightarrow a \in D_i$). In this table, each initial D_i is considered as the integer range $1..|D_i|$. We use the following constant time functions and procedures to handle D_i lists:

  - *last*(D_i) returns the greatest value in D_i if $D_i \neq \emptyset$, else returns 0.
  - if $a \in D_i \backslash last(D_i)$, *next*$(a, D_i)$ returns the smallest value in D_i greater than a.
  - *remove*(a, D_i) removes the value a from D_i. *remove*(a, D_i) can be extended to stop the arc-consistency algorithm if a was the only remaining value in D_i. The CN, indeed, has no solution.

- For all a in D_i, S_{ija} contains all values b in D_j for which (i,a) is assigned as its current support. The *current* support is not necessary the smallest one, as opposed to AC-6.

- In AC6++, we need to record arrays *inf-support*$[(i,j),a]$ which were not needed in AC-6. These arrays are updated by AC6++ to ensure that every b in D_j compatible with (i,a) is greater than or equal to *inf-support*$[(i,j),a]$.

- *Waiting-List* (as in AC-4 or AC-6) contains values deleted from the domain but for which the propagation of the deletion has not yet been processed.

The function *nextsupport* (see Fig. 9.2), which looks for the smallest value in D_j not smaller than b and supporting (i,a) on R_{ij}, is the same as in AC-6 except the addition of the test of line 3 to avoid checking $R_{ij}(a,b)$ when $R_{ji}(b,a)$ has already been checked as false (i.e. when we know that (j,b) has no support in D_i until a value greater than a).

---

[6]Property (3a) held in AC-6 without *inf-support* arrays because we knew that (i,a) was always the smallest support for values in S_{ia}. In AC6++ we lose this strong property.

function nextsupport(**in** i, j, a: integer; **in out** b: integer) : **Boolean**

/* returns true iff a value b is found */

1   **if** $b > \text{last}(D_j)$ **then** *return* **false**;
2   **while not** $M(j, b)$ **do** $b \leftarrow b + 1$;
3   **if** *inf-support*$[(j, i), b] \le a$ **then**
4   **if** $R_{ij}(a, b)$ **then** *return* **true**;
5   **if** $b < \text{last}(D_j)$ **then**
     $b \leftarrow \text{next}(b, D_j)$;
     goto line 3;
6   *return* **false**;

FIGURE 9.2.

Another function, *find-support* (see Fig. 9.3), is used in AC6++ to check whether an S_{ija} set contains values in D_j or not. Every time *find-support* unsuccessfully checks if a value b in S_{ija} is in D_j, b is deleted from S_{ija} to avoid checking it again in the following.

function find-support(**in out** S_{ija} : set; **out** b : *integer*) : **Boolean**

/* returns true iff a value b is found */

1   **if** $S_{ija} = \emptyset$ **then** *return* **false**;
2   $b \leftarrow$ an element of S_{ija};
3   **if** $M(j, b)$ **then** *return* **true**;
4   delete b from S_{ija};
5   **goto** line 1;

FIGURE 9.3.

The algorithm AC6++ roughly looks like AC-6, with an initialization step and a propagation step (see Fig. 9.4). The initialization step looks for at least one support for each value (i, a) on each constraint R_{ij}. But the search of support for (i, a) on R_{ij} is only done if S_{ija} does not contain values in D_j; otherwise, this search is useless: (i, a) has supports on R_{ij} (since values supported by (i, a) are supports for (i, a)). If the search of support is done for a value (i, a) on R_{ij} and a value b is found, a is added to S_{jib} since b is now the current support of (i, a). *inf-support*$[(i, j), a]$ records b as the smallest value in D_j supporting (i, a) on R_{ij} since the search follows the order of D_j.

The propagation step takes values (j, b) from the *Waiting-List* and propagates the consequences of their deletion. It looks for another support for values a in S_{jib} sets if they still belong to D_i and if they have no other known support on R_{ij} ($S_{ija} \cap D_j = \emptyset$).

{initialization}
1. *Waiting-List* ← *Empty-List*;
2. **for** $(i, a) \in \mathcal{D}$ **do** $M(i, a) \leftarrow$ **true**;
3. **for** $(i, j) \in arcs(G)$ **do**
4.   **for** $a \in D_i$ **do**
5. $S_{ija} \leftarrow \emptyset$;
6.   *inf-support*$[(i, j), a] \leftarrow 1$; /* first value of D_j */

7. **for** $(i, j) \in arcs(G)$ **do**
8.   **for** $a \in D_i$ **do**
9.   **if** find-support(S_{ija}, b) /* b is **out** */ **then**
10.   put a in S_{jib}

11.   **else**
12. $b \leftarrow$ *inf-support*$[(i, j), a]$;
13.   **if** nextsupport(i, j, a, b) /* b is **in out** */ **then**
14.   put a in S_{jib};
15.   *inf-support*$[(i, j), a] \leftarrow b$

16.   **else**
17.   remove(a, D_i); $M(i, a) \leftarrow$ **false**;
18.   Add-to(*Waiting-List*, (i, a));

{propagation}
19. **while** *Waiting-List* $\neq \emptyset$ **do**
20.   pick (j, b) from *Waiting-List*;
21.   **for** $i \in \Gamma(j)$ **do**
22.   **for** $a \in S_{jib}$ **do**
23.   delete a from S_{jib};
24.   **if** $M(i, a)$ **then**
25.   **if** find-support(S_{ija}, c) /* c is **out** */ **then**
26.   put a in S_{jic}

27.   **else**
28. $c \leftarrow$ *inf-support*$[(i, j), a]$;
29.   **if** nextsupport(i, j, a, c) /* c is **in out** */ **then**
30.   put a in S_{jic};
31.   *inf-support*$[(i, j), a] \leftarrow c$

32.   **else**
33.   remove(a, D_i); $M(i, a) \leftarrow$ **false**;
34.   Add-to(*Waiting-List*, (i, a));

FIGURE 9.4. AC6++

During the whole algorithm, every time a value is found without support on a constraint, it is removed from D and put in the *Waiting-List*.

In the example, after the processing of arc *(1,2)*, the data structure of AC6++ is in the following state: $S_{12v} = \emptyset$, $\forall v \in D_1$; $S_{21a} = \emptyset$; $S_{21b} = \{a\}$; $S_{21c} = \{b\}$; *inf-support*$[(1,2),a] = b$; *inf-support*$[(1,2),b] = c$; *inf-support*$[(2,1),v] = a$, $\forall v \in D_2$. After the processing of arc *(2,1)* some changes appear: $S_{12a} = \{b\}$; $S_{12b} = \{c\}$; a is removed from D_2; $\forall v \in D_2$, *inf-support*$[(2,1),v]$ is unchanged.

9.3.3   PROOF OF CORRECTNESS OF AC6++

AC6++ is similar to AC-6 except that it does not always ensure to know the smallest support for a value on a constraint, but only the existence of a support and an inferior bound below which no support exists. After the initialization step, the following property holds until the end of the algorithm:

$$(\alpha) \; \forall (i,a) \in D, \forall R_{ij}, \forall (j,b) \in D : R_{ij}(a,b) \Rightarrow b \geq \textit{inf-support}[(i,j),a]$$

Hence, when (i,a) has no current support, and no checked supports in D_j $(S_{ija} \cap D_j = \emptyset)$, we can start looking for another one at *inf-support*$[(i,j),a]$ without forgetting any support of (i,a). Moreover, we do not need to check $R_{ij}(a,b)$ for values b in D_j such that *inf-support*$[(j,i),b] > a$ because of property (α). So, despite line 3 of the function *nextsupport*, an (i,a) support cannot be forgotten. Thus, value (i,a) is only removed from D_i (lines 17 and 33) when it has no support in D_j on a constraint R_{ij}. If all previously removed values are out of $AC(D^0)$ (D^0 being the initial domain), then (i,a) is out of $AC(D^0)$. $AC(D^0)$ is trivially included in D when AC6++ is started (since $D^0 = D$). Then, by induction, (i,a) is out of $AC(D^0)$. Thus, $AC(D^0) \subseteq D$ is an invariable property of AC6++.

Every time a value (j,b) is removed, it is put in the *Waiting-List* until the values it was supporting are checked for other supports. Every time a value (i,a) is found without support on a constraint, it is removed from D. Thus, every value (i,a) in D has at least one support in $D \cup$ *Waiting-List* on each constraint R_{ij}. AC6++ terminates with an empty *Waiting-List*. Hence, after AC6++, every value in D has a support in D on each constraint. Thus, D is arc-consistent.

$AC(D^0) \subseteq D$ and D arc-consistent at the end of AC6++ implies that D is the maximal arc-consistent domain $AC(D^0)$ at the end of AC6++.

9.3.4   PROOF OF OPTIMALITY

In this section, we will show that the properties (1), (2), (3a), and (3b) of section 9.3.1 are kept true by AC6++.

With the same principle as AC-6, properties (1) and (3a) hold. Indeed, we stop looking for supports for a value (i, a) on R_{ij} as soon as we find the first support, and an $R_{ij}(a, b)$ cannot be checked twice since we start looking for a new support for (i, a) on R_{ij} where we stopped the previous time.

Every time a constraint check $R_{ji}(b, a)$ is successfully performed (when looking for a support for (j, b)), AC6++ records b in S_{ija}. Since AC6++ only looks for a support for (i, a) on R_{ij} if $S_{ija} \cap D_j = \emptyset$, we are sure that $R_{ij}(a, b)$ is only checked when none of the previously done constraint checks on R_{ji} can prove that (i, a) has a support in D_j. Property (2) holds.

Finally, we have to prove that when we check $R_{ij}(a, b), R_{ji}(b, a)$ has never been checked before. If $R_{ji}(b, a)$ has already been successfully checked, b must be in S_{ija} or out of D, and $R_{ij}(a, b)$ cannot be checked. If $R_{ji}(b, a)$ has been checked as false, that means that we have looked for a support for (j, b) in D_i and that (i, a) was not a support. So, if $b \in D_j$, inf-support$[(j, i), b]$ is greater than a, and line 3 of function nextsupport avoids checking $R_{ij}(a, b)$. Property (3b) holds.

9.3.5 TIME AND SPACE COMPLEXITY

The two inner loops of AC6++ are in nextsupport and find-support. Since each $R_{ij}(a, b)$ is checked at most once, in nextsupport, complexity due to the calls to this function is bounded above by $O(ed^2)$, as in AC-6. During the whole algorithm, a value $a \in D_i$ is put at most once in S_{jib}: when (j, b) is assigned as the current support of (i, a). find-support, which contains the second inner loop of AC6++, is called at most d times for each S_{ija} (when a value b current support of (i, a) is removed from D_j), for a total work of at most d deletions in each S_{ija}. find-support performs $O(d)$ on each S_{ija}, and so, complexity due to the calls to this function is bounded above by $2ed \times O(d)$ i.e. $O(ed^2)$. Thus, $O(ed^2)$ is the worst-case time complexity for AC6++, as for AC-6.

The worst-case space complexity of AC-6 was $O(ed)$ because of the size of S_{jb} sets. In AC6++, S_{jb} sets of AC-6 are split into S_{jib} sets. This does not increase their total size: each arc-value pair $[(i, j), a]$ has at most one current support (j, b) (i.e. a belonging to S_{jib}). Hence, the total size of the S_{jib} sets is bounded above by $O(ed)$.

Since all supports already found for a value are recorded (to avoid useless checks), this is not a trivial result, the intuition leading us to expect $O(ed^2)$. This result is based on the fact that in AC6++, as in AC-6, during the whole algorithm, the number of $R_{ij}(a, b)$ successfully checked with (i, a) and (j, b) still in $D \cup$ Waiting-List is bounded above by $O(ed)$. We have to add arrays inf-support, which take a $2ed$ space. Thus, the total space complexity of AC6++ remains $O(ed)$.

9.4   Experimental results

We tested the performances of the two algorithms on the same problems as in [2]. For each problem, we counted the number of constraint checks performed by each algorithm, as opposed to [2]. Moreover, the two algorithms use the extension of the procedure *remove* defined in 9.3.2 (i.e. exit from the algorithm as soon as a domain D_i is empty, which is called domain "wipe-out" by Wallace [13]).

The first comparison was the zebra problem [5]. We obtained the following results:

AC-6   :   1025   constraint checks
AC6++   :   734   constraint checks

In Fig. 9.5, we then compared the two algorithms on the n-queens problem (i.e. a $n \times n$ chessboard on which we want to put n queens, none of them attacked by any other).

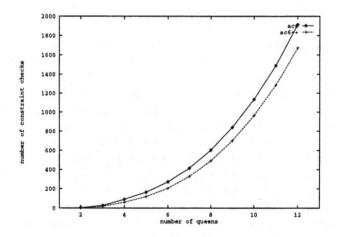

FIGURE 9.5. Comparison of AC-6 and AC6++ on the n-queens problem

Finally, we compared the two algorithms on the classes of randomly generated constraint networks used in [2]. Four parameters were taken into account: n the number of variables, d the number of values per variable, pc the probability that a constraint R_{ij} between two variables exists, and pu the probability in existing relations R_{ij} that a pair of values $R_{ij}(a, b)$ is allowed. The result given for each class is the average of thirty instances of problems in the class so as to be more representative of the class. In Fig. 9.6, 9.7, and 9.8, a vertical line shows the borderline between problems where wipe-out is generally produced (located on the left of the line), and problems where arc-consistency is produced (on the right).

In average, on the tested problems, AC6++ is around 20% better than AC-6 in the number of constraint checks performed. The interesting remark we made is that in these 20%, $R_{ij}(a, b)$ checks avoided because $R_{ji}(b, a)$ has already been checked only represent about 10%. The other 10% are $R_{ij}(a, b)$ checks avoided because there exists $b \neq b'$ such that $R_{ji}(b', a)$ has already been successfully checked.

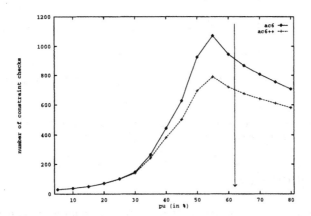

FIGURE 9.6. AC-6 and AC6++ on randomly generated CNs with 20 variables having 5 possible values, where the probability pc to have a constraint between two variables is 30%

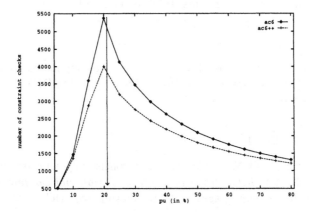

FIGURE 9.7. AC-6 and AC6++ on randomly generated CNs with 12 variables having 16 possible values, where the probability pc to have a constraint between two variables is 50%

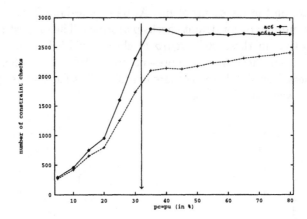

FIGURE 9.8. AC-6 and AC6++ on randomly generated CNs with 18 variables
having 9 possible values

9.5   Conclusion

We have provided an algorithm, AC6++, which achieves arc-consistency in
binary constraint networks where constraints are bidirectional. It uses this
property to avoid useless constraint checks. It performs a minimal number
of constraint checks w.r.t. the variable, value, and arc ordering, without
increasing the $O(ed)$ worst-case space complexity of AC-6. Its worst-case
time complexity is $O(ed^2)$ as for AC-6. Experimental comparison shows
that it significantly outperforms AC-6 in the number of constraint checks
performed.

Acknowledgements: The work of J.C. Régin was supported by SANOFI-
CHIMIE. Moreover, we want to thank Christophe FIORIO for his LaTeX
algorithm style.

9.6   References

[1]   C. Bessière and M.O. Cordier. Arc-consistency and arc-consistency
again. In *AAAI-93, Proceedings Eleventh National Conference on Artificial Intelligence*, pages 108–113, Washington, DC, 1993.

[2]   C. Bessière. Arc-consistency and arc-consistency again. *Artificial Intelligence*, 65(1):179–190, 1994.

[3]   C. Bessière. A fast algorithm to establish arc-consistency in constraint
networks. Technical Report TR 94-003, LIRMM University of Montpellier II, France, January 1994.

[4] C. Bessière and J.C. Régin. An arc-consistency algorithm optimal in the number of constraint checks. In *ECAI'94, Proceedings of the Workshop on Constraint Processing*, pages 9–16, Amsterdam, The Netherlands, 1994.

[5] R. Dechter. Enhancement schemes for constraint processing : Back-jumping, learning, and cutset decomposition. *Artificial Intelligence*, 41:273–312, 1990.

[6] E.C. Freuder. Using metalevel constraint knowledge to reduce constraint checking. In *ECAI'94, Proceedings of the Workshop on Constraint Processing*, pages 27–33, Amsterdam, The Netherlands, 1994.

[7] R.M. Haralick and G.L. Elliot. Increasing tree search efficiency for constraint satisfaction problems. *Artificial Intelligence*, 14:263–313, 1980.

[8] A.K. Mackworth. Consistency in networks of relations. *Artificial Intelligence*, 8:99–118, 1977.

[9] A.K. Mackworth and E.C. Freuder. The complexity of some polynomial network consistency algorithms for constraint satisfaction problems. *Artificial Intelligence*, 25:65–74, 1985.

[10] R. Mohr and T.C. Henderson. Arc and path consistency revisited. *Artificial Intelligence*, 28:225–233, 1986.

[11] M. Perlin. Arc consistency for factorable relations. *Artificial Intelligence*, 53:329–342, 1992.

[12] P. Van Hentenryck, Y. Deville, and C.M. Teng. A generic arc-consistency algorithm and its specializations. *Artificial Intelligence*, 57:291–321, 1992.

[13] R. J. Wallace. Why AC-3 is almost always better than AC-4 for establishing arc consistency in CSPs. In *IJCAI'93, Proceedings Thirteenth International Joint Conference on Artificial Intelligence*, pages 239–245, Chambéry, France, 1993.

[14] R.J. Wallace and E.C. Freuder. Ordering heuristics for arc consistency algorithms. In *Proceedings Ninth Canadian Conference on Artificial Intelligence*, pages 163–169, Vancouver, Canada, 1992.

10

Using Metalevel Constraint Knowledge to Reduce Constraint Checking

Eugene C. Freuder[1]

ABSTRACT Constraint satisfaction problems are widely used in artificial intelligence. They involve finding values for problem variables subject to constraints that specify which combinations of values are consistent. Knowledge about properties of the constraints can permit inferences that reduce the cost of consistency checking. Specifically, such inferences can be used to reduce the number of constraint checks required in establishing arc consistency, a fundamental constraint-based reasoning technique. A general AC-Inference schema is presented and various forms of inference discussed. Some of these apply only to special classes of contraints. However, a specific new algorithm, AC-7, is developed that takes advantage of a simple property common to all binary constraints to eliminate constraint checks that other arc consistency algorithms perform.

10.1 Introduction

Constraint satisfaction problems (*CSPs*) occur widely in artificial intelligence. They involve finding values for problem variables subject to constraints on which combinations are acceptable. For simplicity we restrict our attention here to *binary* CSPs, where the constraints involve two variables.

Binary constraints are binary relations. If a variable U has a domain of potential values DU and a variable V has a domain of potential values DV, the constraint on U and V is a subset of the Cartesian product of DU and DV. If the pair of values v for V and u for U is acceptable to the constraint C between V and U, i.e. a member of the Cartesian product, we will call the values *consistent* (with respect to C). Asking whether a pair of values is consistent is called a *constraint check*.

Constraints can be represented *implicitly*, where a computation, or a real-world process is needed to explicitly constraint check questions, or *ex-*

---

[1]Department of Computer Science, University of New Hampshire, Durham, NH 03824 USA, e-mail: ecf@cs.unh.edu

plicitly, where the answer is already recorded in a data base, e.g. a boolean matrix representation of a constraint C, where the matrix entry C(i,j) is true iff the combination of i and j is acceptable to C. Implicit constraint checks could be very costly to compute. Even if the constraints are represented explicitly in a form that permits quick computation there may be an enormous number to compute, along with associated decisions about which checks to make and how to use the results. As a result much of the work on constraint reasoning has focused on ways to reduce the number of constraint checks required.

Contraint algorithms often seek to establish *support* for a value u, i.e. to find a value for a variable V that is consistent with u (or to determine that no such value exists). Traditionally constraint checks have been used to establish support. This paper proposes to reduce constraint checks by using metalevel knowledge to *infer* support. I will demonstrate that one such inference can save many additional constraint checks, ensuring that the benefits of these inferences can more than offset the costs associated with making and exploiting them.

I apply this approach to building a schema for arc consistency algorithms. Arc consistency is one of the most basic and useful constraint reasoning processes. Thus arc consistency algorithms have been the subject of much interest [6]. For some time the state of the art resided in two algorithms, AC-4 [7], which has optimal worst-case behavior, and AC-3 [5], which often exhibits better average-case behavior [11]. Two AC-5 algorithms, one by Deville and Van Hentenryck [2] and another by Perlin [8], permit exploitation of specific constraint structures, but reduce to AC-3 or AC-4 in the general case. Recently Bessière and Cordier have developed AC-6, which retains the optimal worst-case behavior of AC-4 while improving on the average-case behavior of AC-3 [1].

The new algorithm schema, AC-Inference, owes something to all these predecessors, but permits use of inferred support. I use this schema to build a specific, new algorithm AC-7. AC-7 is a *general* arc consistency algorithm; it does not depend on special properties of a limited class of constraints. It simply utilizes the knowledge that support is *bidirectional*: u supports v if and only if v supports u. (It is tempting to assume that a special class of undirected constraints is required here; but a careful reading of [5] should demonstrate that this is not the case.)

I also identify two simple properties that constraints may have that permit additional inferences. Inferences can be based on metaknowledge that the constraints are irreflexive or commutative. I hope that AC-Inference will permit the exploitation of many other generic and problem domain specific properties of constraints. Furthermore, the metaknowledge inference approach should also be extensible to higher order consistency [3].

The potential redundancy in processing of bidirectional support has been recognized before. When AC-3 removes a value from the domain of variable X because it has no support in variable Y, it realizes that this cannot cause a value of Y to become bereft of support at X. DEEB [4] uses a "revise-both" procedure that more directly anticipates AC-7. After the values for X are checked for support at Y, values for Y are immediately checked for support at X, but only those Y values that have not just provided support for X values are checked. Gaschnig points out that this avoids unnecessary checks performed by AC-3 the first time the domains of X and Y are checked against each other; but he incorrectly, it seems to me, concludes that DEEB also avoids all the checks that AC-3 avoids by utilizing bidirectionality.

Neither algorithm, however, has any long term memory of inferences based on bidirectionality. For example, suppose that the first value, x_1, and last value, x_{100}, among a hundred values for X are found to be supported by a value y for Y. If later x_1 is deleted during the constraint propagation process, neither AC-3 nor DEEB will remember that y still is supported by x_{100}. In fact they may need to look at the other 98 values for X before "rediscovering" that y is supported by x_{100}.

More generally, both AC-3 and DEEB are "arc revision" oriented, while AC-7 is "support maintenance" oriented, in the spirit of AC-6. As a result, AC-7 will have the same sort of constraint check advantage over AC-3 that has been demonstrated for AC-6, plus the additional advantage provided by inferences based on bidirectionality.

I emphasize that the saving that AC-7 can achieve is not simply to avoid *redundant* checks, rechecking that u and v are consistent. AC-7 may avoid *initial* checks: it may never check whether u and v are consistent, while other algorithms do. I will show that there are problems for which AC-7 can avoid a quadratric number of such checks.

We compare AC-7 with AC-3, AC-4 and AC-6 (the AC-5 algorithms achieve their advantages for specific classes of constraints). In terms of constraint checks, AC-7 is capable of considerable improvement over AC-3, AC-4 and AC-6. AC-7 does require space quadratic in the maximum number, d, of values associated with any single variable, whereas AC-6 is linear in d; however, explicit *representation* of the constraints is already quadratic in d.

Of course, constraint checks alone do not tell the whole story. However, if we either assume a large enough cost per constraint check, or demonstrate a large enough savings in the number of constraint checks, the constraint check count will dominate overhead concerns.

In summary, the contributions of this paper are:

- A new approach to utilizing constraint metaknowledge: inferring support

- An algorithm schema, AC-Inference, that supports this approach

- A general-purpose arc consistency algorithm, AC-7, that exploits this approach

- Analytical evidence of the advantages of AC-7, specifically refuting the optimality of AC-6

- Identification of additional, specific constraint properties that permit additional inferences

Section 2 discusses the general theme of meta-level inference and presents the general algorithm schema. Section 3 focuses on the the specific AC-7 algorithm. Section 4 is a brief conclusion.

10.2   Inferring Support

10.2.1   PRINCIPLE

Coloring problems are classic combinatorial problems and have applications, e.g. to scheduling. Consider a trivial one for illustration purposes. The problem is to assign a color, a (aquamarine), b (blue) or c (coral), to each of two countries, A and B, such that A and B have different colors (in general countries which share a border require different colors).

As a CSP, the countries are the variables, the colors the values. The constraint between the two variables specifies that the two countries cannot have the same color (i.e. it is a not-equal constraint).

A value, v, is *arc inconsistent* if there is a variable for which there is no value that supports v. We achieve *arc consistency* by removing all arc inconsistent values—or in this simple coloring problem by verifying that there are no arc inconsistent values. In general, removing one value may make another value arc inconsistent, so we say that achieving arc consistency can involve a *constraint propagation* process. However, in this simple example we do not have to worry about that. Processing order can make a significant difference in arc consistency effort [12]. However, for purposes of illustration in this paper we will assume that variables and values are processed in lexicographic order initially.

The AC-4 arc consistency algorithm operates by first checking for all possible support. It stores summary information in support counters, and is later able to implement constraint propagation efficiently when propagation is required, by updating the counters rather than by performing further constraint checks. However, its brute force initial processing is costly; it performs all possible constraint checks twice (this total can be reduced when values are deleted during initial processing). Eighteen constraint checks are required for this little problem.

These are shown in Figure 10.1a. The values for country A are on the left, for country B on the right. An arrow from a value, i, for A to a value, j, for B indicates that a check of the consistency of i with j has been computed while seeking support for i. The double ended arrows indicate that redundant checks were made, while seeking support for both i and j.

A solid arrow indicates that the check established consistency; a dashed arrow indicates that the check established inconsistency.

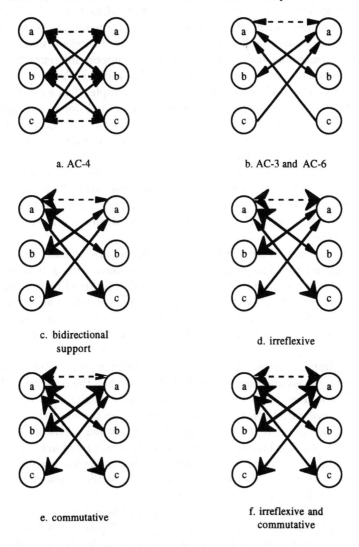

a. AC-4

b. AC-3 and AC-6

c. bidirectional
support

d. irreflexive

e. commutative

f. irreflexive and
commutative

FIGURE 10.1. Making inferences.

AC-3 seeks only to establish that each value has a supporting value (at every other variable). This only requires 8 constraint checks here (Figure 10.1b), but some of them are redundant. In general, AC-3 propagation can involve additional redundant checking, but this does not enter in here.

AC-6 can improve on AC-3 by avoiding some redundant checking during propagation. If the support it finds initially is deleted, it proceeds on from that point to look for another support; it does not need to "start over" as

AC-3 does. However, in this simple example, AC-6 has no opportunity to exhibit this additional intelligence. It too requires 8 constraint checks.

AC-3 may check pairs once, twice, or more than twice. AC-4 checks each pair at most twice. AC-6 was said to be optimal in the sense that it only made necessary checks. (The actual number of checks it makes is still subject to processing order effects.) However, support inference based on the bidirectionality of support can reduce constraint checks further.

AC-6 (AC-3 and AC-4 as well) checks, for example, that a for A is supported by b for B, and then separately checks that b for B is supported by a for A. These algorithms can not say: "oh, I already know b for B is supported; I just found that out while looking for support for a for A".

The AC-7 algorithm that I propose here *can*, in effect, say this. After it checks a for A against b for B and finds that the latter supports the former, it *infers* that the former also supports the latter. This inference is based upon the simple metaknowledge that support is bidirectional. Utilizing such inferences, AC-7 only requires 5 constraint checks to establish arc consistency.

This is shown in Figure 10.1c. Large barbed arrowheads are used to indicate inferences. The double-ended arrows here, with a barb on one end, indicate a constraint check in one direction followed by a constraint inference in the other. Notice that negative support information can also be inferred: after performing a constraint check to determine that a for B does not support a for A, we can infer that a for A does not support a for B.

In this simple example, AC-7 only saves redundant constraint checks; in fact, one might assume that at best it will require half the constraint checks of AC-6 on a given problem. However, in the next section we will see that AC-7 can save initial constraint checks and require far fewer than half the constraint checks of AC-6 for appropriately structured problems.

Moreover, AC-7 is but one instance of the general principal of using constraint metaknowledge to infer or avoid constraint checks. I will illustrate this point with a couple of further examples, and then present a general algorithmic schema that supports this principle.

Suppose we have further metaknowledge of these constraints. Suppose we know that they are also *irreflexive*: $C(i,i)$ and $C(i,i)$ do not hold for any i. Then the number of checks can be reduced to 4. Irreflexivity allows us to immediately infer that a for A is inconsistent with a for B, making it unnecessary to check this (Figure 10.1d).

Suppose we know that the constraints are *commutative*: $C(i,j) = C(j,i)$. This permits us to reduce the number of constraint checks to 3. For example, after checking $C(a,b)$ we can infer $C(b,a)$. See Figure 10.1e. If we know they are irreflexive and commutative, we are down to two checks, Figure 10.1f.

Finally, suppose we know that the constraints are inequality constraints. What does it mean to know that they are inequality constraints? Well one thing it could mean is that we have an inference rule that says simply: if the constraints are inequality constraints, and the domains contain more than one element, forget arc consistency processing—the problem is already arc consistent. This reduces the processing to zero constraint checks.

Notice that different inferences can be combined, and we can get inference chaining. However, as we increase our inferential power we have to make decisions about how much inferencing is cost effective. We can find ourselves making inferences we never use, or inferring the same constraint check repeatedly.

On the other hand, in evaluating the significance of inferred support we should bear in mind several factors that could increase the importance of utilizing such inferences:

- First, computing constraint checks could be costly.

- Second, inferring one support may permit us to avoid a number of additional constraint checks. I will discuss this further in connection with AC-7.

- Third, it may be that some support can only be determined by inference, at least within given time constraints.

- Fourth, even obviously unnecessary constraint checks may not be obvious to unintelligent automated systems.

Even the simple inferences associated with bidirectional support represent a form of common sense that must be implemented explicitly in our reasoning system. Accomodating inference can substitute intelligent observation for brute force examination.

10.2.2 SCHEMA

The key to the inference schema, as it is to AC-3, AC-4 and AC-6, is maintaining appropriate information. AC-3 determines which values need to be rechecked to see if they are still supported. AC-4 computes a total support count initially and then updates it as values are deleted. If AC-7 needs to find support for value v at variable U, it looks through an ordered list of U values for a single supporting value, u. If u is deleted, AC-7 looks for another supporting value later in the list.

The schema data structures are something of a hybrid of AC-4 and AC-6. Conceptually, for each value, v, for each variable, V, and each other variable U, which shares a constraint with V, AC-7 maintains a *support set* of values from the domain of U that support v, and the *unchecked set* of values from the domain of U that have not yet been checked to see if they support v. (Values that have been checked and found not to support v appear in neither set.)

Maintaining these sets enables the schema to remember inferred constraint check information. Positive results are remembered by adding to the support sets. Negative results are remembered by deleting from the unchecked sets. Like AC-6 we only have to work through the unchecked sets once; unlike AC-6 we can avoid some of those values via inference.

The detailed data structures to implement the schema are beyond the scope of this paper, and may well best vary depending on the specific instantiation of the schema and the structure of the problems being addressed. For our purposes here it is sufficient to note that the types of data structures used in AC-4 and AC-6 can be adapted for the schema.

The support data structures of AC-4 accept additional support during the initialization phase and can be modified to reflect deletion of support. For the schema, support can be both added and deleted throughout the processing. AC-6 proceeds through the variable domains as necessary looking for support, ignoring deleted values. The schema does the same, ignoring also values whose support status has already been inferred. The number of supporting and unchecked values can be maintained to facilitate deletion decisions.

The schema can be expressed as a processor for two streams.

```
Initialize the seek-support stream
Establish the initial support and unchecked sets,
    using any initial inferences
    Repeat until done:
    If process-deletion stream is not empty,
        process its first element
    else if seek-support stream is not empty,
        process its first element
    else done
```

FIGURE 10.2. AC-Inference Schema

The *seek-support* stream contains value-variable pairs. If v is a value for a variable V and the variable U shares a constraint with V, (v,U) will appear on the initial seek-support stream. Processing an element of this stream involves looking for support for the value in the unchecked set of the variable. After each constraint check a set of inferences is made, based on the outcome. The specific set of inferences chosen instantiates the schema.

The *process-deletion* stream consists of values whose support and unchecked sets at some variable are both empty. Processing a deletion involves removing it, at least conceptually, from the domain of values for its variable, and the support and unchecked sets in which it appears.

When both the support and unchecked sets for a value with respect to a variable become empty, that value enters the process-deletion stream. This can happen either as the result of seeking support or processing deletion.

When only the support set for a value with respect to a variable becomes empty, that value enters the seek-support stream. This can happen as the result of processing a deletion.

We saw earlier that inference can in fact make it unnecessary to perform any constraint checks. There is another sense in which AC-Inference can require zero constraint checks. If the constraints are being entered explicitly into the knowledge base, it may be reasonable to ask that they be entered directly in the form of support sets. In that case we can proceed directly to the constraint propagation phase for values without support.

This is not an inference issue; a similar observation could be made for AC-4. However, if some support set information was available explicitly and some was not, with AC-Inference we could use the former to establish initial support sets, and the latter for initial unchecked sets.

10.3   AC-7

The AC-7 algorithm exploits the bidirectionality of support. It instantiates the AC-Inference schema by inferring that v supports u whenever it determines that u supports v, and by inferring that v does not support u whenever it determines that u does not support v. Figure 10.1c in fact has already illustrated the operation of AC-7 on our initial example.

I will sketch several propositions regarding AC-7 performance. The comparisons made are in terms of constraint checks versus AC-3, AC-4 and AC-6.

Proposition 1 *AC-7 has a worst-case time and space bound quadratic in the number of variables and the maximum domain size.*

First we observe that the space requirements of AC-7 are quadratic as with AC-4. The space needed to represent the support and unchecked sets is of the same order of magnitude as that needed to represent the constraints themselves explicitly. AC-6 is more parsimonious in its space requirements, but unless the constraints are to be represented implicitly this does not seem to be a significant issue. Even with implicit constraints, we may need a quadratic amount of space to store constraint checks once computed, to avoid computing them redundantly during search.

The worst case time bound is similarly quadratic, as it is for the other algorithms. Each of the quadratic number of possible constraint checks is performed at most once. In terms of overall effort, beyond constraint check counts, we might have a concern in comparing worst-case bounds with AC-4 and AC-6 about the effort involved in updating the support and unchecked sets. However, recall that these can be implemented using similar data structures to those employed in AC-4 and AC-6.

We will now look at a number of sample problems, problem structures really, to demonstrate the different levels of savings that are possible for AC-7 as compared to these other algorithms. Figure 10.3 shows the microstructure of these problems in the form of a *consistency graph*, where each consistent pair of values is joined by an edge. Each of these problems will just involve two variables, and we will put the values for each variable in a separate column, assuming the unlabeled values are ordered lexicographically from top to bottom, and the unlabeled variables are ordered lexicographically from left to right.

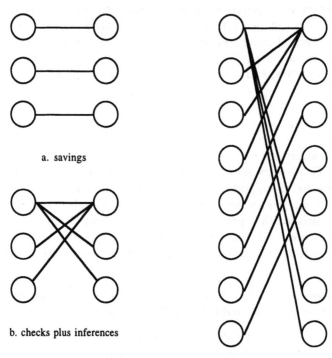

a. savings

b. checks plus inferences

c. more savings

FIGURE 10.3. Analysis.

Note first that AC-7 is unlikely to make matters worse. AC-4 always computes all checks twice, AC-7 at most twice. (Both can avoid some checks by deleting unsupported values.) AC-3 and AC-6 look for a support and then look for additional support only as needed, when current support is deleted, AC-6 avoiding some redundant checks made by AC-3. The same is true of AC-7, including the avoidance of redundant checks, but inferences further reduce redundant checking and may reduce the need to look for support.

Of course, specific case performance of these algorithms depends in part on the order in which constraint checks are made (and may benefit from ordering heuristics). AC-4 and AC-6 complete an initialization phase before turning their attention to deletions. A queue-based implementation of AC-3 will as well. The stream-oriented implementation of the inference schema is potentially profitable in its priority handling of deletions.

On the other hand, we could add bidirectional support inference more directly to AC-6, as AC-6 built on the structure of AC-4, to guarantee fewer constraint checks. Moreover the results we will now establish demonstrating the potential savings of AC-7 would also hold for this algorithm. However, the stream implementation seems likely to be more efficient in practice (as well as more elegant in expression).

Proposition 2 *AC-7 can save d checks for any constant d.*

Consider the problem in Figure 10.3a. (This could be regarded as representing an equality constraint, as opposed to the inequality constraints we focused on earlier in the context of coloring problems.) The support for the third value of the second variable that is inferred by AC-7 requires 3 constraint checks to find for the other algorithms. If we construct a similar problem where each variable has d values rather than 3, AC-7 will save at least d constraint checks.

It might seem at first glance that AC-7 can only avoid computing redundant checks that establish whether u supports v after establishing whether v supports u. If this were the case one might argue that it would be no more costly, when we have explicitly represented constraints, to make the redundant check than it would be to infer the support; and for costly, implicitly represented constraints we could store the result of the initial constraint check explicitly and then look it up if it was required redundantly.

In fact, one might be be concerned that the number of checks *plus* the number of inferences, for AC-7, (one per check) could exceed the number of checks for another algorithm. This can happen; see Figure 10.3b in which AC-7 uses 5 checks and 5 inferences, while AC-3 or AC-6 only requires 6 checks. (More concretely there is the issue of the cost associated with utilizing inferences.)

However, first, bear in mind that inferring non-support and utilizing it immediately can justify the deletion of values. Early deletions of values can lead to further savings, as we no longer have to seek support for these deleted values, or consider them as possible supports for other values. It may even lead to early discovery of unsolvability.

Second, AC-7 can save more than redundant checks.

Proposition 3 *AC-7 can avoid initial constraint checks.*

In fact the problem in Figure 10.3a also demonstrates this. The savings noted earlier included avoiding checks that were not computed earlier.

Even in this example, however, the number of checks for AC-7 is only half the number of checks for AC-3 and AC-6. Thus the total of checks plus inferences for AC-7 equals the number of checks for these algorithms. We can argue that this advantage could be greater than it first appears, if some of the checks AC-7 avoids are very costly, perhaps even impossible, to compute. We can go further, however, and show that AC-7 can, in fact, more than cut in half the number of constraint checks, thus guaranteeing that checks plus inferences for AC-7 will still be less than the number of checks for the other algorithms.

Proposition 4 *AC-7 can more than cut in half the number of constraint checks.*

Figure 10.3c presents an example in which the number of checks for AC-7 is 21; for AC-3 or AC-6, 48.

Observe that this example generalizes to show that AC-7 can save a quadratic number of initial checks. (The total number of different possible checks is only quadratic itself.)

Proposition 5 *AC-7 can save a quadratic number of initial constraint checks.*

The previous example can be generalized from domain sizes of 8 to domain sizes of d, where $O(d^2)$ checks are saved. Observe that it is constructed so that d/2 of the values in the second domain must be checked (and fail) against from d/2-1 to d-1 of the values in the first domain with AC-3 or AC-6, while AC-7 avoids these checks entirely.

Notice that we have established these various propositions without even considering constraint propagation, where further savings may be realized. We would expect AC-7 to show to best advantage on problems with structures such as those above, that can especially benefit from the undirected constraint inferences. We would expect AC-7 to show to better advantage on more tightly constrained problems, where one has to look harder to find support, and thus can benefit more when inferences preclude the need to look for support. Of course, we would expect AC-7 to show to better advantage on problems where individual constraint checks are costly.

Changing the order in which values are considered can increase (or reduce) the advantage of AC-7, but since these advantages are tied to the structure of the consistency graph, and since determining consistency graph structure involves performing the very constraint checks we are trying to avoid, it is difficult to argue strongly for or against AC-7 based on such ordering considerations. However, in specific cases, we might be able to utilize metaknowledge of the consistency graph structure for effective value-ordering heuristics.

One of the most important uses of arc consistency may be in combination with backtrack search where arc consistency is dynamically maintained as search choices are made [9]. In this situation AC-4 may normally prove superior to both AC-6 and AC-7. However, one might still want to employ the basic insight of this paper, modifying AC-4 to make inferences based on bidirectional support or problem-specific constraint properties. Ultimately the significance of AC-7 may lie in its extension to higher order consistency, and as a simple example of the potential of AC-Inference.

10.4   Conclusion

Metaknowledge about constraints can be used to infer, rather than compute, support information, and to both infer and avoid constraint checks. A variety of basic properties of constraint relations can be exploited in this way. The AC-Inference schema permits exploitation of inferences in establishing arc consistency. AC-7 is an instance of that schema that exploits only the bidirectionality of support; thus is a fully general arc consistency algorithm. AC-7 can exhibit significant savings over previous general arc consistency algorithms. AC-Inference may prove especially useful when constraint checks are costly to compute, and when constraints have strong structural features. More generally this line of inquiry provides an opportunity to synergistically meld constraint-based and rule-based reasoning (see also [10]), and to take advantage of domain specific constraint metaknowledge.

Acknowledgements: This material is based on work supported by the National Science Foundation under Grant No. IRI-9207633. I would like to thank Alan Mackworth for a very helpful discussion.

10.5   References

[1] C. Bessière and M. O. Cordier. Arc consistency and arc consistency again. In *Proceedings of the Eleventh National Conference on Artificial Intelligence*, pages 108–113, 1993.

[2] Y. Deville and P. Van Hentenryck. An efficient arc consistency algorithm for a class of csp problems. In *Proceedings of the Twelfth International Joint Conference on Artificial Intelligence*, pages 325–330, 1991.

[3] E. Freuder. Synthesizing constraint expressions. *Communications of the ACM*, 21:958–966, 1978.

[4] J. Gaschnig. Experimental case studies of backtrack vs waltz-type vs new algorithms for satisficing assignment problems. In *Proceedings of the Second National Conference of the Canadian Society for Computational Study of Intelligence*, pages 268–277, 1978.

[5] A. Mackworth. Consistency in networks of relations. *Artificial Intelligence*, 8:99–118, 1977.

[6] A. Mackworth and E. Freuder. The complexity of constraint satisfaction revisited. *Artificial Intelligence*, 59:57–62, 1993.

[7] R. Mohr and T. Henderson. Arc and path consistency revisited. *Artificial Intelligence*, 28:225–233, 1986.

[8] M. Perlin. Arc consistency for factorable relations. *Artificial Intelligence*, 53:329–342, 1992.

[9] D. Sabin and E. Freuder. Contradicting conventional wisdom in constraint satisfaction. In *Proceedings of the Eleventh European Conference on Artificial Intelligence*, pages 125–129, 1994.

[10] S. Subramanian and E. Freuder. Compiling rules from constraint-based experience. *International Journal of Expert Systems: Research and Applications*, 6:401–418, 1993.

[11] R. Wallace. Why ac-3 is almost always better than ac-4 for establishing arc consistency in csps. In *Proceedings of the Thirteenth International Joint Conference on Artificial Intelligence*, pages 239–245, 1993.

[12] R. Wallace and E. Freuder. Ordering heuristics for arc consistency algorithms. In *Proceedings of the Ninth Canadian Conference on Artificial Intelligence*, pages 163–169, 1992.

11

Forward Checking with Backmarking

Patrick Prosser[1]

ABSTRACT The forward checking routine (FC) of Haralick and Elliott attempts to encourage early failures within the search tree of constraint satisfaction problems, leading to a reduction in nodes visited, which tends to result in reduced search effort. In contrast, Gaschnig's backmarking routine (BM) attempts to avoid performing redundant consistency checks. These two algorithms are combined to give FC-BM, an algorithm that attempts to minimise the number of nodes visited, while avoiding redundant consistency checks. This algorithm is further enhanced such that it incorporates conflict-directed backjumping (CBJ) to give FC-BM-CBJ. A series of experiments are then carried out on really hard problems in an attempt to position these new algorithms with respect to the known algorithms.

11.1 Introduction

In the binary constraint satisfaction problem we are given a set of variables, where each variable has a domain of values, and a set of constraints, where a constraint acts between a pair of variables. The problem is then to find an assignment of values to variables, from their respective domains, such that the constraints are satisfied [5, 11, 12, 13]. Typically these problems may be addressed by backtracking search, such as naive backtracking (BT) [1], backmarking (BM) [7], backjumping (BJ) [8], forward checking (FC) [10], graph-based backjumping (GBJ) [4], conflict-directed backjumping (CBJ) [17], dynamic backtracking (DB) [9], and the hybrid algorithms reported in [18]. All of these algorithms are *complete*, in that if the csp is satisfiable they will eventually find a solution, and if the csp is over-constrained they will terminate.

Most empirical studies, so far, have considered FC to be the best algorithm of the set {BT, BM, BJ, GBJ, FC} with BM a close competitor, and some have gone so far as to suggest that a significant improvement could be brought about by combining FC with BM [14, 6]. In this paper

[1]Department of Computer Science, University of Strathclyde, Glasgow G1 1XH, Scotland

we present such an algorithm, namely FC-BM, and enhance it such that it also incorporates conflict-directed backjumping (FC-BM-CBJ). A series of experiments are then carried out to position these new algorithms with respect to the existing algorithms.

The algorithms are presented in unstructured English (although pseudo code is given in the appendix) but the variable names and descriptions are compatible with those in [16, 17, 18]. We assume that we have the following global variables; an array of n variables, such that $v[i]$ is the ith variable; each variable has a discrete domain of values $domain[i]$, such that $domain[i]$ has cardinality m; each variable also has a *working* domain, namely $current - domain[i]$. When a variable is instantiated with a value $v[i] := k$, that value k is selected from $current - domain[i]$. If that instantiation is discovered to be infeasible then k is removed from $current - domain[i]$, and when backtracking takes place from i to h (where $h < i$) $current - domain[i]$ will be reset to $domain[i]$. We have a constraint matrix C, such that $C[i, j]$ is a constraint relation between $v[i]$ and $v[j]$. If there is no constraint between $v[i]$ and $v[j]$ then $C[i, j]$ will be *nil*.

11.2   BackMarking (BM)

Backmarking [7] attempts to avoid the execution of redundant consistency checks. There are two scenarios where consistency checks can be shown to be redundant. The first is when we know that checking will fail, and the second is when we know that checking will succeed. In backmarking (BM), or in fact any backward checking algorithm, we instantiate the current variable $v[i]$ with a value k and check (backwards) against the instantiated variables (the past variables). That is, we check $v[i] := k$ against $v[1]$. If this test succeeds we then check $v[i] := k$ against $v[2]$, and so on to $v[i - 1]$, so long as no consistency check fails. Assume that consistency checking between $v[h]$ and $v[i]$ failed (where $h < i$). We can now deduce two pieces of search knowledge. The next time that $v[i]$ becomes the current variable we may again try the instantiation $v[i] := k$. If $v[h]$ has not been re-instantiated with a new value then we can be sure that the consistency check between $v[h]$ and $v[i] := k$ will again fail. Therefore we do not have to attempt this instantiation. Nadel refers to this as a type (a) saving [14].

Conversely assume that since we last visited $v[i]$ we have backtracked to $v[g]$ (where $g < h$), and that we have reinstantiated $v[g]$ and $v[g + 1]$, right up to $v[i - 1]$. We can now be certain that $v[i]$ will again pass consistency check with $v[f]$, for all $f < g$, because these variables have not changed values. Therefore we need only perform consistency checks between $v[h]$ and the instantiation $v[i] := k$, for all h, where $g \leq h < i$. Nadel calls this a type (b) saving.

These tests can be implemented by using two arrays, namely mcl and mbl. mcl is an n by m array. When a consistency check is performed between $v[h]$ and $v[i] := k$ the array element $mcl[i, k]$ is set to h. That is, mcl is the 'maximum checking level' performed for a given instantiation (and initially $mcl[i, k]$ is set to zero for all i and all k). mbl is an n element one dimensional array, and corresponds to the 'minimum backtracking level'. $mbl[i]$ records the shallowest variable in the search tree that has been re-instantiated since we last visited $v[i]$. Initially $mbl[i]$ is set to zero, for all i. When we backtrack from $v[i]$ to $v[i-1]$ we set $v[i]$ to $i-1$, and set $mbl[j]$ to the minimum of $mbl[j]$ and $i-1$, for all j where $i < j \le n$. Therefore, when we again attempt to instantiate $v[i] := k$ we perform the following tests:

(a) if $mcl[i, k] < mbl[i]$ we know that the consistency check has failed in the past against some variable $v[h]$, where $h < mbl[i]$, and since this variable has not changed value the test will fail again.

(b) if $mcl[i, k] \ge mbl[i]$ we know that the instantiation has passed consistency checks with all variables $v[g]$, where $g < mbl[i]$, and that these variables have not changed values. Therefore these tests will again succeed, and we only need to test $v[h]$ against $v[i] := k$, for all h, where $mbl[i] \le h < i$.

11.3   Forward Checking (FC)

In forward checking [10] we instantiate the current variable $v[i] := k$ and then check forwards against the uninstantiated (future) variables. In doing this we remove from the current domain's of variables values which are incompatible with $v[i] := k$. That is, we instantiate $v[i] := k$ and check against all remaining instantiations for $v[i + 1]$ (assuming of course that there is a constraint $C[i, i+1]$ between $v[i]$ and $v[i+1]$). Any incompatibilities are then removed from $current - domain[i+1]$. If there are still values remaining for $v[i + 1]$ we then check forwards from $v[i]$ to $v[i + 2]$ (again assuming the existence of constraint $C[i, i + 2]$), and so on until we check from $v[i]$ to $v[n]$. If any forward checking from $v[i]$ to $v[j]$ (where $i < j$) removes all values from $current - domain[j]$ (ie. annihilates the current domain) then we undo the effects of forward checking and attempt a new instantiation for $v[i]$, and if there are no values remaining to be tried we then re-instantiate $v[i - 1]$.

11.4   Forward Checking with BackMarking (FC-BM)

We can incorporate the type (a) savings of BM into FC, and we do this by making the effects of forward checking explicit. Assume that we instantiate

$v[i] := k$ and check forwards against $v[j]$. Assume that this results in the removal of incompatible values from $current - domain[j]$. We can record the fact that $v[i]$ removes values, and we do this in the array element $past - fc[j]$. That is, $past - fc[j]$ is a set of variables indices, such that if $v[i]$ checks against $v[j]$ then $i \in past - fc[j]$. We initialise $past - fc[i]$ to be $\{0\}$ for all i. That is, we assume that the pseudo variable $v[0]$ checks forwards against all other variables, and that it removes no values from the current domain's of future variables (there are a number of reasons why this is done, and these are explained later on).

Assume that when we attempt the instantiation of $v[i] := k$ we check forwards against $v[j]$ and this results in the annihilation of $current - domain[j]$. We then uninstantiate $v[i]$ and undo the effects of forward checking from $v[i]$. We can now be sure that if we do not re-instantiate any of the variables forward checking against $v[j]$ then the instantiation $v[i] := k$ will again annihilate $current - domain[j]$. Conversely, if h is the largest variable index in $past - fc[j]$, and any variable $v[g]$ is re-instantiated (where $g \leq h$) we might be able to re-consider the instantiation of $v[i] := k$.

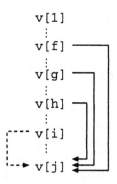

FIGURE 11.1. Forward Checking Scenario 1

Figure 11.1 shows a forward checking scenario that exhibits the above properties. Variable $v[f]$ has been instantiated with a value and forward checking takes place against $v[j]$, filtering $current - domain[j]$. The instantiation of $v[g]$ also checks forwards against $v[j]$ (again removing values from $current - domain[j]$) as does the instantiation of $v[h]$ (where $f < g < h < i < j$). We then attempt an instantiation of the current variable $v[i] := k$ and this checks forwards against $v[j]$ (the dotted line). This instantiation is incompatible with all remaining values in $current - domain[j]$ (ie. it annihilates $v[j]$). The effects of forward checking from $v[i]$ are then undone, and the array element $past - fc[j]$ will then be $\{0, f, g, h\}$. We can now be sure that the instantiation $v[i] := k$ will be infeasible until we backtrack to (or above) $v[h]$.

We can encode this by again using the arrays mcl and mbl. In this case let mcl be initialised such that $mcl[i, k] := i$, for all i and all k. If forward checking from the instantiation $v[i] := k$ annihilates $current-domain[j]$ we then undo the effects of forward checking from $v[i]$ and set $mcl[i, k]$ to the maximum value in $past - fc[j]$. That is, $mcl[i, k]$ is the deepest variable that checks forwards against $v[j]$. Conversely, if $v[i] := k$ is consistent with the current search state (or we have no evidence to believe that the instantiation is inconsistent) then we set $mcl[i, k]$ to i. $mbl[i]$ is as-before, and records the shallowest variable that has been re-instantiated since we last visited v[i] (and $mbl[i]$ is initially 0, for all i). Therefore, we have the type (a) saving for forward checking with backmarking (FC-BM):

(a) If $mcl[i, k] < mbl[i]$ then the instantiation $v[i] := k$ will annihilate the current domain of some future variable. That is, we have not re-instantiated any of the variables that check forward against $v[j]$, and if $v[i]$ is again assigned the value k then (again) $current - domain[j]$ will be annihilated. Therefore, do not consider this instantiation.

Again, we update $mbl[i]$ as in BM, but with one detailed change. Assume that we are backtracking from $v[i]$, and we are about to set $mbl[i] := i - 1$. We must now be careful, for the following reason. Assume that $mbl[i] = f$ and that we are about to set $mbl[i]$ to h, where $0 < f < h$ ($mbl[i]$ is about to increase in value from some non-zero value). This corresponds to a situation where we have previously encountered a search state where we were unable to instantiate $v[i]$ and eventually backtracking took place up to variable $v[f]$ (causing $mbl[i]$ to be set to f). The search process then advanced back down through the search tree to $v[i]$, and no compatible instantiation was found for $v[i]$. It may be the case that we have some $k \in domain[i]$ such that

(1) k has been removed from $current-domain[i]$ due to forward checking from $v[g]$ where $g < h$, and

(2) $mcl[i, k] \geq f$ implying that the instantiation $v[i] := k$ should now be considered as a possibility, due to rule (a) above.

In the above situation, if we blindly set $mbl[i]$ to h then the next time that we visit $v[i]$ we would not consider the instantiation $v[i] := k$ as it would appear that we had not backtracked to $v[f]$. In essence, this complication arises because when we visit $v[i]$ we might not examine all values in $domain[i]$, because some of these values may have been disallowed due to forward checking. Consequently, the information in $mcl[i, k]$ may be out of date. Therefore, when we backtrack from $v[i]$ we must analyse $mcl[i, k]$, for all k, before we set $mbl[i]$ to $i - 1$. That is,

If $0 < mbl[i] < i - 1$ then for all $k \in domain[i]$, if $mcl[i, k] \geq mbl[i]$ then set $mbl[i, k]$ to i

This will allow us to reconsider the instantiation $v[i] := k$ the next time that we visit $v[i]$. If we did not do this we would have an incomplete search algorithm.

FIGURE 11.2. Forward Checking Scenario 2

It is worth noting that FC-BM automatically achieves directed arc consistency [3] during the search process. This is demonstrated in Figure 11.2, the second forward checking scenario. Assume that we attempt the instantiation $v[i] := k$ and this annihilates $current - domain[j]$. Further assume that no other variable forward checks against $v[j]$. Therefore, all values in $current - domain[j]$ are incompatible with $v[i] := k$. When we undo the effects of forward checking from $v[i]$ the array element $past - fc[j]$ will be $\{0\}$, consequently $mcl[i, k]$ will be set to 0 (ie. the largest valued index in $past - fc[j]$). The instantiation $v[i] := k$ will never be attempted again, because $mcl[i, k]$ will always be less than $mbl[i]$ during the search process. It is only when we attempt to backtrack beyond $v[1]$ to $v[0]$ that we would allow this value, and when we backtrack to $v[0]$ the search process terminates as there is no solution to the csp.

11.5   No type (b) saving in FC-BM?

There is no efficient type (b) saving within forward checking. If we know that forward checking from the instantiation $v[i] := k$ to $v[j]$ does not annihilate $current - domain[j]$ we must still go ahead and do it. We must go ahead and filter out the incompatible values from $current - domain[j]$ otherwise we could then make an instantiation of $v[j]$ that was in conflict with the past variables. To be strictly correct we should then call FC-BM, FC-PBM (Forward Checking with Partial BackMarking).

11.6   FC with Conflict-directed BackJumping (FC-CBJ)

If we assume that we have made the effects of forward checking explicit, via $past - fc[j]$ then we can exploit this information to allow conflict-directed backjumping (CBJ) within forward checking [17, 18]. Assume that $v[i] := k$ annihilates $current - domain[j]$ and that we then undo the effects of forward checking from $v[i]$ to $v[j]$. Further assume that k was the only value in $current - domain[i]$ (only to simplify this explanation).

In order to resolve this conflict we have 2 options open to us. First, we may uninstantiate some variable that forward checks against $v[j]$ such that $current - domain[j]$ is relaxed, or we can uninstantiate some variable that forward checks against $v[i]$. That is we should jump back to the largest indexed variable in $past - fc[i] \cup past - fc[j]$ (ie. jump back to the variable deepest in the search tree that checks forward against $v[i]$ or $v[j]$).

In fact we can maintain a conflict set [4] for each variable, $conf - set[i]$ (where initially $conf - set[i]$ is set to $\{0\}$ for all i, corresponding to a conflict with the pseudo variable $v[0]$). If an instantiation of $v[i]$ annihilates $current - domain[j]$ we undo the effects of forward checking and update $conf - set[i]$ such that it becomes $conf - set[i] \cup past - fc[j]$. When there are no values remaining to be tried in $current - domain[i]$ we then jump back to $v[h]$ where h is the highest valued index in $past - fc[i] \cup conf - set[i]$, and we update $conf - set[h]$ to become $conf - set[h] \cup conf - set[i] \cup past - fc[i] - h$.

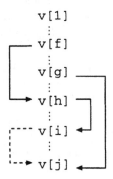

FIGURE 11.3. Forward Checking Scenario 3

In Figure 11.3, the third forward checking scenario, $v[f]$ checks forwards against $v[h]$, $v[g]$ checks forwards against $v[j]$, and $v[h]$ checks forwards against $v[i]$. The instantiation $v[i] := k$ annihilates $current - domain[j]$. Consequently $conf - set[i]$ becomes $\{0,g\}$. If there are no more values to be tried in $current - domain[i]$ we then jump back to the largest index in $conf - set[i] \cup past - fc[i]$ (ie. largest element of $\{0,h,g\}$), namely $v[h]$, and $conf - set[h]$ becomes $\{0,g\}$. If there are no values remaining to be tried for $v[h]$ we then jump back to $v[g]$, and $conf - set[g]$ becomes $\{0,f\}$. We might then jump back from $v[g]$ to $v[f]$, setting $conf - set[f]$ to $\{0\}$, and ultimately jumping from $v[f]$ to the pseudo variable $v[0]$ (where the search process would terminate).

11.7   FC with BM and CBJ (FC-BM-CBJ)

Just as we can combine backjumping with backmarking (to give BMJ) [16], and conflict-directed backjumping with backmarking (BM-CBJ) [18], we can also incorporate backmarking into FC-CBJ (with minor surgery). When an instantiation $v[i] := k$ annihilates $current - domain[j]$ we remember that $v[j]$ was in fact the "victim" of forward checking. That is, if $v[i] := k$ annihilates $current - domain[j]$ we undo the effects of forward checking from $v[i]$, update $mcl[i, k]$ such that it becomes the highest valued index in $past - fc[j]$, and update the array element $victim[i, k] := j$ (where $victim$ is an n by m array, each element initialised to some 'dont care' value). We also update $conf - set[i]$ to maintain the backjumping information required by the CBJ component of FC-CBJ.

When we re-visit $v[i]$, and are about to make the instantiation $v[i] := k$ we make a type (a) saving because $mcl[i, k] < mbl[i]$. However, we still have to update $conf - set[i]$. We do this by setting j to be $victim[i, k]$ and $conf - set[i]$ to be $conf - set[i] \cup past - fc[j]$. If there are no values remaining to be tried for $v[i]$ we then jump back to $v[h]$ where h is the largest valued index in $conf - set[i] \cup past - fc[i]$. When we jump back from $v[i]$ to $v[h]$ we update $mcl[i, k]$ in a manner similar to that described for FC-BM; set $mbl[i]$ to h, and set $mbl[j]$ to the minimum value of $mbl[j]$ or h, for all j, where $h < j \leq n$.

In fact the updating of $mcl[i, k]$, on jumping back from $v[i]$ to $v[h]$, is a bit more involved than in FC-BM. This is because we might have jumped over $v[i]$ at some earlier stage in the search process when $mbl[i] = 0$. The following scenario is possible.

(1) The array element $mbl[i] = 0$, and the instantiation $v[i] := k_1$ fails. Consequently $mcl[i, k_1]$ is set to f (where f is the highest valued index in $past - fc[j]$).

(2) The instantiation $v[i] := k_2$ succeeds, $mcl[i, k_2] := i$, and the search process proceeds to $v[j]$.

(3) No consistent instantiation can be found for $v[j]$, and the search process jumps back to $v[f]$. Note that $mbl[i]$ retains the value 0.

(4) Variable $v[f]$ is assigned a new value (and this is consistent with the current search state). Consequently, the instantiation $v[i] := k_1$ should be considered when $v[i]$ becomes current.

(5) The search process proceeds from $v[f]$ to $v[g]$, and $v[g] := k_g$ forward checks against $v[i]$, and removes k_1 from $current - domain[i]$.

(6) $v[i]$ again becomes the current variable, no consistent value can be found, and the search process jumps back to $v[h]$ (naively setting $mbl[i]$ to h) and then jumps back from $v[h]$ to $v[g]$. Consequently k_1 is returned to $current - domain[i]$, $mcl[i, k_2] = f$, and (naively) $mbl[i] = g$ (where $f < g$).

(7) When $v[i]$ again becomes current, the instantiation $v[i] := k_2$ will be (wrongly) disallowed (because $mcl[i, k_2]$ is out of date).

Therefore when jumping back from $v[i]$ we need to do as follows.

If $mbl[i] < h$ then for all $k \in domain[i]$, if $mcl[i, k] \geq mbl[i]$ then set $mcl[i, k]$ to i

Consequently, when $mbl[i] = 0$, and the search process jumps back from $v[i]$, all the backmarking information in $mcl[i, k]$ is lost. The backmarking information in $mcl[i, k]$ is therefore only of value on (at best) the third visit to $v[i]$ (rather than the second visit, as in BM and FC-BM).

11.8 FC-BM-CBJ might not be as good as FC-CBJ

We might expect, intuitively, that FC-BM-CBJ will never perform more consistency checks, nor will it visit more nodes than FC-CBJ. We shouldn't trust intuition here. It may be the case that even though FC-BM-CBJ attempts to avoid performing redundant consistency checks this may result in a loss of search knowledge, and this may degrade search performance. There are two scenarios to consider.

(1) Assume that FC-BM-CBJ is about to make a type (a) saving on the instantiation $v[i] := k$ because it has previously been discovered that it will result in domain annihilation for $current - domain[j]$ (ie $victim[i, k] = j$). FC-BM-CBJ will not perform any forward checking from this instantiation, but will update $conf - set[i]$ to be $conf - set[i] \cup past - fc[j]$. Assume that h is the deepest variable forward checking against $v[j]$ and that FC-BM-CBJ then jumps back to $v[h]$.

(2) FC-CBJ makes the instantiation $v[i] := k$ and checks forwards to $v[i + 1]$, then to $v[i + 2]$, and so on till $v[j']$, where $j' < j$. Assume that this results in the annihilation of $current - domain[j']$. That is, instantiations have changed for some $v[h']$, where $mbl[i] < h' < i$, such that $v[h']$ now checks against $v[j']$, and $v[i] := k$ now annihilates $current - domain[j']$. We would then update $conf - set[i]$ to become $conf - set[i] \cup past - fc[j']$, and we may then jump back to $v[h']$, where $h < h'$.

Therefore FC-BM-CBJ may jump back to $v[h]$ as a result of the type (a) saving, whereas FC-CBJ jumps back to $v[h']$, where $h < h'$. FC-CBJ might then jump back from $v[h']$ to $v[g]$, where $g < h$, and therefore visit less nodes in the search tree than FC-BM-CBJ. However, it is equally likely that FC-BM-CBJ will jump back from $v[h]$ to $v[f]$, where $f < g$. In summary, adding backmarking to FC-CBJ can result in an increase in search effort due to search knowledge ignored due to the type (a) saving, or it can lead to a reduction in search effort due to the the type (a) saving combined with the preservation of search knowledge. In some respects, this phenomenon is similar to the *bridge* described in [17].

11.9   Empirical Analysis

Experiments were performed over a range of csp's, randomly generated in a manner similar to that of [4, 6, 19]. An instance of the binary constraint satisfaction problem (csp) can be classified as a four-tuple $< n, m, p_1, p_2 >$ where n is the number of variables in that csp, there is a uniform domain size m, p_1 is the probability of a pair of symmetric constraints existing between any two variables, and p_2 is the probability of a conflict between a labelling of a pair of variables (where there are constraints between that pair of variables).

In [2] it is noted that many instances of NP-complete problems are easy to solve, and that computationally hard problems are rare. For csp's these *really* hard problems appear to exist at the critical point that separates under-constrained problems from over-constrained problems. That is, if we are given values for n, m, and p_1, there will be a value for p_2, call it p_{2crit}, that corresponds to a *phase transition*. For a csp $< n, m, p_1, p_2 >$, if p_2 is less than p_{2crit} the probability that the csp is satisfiable is close to 1, and the problem tends to be easy. Conversely, if p_2 is greater than p_{2crit} the probability of satisfiability is close to zero, and again the problem is easy. However, when p_2 is close to p_{2crit} the problem tends to be hard [19, 21][2]. This feature has been exploited in the experiments, such that the algorithms were applied only to hard problems.

The algorithms were encoded in Sun Common Lisp, SCLisp version 4.0, compiled, and then run on SUN SPARCstation IPC's with 16MB of memory.

The algorithms BM, FC, FC-BM, FC-CBJ, and FC-BM-CBJ were applied to 90 randomly generated csp's. That is, 10 hard csp's were generated at each parameter point $< 15, 5, p_1, p_2 >$, where p_1 and p_2 took the pairs of values $< 0.1, 0.7 >$, $< 0.2, 0.6 >$, $< 0.3, 0.5 >$, $< 0.4, 0.4 >$, $< 0.5, 0.3 >$, $< 0.6, 0.3 >$, $< 0.7, 0.25 >$, $< 0.9, 0.2 >$, and $< 1.0, 0.2 >$. The algorithms were then applied to each of the problems, and a measure was taken of the number of consistency checks performed on each problem (Table 11.1), the number of nodes visited in the search tree (Table 11.2), and the amount of CPU seconds consumed (Table 11.3). In Table 11.1 (and subsequent tables) column μ is the average, σ is the standard deviation, *min* is the minimum, and *max* the maximum. If we take consistency checks as a measure of search effort we see that FC is better than BM, and that adding BM

---

[2]... and it should be noted that Smith has developed a theory that predicts p_{2crit} with some accuracy

TABLE 11.1. Consistency checks for 90
hard csp's at $< 15, 5 >$

Algorithm	μ	σ	min	max
BM	13.5	21.4	.03	162.2
FC	5.8	7.5	.04	59.9
FC-BM	5.1	6.8	.04	56.3
FC-CBJ	4.1	6.3	.04	53.3
FC-BM-CBJ	3.9	6.0	.04	50.4

Measured in 1,000's of checks

to FC gives a marginal improvement to FC. It also appears that adding
conflict-directed backjumping gives a further improvement, but over these
problems the improvement is not significant.

TABLE 11.2. Nodes visited for 90 hard
csp's at $< 15, 5 >$

Algorithm	μ	σ	min	max
BM	47.9	170.5	0.02	1,391
FC	0.6	1.2	0.002	6.7
FC-BM	0.6	1.2	0.002	6.7
FC-CBJ	0.2	6.3	0.002	5.4
FC-BM-CBJ	0.2	6.0	0.002	5.4

Measured in 1,000's of nodes visited

Table 11.2 shows the number of nodes visited, ie the number of times an
attempt was made to instantiate a variable. BM performs very poorly in
this respect (the same as chronological backtracking). Over the 90 problems
there were 14 cases where BM performed less checks than FC, but only 3
cases where BM took less CPU time than FC. There were 9 cases where BM
performed less checks than FC-BM, but only 2 cases where BM took less
CPU time than FC-BM. FC-BM never performed more consistency checks
than FC (as expected), although there were 33 cases where FC took less
CPU time than FC-BM. FC-CBJ never performed more consistency checks
than FC (as expected). There were 2 cases where FC-BM performed better
than FC-BM-CBJ. This was not initially expected, but can be explained
due to the possible loss of backmarking information during backjumping.
This phenomenon has already been observed for other algorithms that combine BM with backjumping [16]. That is, when FC-BM-CBJ jumps back
from $v[i]$ to $v[g]$ over $v[h]$ where $g < h$, if $mbl[h] < g$ useful information

may be lost in $mcl[h, k]$ (a fuller explanation is given in [16]).

TABLE 11.3. CPU time for 90 hard csp's
at $< 15, 5 >$

Algorithm	μ	σ	min	max
BM	14.8	48.7	0.01	355
FC	0.94	1.38	0.01	10.5
FC-BM	0.90	1.34	0.01	10.9
FC-CBJ	0.63	1.12	0.01	10.2
FC-BM-CBJ	0.63	1.12	0.01	10.2

Measured in seconds

In Table 11.3 we have the CPU time, measured in seconds. BM is the most expensive algorithm to run. Even though BM performs approximately 3 times as many consistency checks as any of the other algorithms, it takes on average 15 times as long to run. This is due to the computational effort in maintaining the array elements in *mbl* during backtracking. As can be seen, over these problems, there is little if anything to choose between FC, FC-BM, FC-CBJ, and FC-BM-CBJ. In conclusion, problems at $n = 15$ and $m = 5$ do not appear to be hard enough to discriminate between the algorithms.

The problem size was then increased to $n = 20$ and $m = 5$. Unfortunately these problems were just too hard for BM, and the experiments were abandoned after a number of hours. Table 11.4 gives anecdotal evidence of just why this was so.

TABLE 11.4. *Really* hard problems for BM
at $< 20, 5 >$

Algorithm	checks	nodes	CPU
$< 20, 5, 0.1, 0.3 >$			
BM	13,251	58,227	19,787
FC	74.2	4.8	17.09
FC-CBJ	0.28	0.03	0.03
$< 20, 5, 0.1, 0.4 >$			
BM	1,320	2,571	1,074
FC	319.9	80.4	92
FC-CBJ	0.163	0.03	0.02

1,000's of checks and 1,000's of nodes visited

As can be seen (Table 11.4), in the first problem $< 20, 5, 0.1, 0.3 >$ BM took in excess of 5 hours CPU time, FC took about 17 seconds, and FC-

CBJ took about a fiftieth of a second. FC-CBJ was more than half a million times faster than BM. In the second problem BM took about 18 minutes, FC took a minute and a half, and again FC-CBJ took a fiftieth of a second. It appears that backmarking is practically useless when we move towards relatively large sparse problems, and that we should use the FC based algorithms.

The problem size was then increased to $n = 25$ and $m = 5$, and 500 problems were generated at $p_1 = 0.2$ and $p_2 = 0.4$. The forward checkers FC, FC-BM, FC-CBJ, and FC-BM-CBJ were then applied to each of these problems. Of the 500 problems, 238 were satisfiable. That is, the parameters correspond to the phase transition point, where hard problems exist [2, 19, 21]. Table 11.5 gives the performance of the algorithms with respect to consistency checks performed and CPU time in seconds. We can see

TABLE 11.5. 500 csp's at $< 25, 5, 0.2, 0.4 >$

Algorithm	μ	σ	min	max
Checks				
FC	225.4	623.2	0.17	7,458.
FC-BM	167.3	461.3	0.17	5,721
FC-CBJ	39.7	88.9	0.17	1,232
FC-BM-CBJ	34.3	76.3	0.17	1,108
CPU seconds				
FC	44	123	0.02	1,427
FC-BM	38	108	0.02	1,246
FC-CBJ	7.4	17	0.02	241
FC-BM-CBJ	6.8	15	0.03	230

1,000's of checks, and CPU seconds

that adding backmarking to forward checking gives a marginal improvement (difference between FC and FC-BM, and difference between FC-CBJ and FC-BM-CBJ), typically about 10% measured in checks and cpu seconds. Adding conflict-directed backjumping gives a significant improvement (difference between FC and FC-CBJ, and FC-BM and FC-BM-CBJ), typically an improvement of about a factor of 5. Therefore it appears that the chronological backtrackers, FC and FC-BM, should be dispensed with.

The problem size was increased once more, and 100 problems were generated at $< 30, 7, 0.5, 0.2 >$. FC and FC-BM were dropped from the experiments. As can be seen (Table 11.6) these problems are *really* hard. Collectively, more than 81 hours CPU time was spent running these experiments. Of the 100 problems, 90 were satisfiable. FC-CBJ never performed less checks than FC-BM-CBJ, although there were 2 cases where FC-BM-CBJ visited more nodes than FC-CBJ (and this was anticipated).

There were 2 cases where FC-BM-CBJ took more CPU time than FC-CBJ, but this difference was measured in hundredths of seconds. The perfor-

TABLE 11.6. 100 csp's at $< 30, 7, 0.5, 0.2 >$

Algorithm	μ	σ	min	max
Checks				
FC-CBJ	4,933	7,536	1.04	36,238
FC-BM-CBJ	4,375	6,631	1.04	32,242
CPU				
FC-CBJ	760	1,175	0.14	5,695
FC-BM-CBJ	705	1,081	0.15	5,336

1,000's of checks and CPU seconds

mance improvement brought about by adding BM to FC-CBJ should be viewed in context. In the problems generated, a constraint was represented as a set of conflicting pairs of values. Therefore, to determine if a pair of values were consistent, a set membership function was performed. For the $< 25, 5, 0.2, 0.4 >$ problems a constraint $C[i, j]$ would typically contain $p_2 . m^2$ pairs, ie. 10 pairs for this problem, and for $< 30, 7, 0.5, 0.2 >$ 10 pairs again. Therefore, the cost of checking a constraint is very small. If the cost of checking constraints is high then we should expect that FC-BM-CBJ becomes even more attractive.

11.10   Conclusion

Forward checking and backmarking have been combined to give FC-BM (although only half of BM's savings have been incorporated). This has brought about a saving in search effort (consistency checks and nodes visited) and run time. BM has also been added to FC-CBJ, to give FC-BM-CBJ. It was anticipated that in unusual circumstances FC-BM-CBJ could perform worse than FC-CBJ. Out of 790 problems, no such cases were encountered.

All the experiments were carried out using hard problems, although some of these were harder than others. The chronological backtrackers (BM, FC, FC-BM) were quickly overwhelmed by even moderately large, hard problems ($n = 20$, $m = 5$), whereas the backjumpers (FC-CBJ and FC-BM-CBJ) could handle larger, really hard problems ($n = 30$, $m = 7$). For all practical purposes chronological backtracking should be considered as obsolete[3]. Forward checking should always be combined with conflict-

---

[3] ... and maybe even carry a government health warning!

directed backjumping, and this algorithm may be improved with (partial) backmarking. It remains to be seen if FC-BM-CBJ can exploit variable ordering heuristics without corrupting the backmarking information in mcl and mbl.

From a subjective point of view, it may be argued that FC-BM and FC-BM-CBJ are overly complicated, and probably unnatural (if we allow ourselves to consider FC, BM, CBJ, as natural). This is because FC and BM are unwilling bed-fellows. Backmarking, to be effective, needs to explore all values in the domain of the current variable, whereas in forward checking some of the values in the domain of the current variable may be filtered out and thus not explored. Consequently the backmarking information is compromised. Ideally we need to collect richer information in order to make better use of knowledge discovered during the search process, but in doing so we must incur the overhead of maintaining that information. Just where the break even point is, between exploitation (which involves explicating and maintaining search knowledge) and exploration is unclear, but at least we know that there is a spectrum. FC-CBJ would be at the origin, exploiting minimal information; next up would be FC-BM-CBJ; then FC-DDB [15], and finally FC with deKleer's ATMS [20]. A similar spectrum might exist for backward checking algorithms, with BT at the origin, then GBJ, BJ, CBJ, DB, and finally full dependency-directed backtracking (DDB).

Appendix. Pseudo-code for the Algorithms

The pseudo-code for FC-BM and FC-BM-CBJ is given below. The algorithms are described using the same conventions as those in [18], but with the following exceptions. The assignment operator $\leftarrow$ has been replaced with :=, the not equals operator $\neq$ is replaced with /=, less than or equal $\leq$ is replaced with <=.

Forward checking may be made explicit as follows. When the instantiation $v[i] := k$ is attempted $current - domain[j]$ is filtered, for all j, where $i < j \leq n$. The effects of filtering, from $v[i]$ to $v[j]$, are recorded explicitly within the (global) array elements $reductions[j]$, $future - fc[i]$, and $past - fc[j]$. The array element $reductions[j]$ is a sequence of sequences, and is initialised to nil. Let $reduction \in reductions[j]$; $reduction$ is then a sequence of values that are disallowed in $current - domain[j]$ due to the instantiation of one of the past variables. The array element $future - fc[i]$ is a set (and is treated as a stack, initialised to nil) representing the subset of the future variables that $v[i]$ checks against. Let $j \in future - fc[i]$. This is interpreted as follows: the current instantiation of $v[i]$ forward checks against the future variable $v[j]$ and disallows a sequence of values in $current - domain[j]$. The array element $past - fc[j]$ is a set (and is treated as a stack, initialise to $\{0\}$) representing the subset of the past variables that check against $v[j]$. Let $i \in past - fc[j]$. This is interpreted as follows: the current instantiation of $v[i]$ forward checks against $v[j]$ disallowing a sequence of values from $current - domain[j]$.

The function below, $check - forwards$, is called when the variable $v[i]$ is instantiated with a value. It removes all values from $current - domain[j]$ which are inconsistent with the current instantiation of $v[i]$, where $i < j$. It returns a result of *true* if there are values remaining in $current - domain[j]$, otherwise it delivers *false*.

```
1 FUNCTION check-forwards(i,j): BOOLEAN
2 BEGIN
3    reduction := nil;
4    FOR v[j] := EACH ELEMENT OF current-domain[j]
5    DO IF not check(i,j)
6      THEN push(v[j],reduction);
7    IF reduction /= nil
8    THEN BEGIN
9       current-domain[j] := set-difference(current-domain[j],reduction);
10      push(reduction,reductions[j]);
11      push(j,future-fc[i]);
12      push(i,past-fc[j])
13      END;
14   return(current-domain[j] /= nil)
15 END;
```

On termination of the FOR loop the local variable *reduction* will contain the sequence of values in $current - domain[j]$ that are inconsistent with respect to $v[i]$. In lines 9 to 12 a record is maintained of the effects of forward checking. The function call $check(i, j)$ in line 5 tests the compatibility of the instantiations of $v[i]$ and $v[j]$. The function delivers *true* if no constraint exists, otherwise it tests compatibility (and is counted as a consistency check).

The procedure below, $undo - reductions$, is called whenever the variable $v[i]$ is uninstantiated. The procedure undoes all effects of forward checking from $v[i]$.

```
1  PROCEDURE undo-reductions(i)
2  BEGIN
3  FOR j := EACH ELEMENT OF future-fc[i]
4  DO BEGIN
5     reduction := pop(reductions[j]);
6     current-domain[j] := union(current-domain[j],reduction);
7     pop(past-fc[j])
8     END;
9  future-fc[i] := nil
10 END;
```

The statement in line 5, $pop(reduction[j])$, removes the most recent *reduction* from $reductions[j]$, and line 7 removes the backward reference from $v[j]$ to $v[i]$. In line 9 $future - fc[i]$ is set to *nil* because $v[i]$ no longer forward checks against any variable.

The procedure below, $update - current - domain$, recomputes $current - domain[i]$ to be $domain[i]$ less all values disallowed by forward checking (namely $reductions[i]$). This procedure is called whenever $v[i]$ is the current variable and there are no values remaining in $current - domain[i]$.

```
1   PROCEDURE update-current-domain(i)
2   BEGIN
3    current-domain[i] := domain[i];
4    FOR reduction := EACH ELEMENT OF reductions[i]
5    DO current-domain[i] := set-difference(current-domain[i],reduction)
6   END;
```

The main body of the forward checking with backmarking procedures can now be presented.

```
1 FUNCTION fc-bm-label(i,consistent): INTEGER
2 BEGIN
3 consistent := false;
4 FOR k := EACH ELEMENT OF current-domain[i]
  WHILE not consistent
5 DO BEGIN
6    consistent := mbl[i] ¡= mcl[i,k];
7    IF consistent
8    THEN BEGIN
9       v[i] := k;
10      FOR temp := i+1 TO n WHILE consistent
11      DO BEGIN
12         j := temp;
13         consistent := check-forwards(i,j)
14         END;
15      IF not consistent
16      THEN BEGIN
17         current-domain[i] := remove(k,current-domain[i]);
18         undo-reductions(i);
19         mcl[i,k] := max-list(past-fc[j])
20         END
21      ELSE mcl[i,k] := i;
22      END
23   ELSE current-domain[i] := remove(k,current-domain[i])
24   END
25 IF consistent THEN return(i+1) ELSE return(i)
26 END;
```

```
1 FUNCTION fc-bm-unlabel(i,consistent): INTEGER
2 BEGIN
3 h := i-1;
4 undo-reductions(h);
5 update-current-domain(i);
6 IF 0 ¡ mbl[i] and mbl[i] ¡ h
7 THEN FOR k := EACH ELEMENT OF domain[i]
8    DO IF mbl[i] ¡= mcl[i,k]
9       THEN mcl[i,k] := i;
10 mbl[i] := h;
11 FOR j := i+1 TO n
12 DO mbl[j] := min(mbl[j],h);
13 current-domain[h] := remove(v[h],current-domain[h]);
14 consistent := current-domain[h] /= nil
15 return(h);
16 END;
```

```
1 FUNCTION fc-bm-cbj-label(i,consistent): INTEGER
2 BEGIN
3 consistent := false;
4 FOR k := EACH ELEMENT OF current-domain[i]
  WHILE not consistent
5 DO BEGIN
6    consistent := mbl[i] ¡= mcl[i,k];
7    IF consistent
8    THEN BEGIN
```

```
9        v[i] := k;
10       FOR temp := i+1 TO n WHILE consistent
11       DO BEGIN
12         j := temp;
13         consistent := check-forwards(i,j)
14         END;
15       IF not consistent
16       THEN BEGIN
17           current-domain[i] := remove(k,current-domain[i]);
18           undo-reductions(i);
19           mcl[i,k] := max-list(past-fc[j]);
20           conf-set[i] := union(conf-set[i],past-fc[j]);
21           victim[i,k] := j
22           END
23       ELSE mcl[i,k] := i;
24       END
25    ELSE BEGIN
26        current-domain[i] := remove(k,current-domain[i]);
27        j := victim[i,k];
28        conf-set[i] := union(conf-set[i],past-fc[j])
29        END
30    END
31 IF consistent THEN return(i+1) ELSE return(i)
32 END;
```

```
1 FUNCTION fc-bm-cbj-unlabel(i,consistent): INTEGER
2 BEGIN
3   cs := union(conf-set[i],past-fc[i]);
4   h := max-list(cs);
5   conf-set[h] := remove(h,union(conf-set[h],cs));
6   IF mbl[i] ¡ h
7   THEN FOR k := EACH ELEMENT OF domain[i]
8        DO IF mbl[i] ¡= mcl[i,k]
9           THEN mcl[i,k] := i;
10  mbl[i] := h;
11  FOR j := i+1 TO n
12  DO mbl[j] := min(mbl[j],h);
13  FOR j := i DOWNTO h+1
14  DO BEGIN
15     conf-set[i] := list(0);
16     undo-reductions(j);
17     update-current-domain(j)
18     END;
19  undo-reductions(h);
20  current-domain[h] := remove(v[h],current-domain[h]);
21  consistent := current-domain[h] /= nil
22  return(h);
23 END;
```

The procedure below, *bcssp*, shows the environment within which the tree search functions will be called.

```
1   PROCEDURE bcssp (n,status,label,unlabel)
2   BEGIN
3     consistent := true;
4     status := "unknown";
5     i := 1;
6     WHILE status = "unknown"
7     DO BEGIN
8       IF consistent
9       THEN i := label(i,consistent)
10      ELSE i := unlabel(i,consistent);
11      IF i ¿ n
12      THEN status := "solution"
```

```
13     ELSE IF i = 0
14        THEN status := "impossible"
15     END
16 END;
```

Procedure *bcssp* addresses the binary constraint satisfaction search problem: *Given a set of variables (where each variable has a discrete domain) and a set of binary relations that act between pairs of variables, find the first consistent instantiation of these variables which satisfies all the relations.* FC-BM is then bcssp(n,status,fc-bm-label,fc-bm-unlabel) and FC-BM-CBJ is bcssp(n,status,fc-bm-cbj-label,fc-bm-cbj-unlabel). The number of nodes visited (in Tables 11.2 and 11.4) is the number of calls made to *label* at line 9 above.

Acknowledgements: I'd like to thank Bernard Nadel and Eugene Freuder for asking such provocative questions.

11.11 REFERENCES

[1] J.R. Bitner and E. Reingold, Backtrack programming techniques, *Commun. ACM* 18 (1975) 651-656

[2] P. Cheeseman, B. Kanefsky, W.M. Taylor, Where the *really* hard problems are. *Proc IJCAI-91* (1991) 331-337

[3] R. Dechter and J. Pearl, Network-based heuristics for constraint-satisfaction problems, *Artif. Intell.* 34(1) (1988) 1-38

[4] R. Dechter, Enhancement schemes for constraint processing: backjumping, learning, and cutset decomposition, *Artif. Intell.* 41 (3) (1990) 273-312

[5] R. Dechter, Constraint Networks, in *Encyclopedia of Artificial Intelligence* (Wiley, New York, 2nd ed., 1992) 276-286

[6] E.C. Freuder and R.J. Wallace, Partial constraint satisfaction, *Artif. Intell.* 58(1-3) (1992) 21-70

[7] J. Gaschnig, A General Backtracking Algorithm that Eliminates Most Redundant Tests, *Proc IJCAI-77* (1977) 457

[8] J. Gaschnig, Performance measurement and analysis of certain search algorithms, Tech. Rept. CMU-CS-79-124, Carnegie-Mellon University, Pittsburgh, PA (1979)

[9] M.L. Ginsberg, Dynamic backtracking, *JAIR* 1 (1993) 25-46

[10] R.M. Haralick and G.L. Elliott, Increasing Tree Search Efficiency for Constraint Satisfaction Problems, *Artif. Intell.* 14 (1980) 263-313

[11] V. Kumar, Algorithms for constraint satisfaction problems: a survey, *AI magazine* 13 (1) (1992) 32-44

[12] A.K. Mackworth, Constraint Satisfaction, In: *Encyclopedia of Artificial Intelligence, Second Edition,* Volume 1, 285-293

[13] P. Meseguer, Constraint satisfaction problems: an overview, *AICOM* 2 (1) (1989) 3-17

[14] B.A. Nadel, Constraint Satisfaction Algorithms, *Computational Intelligence* 5(4): 188-224, 1989

[15] P. Prosser, Distributed asynchronous scheduling, PhD Thesis, Department of Computer Science, Univesrity of Strathclyde, Glasgow, 1990

[16] P. Prosser, BM+BJ=BMJ, *Proc CAIA-93* (1993) 257-262

[17] P. Prosser, Domain filtering can degrade intelligent backtracking search, *Proc IJCAI-93* (1993) 262-267

[18] P. Prosser, Hybrid algorithms for the constraint satisfaction problem, *Computational Intelligence* 9(3) 268-299

[19] P. Prosser, Binary constraint satisfaction problems: some are harder than others, *Proc ECAI-94* (1994) 95-99

[20] B.M. Smith, Forward Checking, the ATMS and search reduction, in Reason maintenance systems and their applications, Editors B.M. Smith and G. Kelleher, Ellis Horwood Series in Artificial Intelligence, pages 155-168

[21] B.M. Smith, Phase transition and the mushy region in constraint satisfaction problems, *Proc ECAI-94* (1994) 100-104

12

Redundant Hidden Variables in Finite Domain Constraint Problems

Francesca Rossi[1]

ABSTRACT We study finite domain constraint problems with hidden variables and the possible redundancy of some of the hidden variables. These are problems where a subset of the variables are chosen to be "visible", and the others are therefore "hidden". Visible variables are the variables of interest from the outside, in the sense that a solution involves only them. For variable redundancy we mean that the elimination of a variable, together with all the constraints connecting it, does not change the set of solutions of the given problem. We propose several sufficient conditions for hidden variable redundancy and we develop algorithms, based on such conditions, which remove the variables found to be redundant. This, combined with other preprocessing techniques which remove other kinds of redundancy (tuple redundancy, such as the local consistency algorithms, or also constraint redundancy), can be very helpful for constraint solving. In fact, the number of variables coincide with the depth of the search tree. Therefore removing variables means shortening the search tree itself.

12.1 Motivations and Main Results

Finite domain constraint satisfaction problems (CSPs) with hidden variables are very natural for many situations. In fact, it is often convenient to use many variables in order to express all the details of the problem, but then to select only a small subset of the variables as those variables which are of interest. All the other variables are then "hidden". That is, they are needed to define the problem, but they are not visible from the outside. Therefore a solution of such CSPs refers only to the visible variables, while of course satisfying the constraints involving all the variables. Concepts similar to that of hidden variables are the local variables in a procedure, the hidden units in the connectionist model, the existentially quantified variables in logic, and the variables not appearing in a (Constraint) Logic

---

[1]Computer Science Department, University of Pisa, Pisa, Italy. E-mail: rossi@di.unipi.it

Programming [8, 6] goal but which are used during its computations.

Usually a CSP, either with or without hidden units, is solved by a non-deterministic search procedure with backtracking which performs a depth-first search in a tree where the nodes are the variable instantiations and each branch from the root to a leaf involves all the variables. It has been widely recognized that such a procedure can perform very badly if the given problem has a lot of syntactic redundancy [29, 5]. Here we mean that an object of a CSP is (syntactically) redundant whenever its removal does not change the solution of the CSP. Many preprocessing algorithms [10, 29, 4, 3, 7] have been developed in order to remove redundancy in the definition of the constraints. In this paper we analyze a different kind of redundancy, over the set of hidden variables, considering the following fact: if a variable can be found to be redundant, then its removal can shorten the depth of the search tree, since the search tree is as deep as the number of variables.

Our main result consists of several sufficient conditions for hidden variable redundancy. The first one relates the degree of the variables and the level of local consistency of the CSP: if a hidden variable has degree smaller than the level of local consistency, then it is redundant and thus removable (together with all the constraints connecting it). Moreover, the removal of some variables may make other variables redundant (since removing variables does not change the level of consistency and may indeed decrease the degree of the remaining variables), therefore the removal process can continue until no variable is found to be redundant. Such removal process can also be interleaved to a phase where the level of local consistency is increased. In fact, by increasing such level, some variable which is not redundant may become so.

Recent results on the relationship among domain size, constraint arity, and local and global consistency [2] may also be useful in determining whether a hidden variable is redundant or not. We use such results to develop other sufficient conditions for variable redundancy, and we combine them with the previous ones to get algorithms where variable removal (either because of their degree or because of their domain size) is interleaved to local consistency increase.

The above sufficient conditions are, however, not necessary. In fact, it is possible to show that, in order to remove a variable with degree k, we do not need $(k + 1)$-consistency over the whole CSP, but just over the part of the CSP which connects the variable to the rest. Due to this observation, we develop a new removal step which allows us to pass from a polynomial complexity to a linear one for the removal of all the hidden variables of degree smaller than k, if k is fixed and much smaller than the number of all the variables of the CSP. As predictable for people who are familiar with the existing local consistency methods, this removal step yields an algorithm which reminds of the adaptive consistency algorithm [3].

Although some of the sufficient conditions we develop follow from previous results on backtrack-free search, the deletion of a variable is usually more efficient than its backtrack-free instantiation. Moreover, the algorithms proposed are interesting for the interaction between variable removal and local consistency, which could be much more involved that what is presented in this paper.

Experimental results on randomly generated problems show that our algorithms are very convenient when the density of the problem is small (up to 10%), and that in denser problems the overhead for redundancy checking is very small. However, we believe that such problems, which have a uniformly distributed density, are not very realistic, and that instead our algorithms could perform much better on real-life problems which, although with many constraints, may have very sparse subproblems.

The paper is organized as follows. The background material on finite domain CSPs with hidden variables and local consistency is contained in Section 12.2. Then, Section 12.3 relates the degree of the hidden variables to the level of consistency of the problem in order to find a sufficient condition for the safe removal of some of the hidden variables, and Section 12.4 compares our work to that on sufficient conditions to have a backtrack-free search. Section 12.5 then discusses the relation between the amount of variable redundancy and the level of consistency of the problem. Section 12.6 develops another sufficient condition for variable redundancy, based on recent results on relating the domain sizes and the level of local consistency, and Section 12.7 describes a more relaxed but still sufficient condition which requires local consistency just where it is needed. Finally, Section 12.8 informally discusses some properties of the proposed algorithms, Section 12.9 summarizes the experimental results obtained by trying some of the proposed algorithms, and Section 12.10 describes some ideas for future work.

12.2   Background

Here we will give the basic notions on finite domain constraint problems, local consistency, and variable redundancy, that will be useful in the following of the paper.

12.2.1   FINITE DOMAIN CONSTRAINT PROBLEMS

A (finite domain) constraint problem consists of a set of variables ranging over a finite domain, a set of constraints, and a subset of the variables, called visible. Any non-visible variable is then called a "hidden variable". A solution to such problem is an instantiation of the visible variables which can be extended to an instantiation of all the variables such that all the constraints are satisfied.

Definition 1 (constraint satisfaction problem) *A   (finite   domain) constraint satisfaction problem (CSP) is a tuple*

$$\langle V, D, C, con, def, VV \rangle$$

where

- *V is a finite set of* variables *(i.e., $V = \{v_1, \ldots, v_n\}$);*

- *D is a finite set of values, called the* domain;

- *C is a finite set of* constraints *(i.e., $C = \{c_1, \ldots, c_m\}$); C is ranked, i.e. $C = \bigcup_k C_k$, such that $c \in C_k$ if c involves k variables;*

- *con is called the* connection function *and it is such that con : $\bigcup_k(C_k \to V^k)$, where $con(c) = \langle v_1, \ldots, v_k \rangle$ is the tuple of variables involved in $c \in C_k$;*

- *def is called the* definition function *and it is such that $def : \bigcup_k(C_k \to \wp(D^k))$, where $\wp(D^k)$ is the powerset of D^k;*

- *$VV \subseteq V$, and it is called the set of* visible variables.   □

Function *con* describes which variables are involved in which constraint, while function *def* gives the meaning of a constraint in terms of a set of tuples of domain elements, which represent the allowed combinations of values for the involved variables. The visible variables in *VV* are the variables of interest, i.e., the variables of which we want to know the possible assignments compatibly with all the constraints.

¿From a designer point of view, the choice of the visible and non-visible (that is, hidden) variables in a CSP can be made once and for all or also dinamically, every time one uses the CSP to represent and solve a specific problem. In this way a single set of constraints can be generated once and for all to describe a complex scenario, and then different users can select different sets of visible variables, thus defining different CSPs.

Other classical definitions of constraint problems do not have the notion of visible variables: they treat all variables as visible ones [10, 29, 3]. However, we choose this definition because, first, the classical definition can be trivially simulated by having $VV = V$, and, second, we think that this definition is much more realistic. In fact, it is reasonable to think that the CSP representation of a problem contains many details (in terms of constraints and/or variables) which are needed for a correct specification of the problem but are not important as far as the solution of the problem is concerned. In other words, the non-visible (or hidden) variables play the role of existential variables: we want to assure that they can be assigned to values consistently with the constraints, but we don't care to know such assignment. The expressive power of the hidden variables has also been studied in [1] and [2].

Then, the solution $Sol(P)$ of a CSP $P = \langle V, D, C, con, def, VV \rangle$ is defined as the set of all instantiations of the variables in VV (seen as tuples of values) which can be extended to instantiations of all the variables which are consistent with all the constraints in C.

Definition 2 (tuple projection and CSP solution) *Given a tuple of domain values $\langle v_1, \ldots, v_n \rangle$, consider a tuple of variables $\langle x_{i1}, \ldots, x_{im} \rangle$ such that $\forall j = 1, \ldots, m$, there exists a k_j with $k_j \in \{1, \ldots, n\}$ such that $x_{ij} = x_{k_j}$. Then the projection of $\langle v_1, \ldots, v_n \rangle$ over $\langle x_{i1}, \ldots, x_{im} \rangle$, written $\langle v_1, \ldots, v_n \rangle|_{\langle x_{i1}, \ldots, x_{im} \rangle}$, is the tuple of values $\langle v_{i1}, \ldots, v_{im} \rangle$.*

The solution $Sol(P)$ of a CSP $P = \langle V, D, C, con, def, VV \rangle$ is defined as the set $\{\langle v_1, \ldots, v_n \rangle|_{VV}$[2] such that

- $v_i \in D$ *for all i;*

- $\forall c \in C$, $\langle v_1, \ldots, v_n \rangle|_{con(c)} \in def(c)\}$.   □

If a tuple $\langle d_1, \ldots, d_k \rangle$ is in the solution of a CSP whose visible variables are $v_1, \ldots, v_k$, then sometimes we will write it as the set of equations $\{v_1 = d_1, \ldots, v_k = d_k\}$.

The structure of a CSP can be easily pictured as a (hyper)graph, which is usually called a *constraint graph* [3], where nodes represent variables and hyperarcs represent constraints. Constraint definitions are instead represented as labels of hyperarcs. The representation of a CSP by a hypergraph is very convenient, because many notions typical of (hyper)graphs can be used in the CSP context. For example, in this paper we will use the concept of *degree* of a node (variable), which is the number of arcs (constraints) incidents in that node (variable), and of CSP *spanned* by a certain set of variables.

As an example, consider the CSP whose constraint graph is in Figure 12.1, where each arc is labelled by the definition of the corresponding constraint, given in term of tuples of values of the domain, and the visible variables are marked by a star. Then, the solution of this problem is the set $\{\langle a, b \rangle\}$, or, alternatively, the set of equations $\{x = a, y = b\}$.

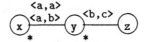

FIGURE 12.1. A CSP.

---

[2] Here we assume to have given an order to the variables in VV.

12.2.2   LOCAL CONSISTENCY

Local consistency algorithms remove from a CSP some domain elements or also some tuples from the constraint definitions if these objects are found to be inconsistent with some other object in the CSP. This is safe (that is, it does not change the set of solutions of the CSP), because local inconsistency implies global inconssistency, and thus such objects would never appear in any solution of the CSP. However, there may be objects (tuples and/or domain elements) which are inconsistent but are not recognized as such and therefore are not removed. Thus only local consistency is achieved (and not global consistency, which would mean that the problem is solved).

The first local consistency algorithms have been called arc-consistency [29] and path-consistency [10]. Later, both of them were generalized to the concept of k-consistency [5]: a CSP is k-consistent if, for each k-1 variables, and values for them which are allowed by all the constraints involving subsets of them, and for each other variable, there is at least a value locally allowed for such k-th variable which is compatible with all the other k-1 variables. In this line, arc-consistency [29] is just 2-consistency and path-consistency is 3-consistency. Formally, k-consistency can be defined as follows:

Definition 3 ((strong) k-consistency [5]) *A   CSP $\langle V, D, C,   con,$ $def, VV \rangle$ is said to be k-consistent if, for all k-1 variables $v_1, \ldots, v_{k-1} \in V$, values $d_1, \ldots, d_{k-1} \in D$, and k-th variable $v_k \in V$, there is at least a value $d_k \in D$ such that, if $v_i = d_i$ for all $i = 1, \ldots, k - 1$ belongs to the solution of the CSP $\langle VK1 = \{v_1, \ldots, v_{k-1}\}, D, C_{|VK1}, con_{|CK1}, def_{|CK1},$ $VK1 \rangle$, then $v_i = d_i$ for all $i = 1, \ldots, k$ belongs to the solution of the CSP $\langle VK = \{v_1, \ldots, v_k\}, D, C_{|VK}, con_{|CK}, def_{|CK}, VK \rangle$. A CSP is said to be* strong k-consistent *whenever it is j-consistent for all $j \leq k$.*   □

For example, consider again the CSP in Figure 12.1. Such CSP is not k-consistent for k=3, since taken the k-1 (that is, 2) variables x and y, and values a and a for them respectively, which satisfy the constraints among them, there is no value for the k-th (that is, 3rd) variable z which satisfies all constraints among x, y and z.

In this paper we are not concerned with how (strong) k-consistency can be achieved. However, we need to know that it can be achieved in $O(n^k)$, where n is the number of variables of the given CSP. Another result that we will use is that, in general, achieving strong k-consistency may involve adding constraints involving at most k-1 variables [4].

This can be easily seen, for example, for 3-consistency (that is, path-consistency [10]). Consider a binary CSP, and suppose there is no constraint connecting variables v_1 and v_2, and there are values d_1 and d_2, for variables v_1 and v_2 respectively, which satisfy the unary constraints connecting v_1 and v_2, but there is no value d_3 for another variable v_3 such that 1) $v_1 = d_1, v_3 = d_3$ satisfies the binary constraint between v_1 and v_3, and 2) $v_2 =$

$d_2, v_3 = d_3$ satisfies the binary constraint between v_2 and v_3. Then the CSP is not path-consistent, and the only way to achieve it is to remove $\langle d_1, d_2 \rangle$ from the pairs of values allowed by the constraint connecting v_1 and v_2. Since such constraint did not exist (explicitly), we would have to add it new, with a definition which allows all pairs but $\langle d_1, d_2 \rangle$.

12.2.3   VARIABLE REDUNDANCY AND REMOVAL

We consider some item of a CSP to be redundant whenever its removal does not change the set of solutions of the CSP. For "item" here we mean either a variable, or a constraint, or a tuple in a constraint definition. Notice however that the removal of a variable is somewhat peculiar, because it implies also the removal of all the constraints involving such variable.

Since CSPs are NP-hard problems, they are usually solved via a back-tracking search, where partial assignments are extended by one variable at a time while checking the satisfiability of the subset of constraints connecting the already assigned variables. Whenever the new variable cannot be assigned to any value compatibly to the constraints, the assignment of the latest variable is backtracked and another value is tried. This search is exponential in the worst case. It can however be improved if 1) some search branches are cut in advance, or if 2) the depth of the search tree (which coincides with the number of variables) is reduced. The first approach is followed by the local consistency algorithms, whose aim is to make constraints stronger while not changing the set of solutions, or, in other words, to remove redundant tuples from the constraint definitions. In fact, if a tuple is removed, then some failure branches are cut from the search tree.

However, no effort towards the removal of variables has ever been undergone, since in the classical definition of CSPs all variables are visible, and thus the removal of any variable always changes the set of solutions of the problem. In our definition of constraint problems, instead, the elimination of a variable does not necessarily change the set of solutions. For example, consider the simple CSP with three variables, x, y, and z, and three binary constraints, depicted in Figure 12.2, where the selected variables are y and z: the removal of variable x, together with all the constraints involving it, does not change the solution of the CSP, which is $\{y = c, z = b\}$.

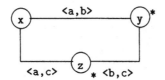

FIGURE 12.2. Variable redundancy.

For further reference, we will now give a formal definition of variable redundancy.

Definition 4 (variable redundancy) *Given a CSP $P = \langle V, D, C, con, def, VV \rangle$, consider any variable $v \in (V - VV)$. Consider also the CSP $P' = \langle V', D', C', con', def', VV' \rangle$, where $V' = V - \{v\}$, $D' = D$, $C' = C - \{c$ such that $v \in con(c)\}$, $con' = con_{|C'}$, $def' = def_{|C'}$, $VV' = VV$. Then v is said to be redundant for P if $Sol(P) = Sol(P')$.*   □

12.3 Variable Degree and Local Consistency

Here we will analyze the interrelation that may exist among the level of local consistency of a CSP, the degree of a variable, and its redundancy. In particular, the main result of this section can be stated as follows: if a CSP is strong k-consistent, then all its variables which are hidden variables and which have degree smaller than k are redundant, and therefore may be removed. The new problem so obtained is still strong k-consistent, so again we can remove all its hidden variables with degree smaller than k, and so on until all variables have degree greater or equal to k.

Consider for example the CSP in Figure 12.3. Assuming that the domain of each variable contains (or it is represented by a unary constraint containing) the values 0 and 1, this CSP is 2-consistent but not 3-consistent, since there is no way to extend any instantiation of any two variables among x, y and z to the third variable. Now, it is easy to see that variable w, which has degree 1, is redundant for such CSP, since its removal does not change the solution of the problem (which is the empty set of values). However, variable y, which has degree 2, is not redundant, since its removal would indeed change the solution of the CSP (it would become the set of values $\{0,1\}$). The same holds for variable z, which has degree 3. Therefore, in this particular problem, only the variable with degree smaller than the level of consistency of the problem is redundant and can thus be safely removed. This is true also in general, as the following theorem states.

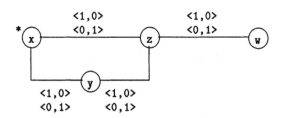

FIGURE 12.3. Redundancy and variable degree.

Theorem 1 (strong k-consistency and variable redundancy)
Consider a strong k-consistent CSP $P = \langle V, D, C, con, def, VV \rangle$, and any of its hidden variables, say $v \in (V - VV)$, such that degree(v) $\leq k - 1$. Then v is redundant for P.

Proof: To show that v is redundant for P we have to show that the solution of the CSP is not changed by the removal of v. Therefore we consider $Sol(P')$, where $P' = \langle V' = V - \{v\}, D, C' = C - \{c \mid v \in con(c)\}, con_{|C'}, def_{|C'}, VV \rangle$. Obviously $Sol(P) \subseteq Sol(P')$, since the removal of some constraints can only enlarge the set of allowed tuples for the visible variables. Consider now any tuple $t \in Sol(P')$: being a solution of P', t can be extended to a tuple t' involving all variables in $V - \{v\}$. Let us now see if t' can be extended to v (while satisfying all the constraints in P). This is indeed so, since P is strong k-consistent, and degree(v) $\leq k - 1$. In fact, consider the projection of t', say tp, to the variables connected to v, say $v_1, \ldots, v_i$, with $i \leq k - 1$. Then, by strong k-consistency, tp can be extended to v while satisfying all constraints involving $v, v_1, \ldots, v_i$, yielding tuple tv. Therefore tv is an extension of t', and thus also of t, which satisfies all constraints in P: that is, t is in the solution of P. Thus, $Sol(P') \subseteq Sol(P')$. As a result, $Sol(P) = Sol(P')$. Therefore v is redundant for P. $\square$

This theorem gives us a way to remove possibly many variables from a given CSP, thus obtaining a new equivalent CSP with a smaller search space. A nice application of Theorem 1 is the problem of coloring a graph with k colors. In fact, it can be proved that such a problem is k-consistent [13], and thus any variable with degree $k - 1$ or less is redundant.

Once all variables of degree smaller than k in the original CSP have been removed, there may be some variables which did not have degree smaller than k in the original problem but have it now. The nice thing is that we can remove them as well, since, as the following theorem states, at any stage during the removal process we still have a strong k-consistent CSP.

Theorem 2 (variable redundancy and strong k-consistency)
Consider a strong k-consistent CSP $P = \langle V, D, C, con, def, VV \rangle$, and any of its hidden variables, say $v \in (V - VV)$, such that degree(v) $\leq k - 1$. Consider also the CSP $P' = \langle V' = V - \{v\}, D, C' = C - \{c \mid v \in con(c)\}, con_{|C'}, def_{|C'}, VV \rangle$. Then P' is strong k-consistent as well.

Proof: Since $v' \subseteq V$, all variables of P' are also in P, and all constraints of P' are also in P. Therefore all the properties of subsets of such variables and constraints, which hold in P, will *a fortiori* hold also in P'. $\square$

An algorithm that removes redundant variables according to the results of Theorem 1 and 2, called It-Remove, can be seen in Table 12.1. As an example of the application of algorithm It-Remove, consider the CSP in Figure 12.3. For this CSP, which as noted above is 2-consistent, the algorithm removes only variable w, which has degree 1, since no other variable gets a degree smaller than 2 after w is removed. Consider now the CSP in Figure 12.2, which is 3-consistent. Here there is only one variable, x, which is hidden and which has degree less than 3. Thus the algorithm removes only this variable. For the CSP in Figure 12.1, if we assume that there are unary constraints stating that $x = a$, $y = b$, and $z = c$, and that Step 1 is preceded by a 2-consistency step which deletes tuple $\langle a, a \rangle$ from the constraint connecting x and y, we have that z is the only variable with degree less than 2, and is therefore removed by the algorithm. Instead, consider the CSP in Figure 12.4 (here unary constraints are denoted by arrows pointing to the involved variable). This problem is not 3-consistent, but it is 2-consistent. In the first iteration algorithm It-Remove removes only variable w, since this is the only variable with degree 1. Then, it removes also v, since v gets degree 1 after the first pass of the algorithm.

Algorithm It-Remove:
Input: a strong k-consistent CSP P.
Step 1: remove from P all hidden variables with degree smaller than k, obtaining P'.
Step 2: If $P \neq P'$, then $P := P'$ and go to Step 1.

TABLE 12.1. Algorithm It-Remove.

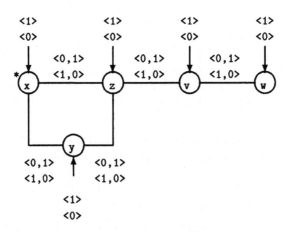

FIGURE 12.4. A CSP with two redundant variables: w and v.

12.4   Width

It has been recognized that the sparseness of the constraint graph and the level of consistency of the CSP have a strong relationship with the fact that a search-based solution algorithm could solve the CSP without backtracking at all or with a bounded amount of backtracking [5]. More precisely, the result which is more related to our work can be stated as follows: if a CSP is strong k-consistent and has "width" less than k, then it is backtrack-free. Here, the width is a notion related to how sparse the CSP is: the sparser it is, the smaller its width is.

Definition 5 (width [5]) *Given a CSP and its constraint graph, consider the ordered graph obtained by putting an order on the nodes of the constraint graph. Then*

- *the width of a node in an ordering O is the number of arcs that connect such node to nodes previous to it in the order O: if $O = v_1, \ldots, v_n$, then the width of v_k in O is the number of arcs a such that $\{v_i, v_k\} \subseteq con(a)$ and $i \in \{1, \ldots, k-1\}$.*

- *the width of an ordering is the maximum of the widths of the nodes in that ordering.*

- *the width of a constraint graph is the minimum of the widths of all the orderings on that graph.*   □

Theorem 3 (width, k-consistency, backtrack-free search [5])
Given a CSP, there exists a backtrack-free search if the level of strong consistency of the CSP is greater than the width of its constraint graph.
□

Now, it is possible to prove that the variables we remove via Algorithm It-Remove in a strong k-consistent CSP, together with the constraints connecting them, constitute a CSP with width less than k.

Theorem 4 (redundancy and width) *Given a strong k-consistent CSP P, consider the CSP P' which is spanned by the variables removed from P by algorithm Remove2 and by the constraints connecting subsets of them. Then, P' has width less than k.*

Proof: To show that P' has width less than k it is enough to find an ordering with width less than k, that is, where all the nodes are connected to at most $k-1$ previous nodes. Consider then the ordering, say O, where the nodes (variables) are ordered as they are removed by algorithm Remove2. In O, each node is connected to at most $k-1$ nodes which are later in the ordering, otherwise it could not be removed by Remove2. Therefore, the reverse of ordering O has the desired feature.   □

Therefore, by the result of Theorem 3, the subgraph spanned by the removed variables and the constraints connecting them has a backtrack-free search. That is, there is an ordering of its variables such that they all can be instantiated without ever needing to backtrack.

Now, since the removed portion is in general just a subpart of the whole CSP, an alternative to removing it would be to instantiate its variables, without backtracking, at the end of the search process, after having instantiated all the other variables. In this way the redundant variables would only bring a linear factor (linear in their number) to the complexity of the search-based solution process. Therefore, our result could be seen as an application of the result in [5] to (dinamically chosen) subCSPs instead of entire CSPs.

However, this is not really true. In fact, even though the search steps devoted to the instantiation of a redundant variable never implies any backtracking, it is still necessary to spend time to find one of the instantiations of such variable which is compatible with the variables connected to it. In fact, we know that there is at least one (because the ordering is backtrack-free), but we do not know which one. Instead, in line with the meaning of hidden variables as "existential" variables, we don't care to find such instantiation. Therefore we don't want to spend such time in finding it. Thus, removing the variables makes more sense in this line of thought. This makes even more sense if one considers that usually the number of visible variables is much smaller than the number of the hidden variables.

12.5   Levels of Local Consistency

Since the removable variables are all those with degree smaller than the level of consistency of the given CSP, the higher this level, the more variables one can remove. Therefore one could think that by increasing the level of consistency of the CSP before applying algorithm It-Remove it would be possible to remove more variables. Unfortunately, this is not always true. In fact, as noted above, in general achieving strong k-consistency may involve adding constraints involving at most k-1 variables [4]. This implies that a CSP may become much less sparse when achieving a higher level of consistency, thus incresing the degrees of its variables. Therefore, variables which are removable in an i-consistent CSP could not be removable any more when the CSP is made j-consistent, with $j \geq i + 1$.

A possible solution to this problem is to combine the removal of variables and the consistency increase, so to remove all the variables which are removable at every current CSP (either the given one or the ones obtained by increasing the level of consistency, up to a desired highest level k'), and base the stop condition on the fact that no more variables are removable or that k'-consistency has been achieved. A version of such algorithm can be seen in Table 12.2. In such version, there is still some choices to be made, mainly in Step 2. In fact, one has to choose the amount of consistency increase to perform at each pass. We believe that only experimental evidence will be able to guide such choice.

Algorithm Level-Remove:
Input: a strong k-consistent CSP P and an integer $k' \geq k + 1$.
Step 1: apply algorithm It-Remove to P, obtaining P'.
Step 2: make P' strong j-consistent, with $k + 1 \leq j \leq k'$, obtaining P''.
Step 3: if $P' \neq P''$, $k := j$, $P := P''$, and go to Step 1.

TABLE 12.2. Algorithm Level-Remove.

12.6   Domain Size

Besides degrees and other topological properties of the CSP, also the size of a variable domain can be of help in determining whether a variable is redundant. The first time domain size was taken into consideration to relate local to global consistency was in [2]. There, domain sizes and arity of the constraints have been used to characterize when CSPs which are only locally consistent are also globally consistent (that is, they have a backtrack-free search-based solution algorithm). The main result is stated by the following theorem.

Theorem 5 ([2]) *Consider a CSP with domains of size at most k and constraints of arity at most r, and which is strong $k(r - 1) + 1$-consistent. Then it is globally consistent.*   □

This result can be used for the goal of this paper, that is, to find out whether a hidden variable is redundant and thus removable. In fact, it is possible to show that a hidden variable whose domain size is smaller than k in a CSP with constraints of arity at most r and which is strong $k(r - 1) + 1$-consistent is redundant.

Theorem 6 (redundancy, domain size, constraint arity)
Consider a CSP with constraints of arity at most r, and which is strong $k(r - 1) + 1$-consistent. Then a hidden variable v with a domain of size at most k is redundant.

Proof: Very similar to the proof of the main theorem in [2].   □

This means that algorithm Level-Remove can be modified in order to remove such redundant variables as well. Better, we modify algorithm It-Remove and then use the new It-Remove into Level-Remove as it is. The new It-Remove algorithm basically removes both the hidden variables with degree smaller than the level of consistency of the CSP, and those which have a domain of size smaller than a certain k if the level of consistency is $k(r-1)+1$. Such algorithm can be seen in Table 12.3. Notice that we do not need to iterate the two removal phases (of the two kinds of variables), since the removal of any variable does not change the domain size of any other variable. The final algorithm, called Remove, which combines the removal of redundant variables (both because of their degree and of their domain size) can be seen in Table 12.4.

Algorithm New-It-Remove:
Input: a strong k-consistent CSP P with constraints of arity at most r, and let $k = k'(r-1)$.
Step 1: remove from P all hidden variables with domain size at most k'.
Step 2: remove from P all hidden variables with degree smaller than k, obtaining P'. If $P \neq P'$, then $P := P'$ and go to Step 2.

TABLE 12.3. Algorithm New-It-Remove.

Algorithm Remove:
Input: a strong k-consistent CSP P with constraints of arity at most r and an integer $k' \geq k + 1$.
Step 1: apply algorithm New-It-Remove to P, obtaining P'.
Step 2: make P' strong j-consistent, with $k + 1 \leq j \leq k'$, obtaining P''.
Step 3: if $P' \neq P''$, then $k := j$, $P := P''$, $r :=$ arity of the largest constraint in P'', and go to Step 1.

TABLE 12.4. Algorithm Remove.

12.7   Partial Local Consistency

Consider a CSP where a variable, say z, has degree 1, and it is connected to the variable x. Then we know that z can be removed if the CSP is (at least) strong 2-consistent. However, even if this is not the case, we can still remove z if we make sure that the constraint c between x and z is arc-consistent. This means that we need to delete from the domain of x all those values v such that there is no value v' in the domain of z with $(v, v') \in def(c)$. In fact, this assures that the constraining information given by the variable z and the constraint c is coded, in some sense, in the domain of the variable x. Therefore, generalizing from 2- to k-consistency, we can state the following result.

Theorem 7 (partial local consistency and redundancy) *Consider a CSP $P = \langle V, D, C, con, def, VV \rangle$, and any of its hidden variables, say $v \in (V - VV)$, such that $degree(v) \leq k - 1$. Consider also the CSP P' spanned by v and the variables of P connected to v. Then, if P' is strong k-consistent, v is redundant for P.*

Proof: Very similar to that of Theorem 1, except for the reason for extending tuple t' to variable v, which is here based on the strong consistency of P' instead of that of the whole CSP P. □

The above theorem basically says that, in order to safely remove all variables with degree smaller than k, we just need k-consistency on the "border" between the removed variables and the remaining ones. In reality, strong k-consistency of P' is sufficient but still not necessary, since it is useless to remove domain elements or tuples in those domains and constraints which are going to be removed by the removal of v. Therefore directional-k-consistency [3] of P' would be enough for the result of the theorem to hold.

In view of this result, the basic removal step can be changed so that, before removing v and the constraints connecting it, we employ a consistency step: consider the variables $v_1, \ldots, v_i$ connected to v (therefore $k - 1 \geq i$), and apply (directional) (i+1)-consistency to the CSP spanned by $v, v_1, \ldots, v_i$. Then remove v and all the constraints connecting it. Such a removal step has a complexity which is $O(|D|^{i+1})$.

Note that this new removal step may create a new constraint connecting $v_1, \ldots, v_i$. Therefore we have to be careful about the order in which variables are removed, since removing a variable of degree h may create a constraint of arity h, thus possibly increasing the degree of variables with a degree even smaller than h. To avoid this problem, we have to first remove variables with smaller degree, and then those with larger degree. We can therefore write a new removal algorithm based on this removal step, called Cons-Remove, which can be seen in Table 12.5. Note that this algorithm takes a CSP and an integer k, and returns a new CSP where all the variables of degree less than k have been removed.

Algorithm Cons-Remove:
Input: a CSP $P = \langle V, D, C, con, def, VV \rangle$, and an integer k.
Step 1: $i := 1$.
Step 2: Choose a variable $v \in (V - VV)$ with degree i. Let $v_1, \ldots, v_i$ the variables connected to v. Apply (directional) i+1-consistency to the CSP spanned by $v, v_1, \ldots, v_i$.
Step 3: remove v. If there are other variables with degree i, go to Step 2.
Step 4: $i := i + 1$.
Step 5: If $i \leq k$, then go to Step 2.

TABLE 12.5. Algorithm Cons-Remove.

The complexity of removing a variable with the new removal step is $O(|D|^{i+1})$. Therefore, the complexity of removing m variables, each with degree at most k, is $O(m|D|^k)$. This can be compared with the complexity of obtaining strong k-consistency, which is $O(n^{k+1})$, and which was needed in the previous algorithms if one wanted to remove variables of degree at most k. Therefore Theorem 7 allowed us to pass from $O(n^{k+1})$ to $O(m \mid D \mid^k)$. Considering that usually the domain size ($\mid D \mid$) is smaller than the number of variables in the CSP (n), this is in practice a significant improvement.

Consider a CSP $P = \langle V, D, C, con, def, VV \rangle$, and assume that $\mid V \mid = n$ and $\mid VV \mid = h$. Then the removal of at most all the hidden variables is $O((n - h) \mid D \mid^k)$. Special cases arise when $h \leq\leq n$, that is, the number of hidden variables is comparable to the number of all the variables (which is often the case, for example in CLP [6] programs). Then, if k is small enough, the complexity becomes linear.

12.8   On the Algorithms

All the proposed algorithms take as input a CSP and return another CSP. The most basic property of such algorithms (without which they do not make sense at all) is that they can be proved to be *sound*, in the sense that they do not change the set of solutions of the given CSP. The formal proofs all rely on the definition of variable redundancy, on the theorems of this paper and on the fact that any local consistency algorithm satisfies such property as well [11].

Moreover, all the algorithms which delete several hidden variables at a time (like in Step 1 of algorithms It-Remove, Level-Remove, New-It-Remove, and Remove, and in Step 2 of algorithm New-It-Remove) could be rewritten so that only one variable at a time is deleted (which would be much closer to what the implemented algorithms do): just choose one elimination order for each set of deletable variables. The nice property is that such order does not influence the resulting CSP produced by the algorithms. That is, the same CSP is obtained for any order and also for the set-at-a-time version. This is especially important for algorithm Cons-Remove, where Step 2 asks for a nondeterministic choice of any hidden variable with degree i. In fact, it is possible to prove that any choice (and thus any order of variable elimination) leads to the same result. The main reason for this result to hold relies on the fact that the elimination of a redundant variable can only increase the number of remaining redundant variables, which in turn implies that the operation that removes a redundant variable is a *closure operator* over the set of CSPs which are obtained from one CSP P by eliminating some of its redundant variables. By classical results on chaotic iteration and on closure operators, one can prove that the order of application of such operations does not matter.

12.9   Some Experiments

We experimented some of the algorithms proposed in this paper on both random and manually generated constraint problems. In particular, we studied the effect of algorithm It-Remove on random binary constraint problems with at least one solution, 50 variables, 5 values for each domain, 5 visible variables, and various densities (i.e., percentage of constraints over the maximun number) and constraint tightnesses (i.e., percentage of allowed pairs).

The behaviour of our algorithm was then compared to the search for a solution via a classical method, employing arc-consistency plus forward checking, on the same problems. The comparison was based on the overall time taken to find the solution, and not on the number of consistency checks (as usually is done for comparing two different solution algorithms). In fact, it would not be significant to look at the number of checks, since our method always uses less checks if the number of variables is smaller (that is, some have been found to be redundant and thus eliminated). Instead, what is important to see is whether the amount of time used to find the redundant variables does not cancel out the advantage of having less variables.

The comparison showed that our method (using algorithm It-Remove) is definitely very convenient when the problem is sparse, that is, with a density ranging from 0 to 10%. At higher densities, our algorithm is more costly than the standard one, but only for a very small factor. In fact, even in those cases where no variable is recognized as redundant, the overhead for redundancy checking is small.

12.10   Future Work

We plan to experiment also with the other algorithms proposed in the previous sections and also with non-binary problems. We conjecture that they will show a different pattern of convenience w.r.t. classical methods. In fact, for such algorithms sparseness is just one among many issues that can increase the number of redundant variables. We also believe that random problems, with a uniformly distributed density, are not very significant for showing the real capabilities of our technique. In fact, there are many real-life problems with a non-uniform sparseness (and maybe also very dense subproblems) and many redundant variables, that therefore could take great advantage of our preprocessing algorithms.

We also plan to investigate the relationship between constraint tightness and variable redundancy, following some recent studies on the relationship between such notion and backtrack-free search [13]. In fact, our conjecture is that, in a CSP which is $(m+2)$-consistent, any variable, which is involved only in constraints with tightness smaller than or equal to m, is redundant.

Our sufficient conditions for hidden variable redundancy could also be used for the detection of "backtrack-free variables" in CSPs where all variables are visible, where for "backtrack-free' variable we mean a variable whose instantiation during a backtracking search (if done after all the others) does not need to be retracted. The two things could also be combined, so that in a CSP with both visible and hidden variables, some hidden variables are removed because found to be redundant, and some visible variables are scheduled later because found to be backtrack-free.

The first field where the removal of redundant variables has been studied and experimented is that of constraint logic programs [8, 6]. In fact, a recent study [12] showed that redundant hidden variables (also called "dead variables" in [12]) occur very often in constraint logic programs, since most local variables are used only during a short span of the computation. They also showed that recognizing and removing such variables, and thus the space allocated for them, generally brings a substantial speed-up and the possibility of solving larger problems. However, they just considered the possibility of making a constraint set arc-consistent, and thus removing only variables of degree 1. Instead, we plan to investigate also the effect of the other results (concerning variables with higher degree, levels of local consistency, and domain sizes) on program execution time.

Acknowledgements: This work has been partially supported by the AC-CLAIM Esprit Basic Research Action Project n.7195. Moreover, we would like to thank Peter Van Beek for providing the C programs implementing the basic search and local consistency algorithms for CSPs, that we used as a base for our algorithms, and Eugene Freuder for many helpful discussions on the subject of this paper.

12.11   REFERENCES

[1] R. Dechter. On the expressiveness of networks with hidden variables. Technical report, Technion, Haifa, Israel, 1991.

[2] Rina Dechter. From local to global consistency. *Artificial Intelligence*, 55:87–107, 1992.

[3] R. Dechter and J. Pearl. Network-Based Heuristics for Constraint-Satisfaction Problems. In Kanal and Kumar, editors, *Search in Artificial Intelligence*. Springer-Verlag, 1988.

[4] E. Freuder. Synthesizing constraint expressions. *Communication of the ACM*, 21(11), 1978.

[5] E. Freuder. Backtrack-free and backtrack-bounded search. In Kanal and Kumar, editors, *Search in Artificial Intelligence*. Springer-Verlag, 1988.

[6] J. Jaffar and J.L. Lassez. Constraint logic programming. In *Proc. POPL*. ACM, 1987.

[7] V. Kumar. Algorithms for constraint satisfaction problems: a survey. *AI Magazine*, 13(1), 1992.

[8] J. W. Lloyd. *Foundations of Logic Programming*. Springer Verlag, 1993.

[9] A.K. Mackworth. Consistency in networks of relations. *Artificial Intelligence*, 8(1), 1977.

[10] U. Montanari. Networks of constraints: Fundamental properties and application to picture processing. *Information Science*, 7, 1974.

[11] U. Montanari and F. Rossi. Constraint relaxation may be perfect. *Artificial Intelligence Journal*, 48:143–170, 1991.

[12] A. D. Macdonald, P. J. Stuckey, and R. H. C. Yap. Redundancy of Variables in clp(r). In *Proceedings ILPS93*. MIT Press, 1993.

[13] P. van Beek and R. Dechter. Constraint tightness versus global consistency. In *Proc. KR94*. Morgan Kaufmann, 1994.

13

Semantic Properties of CHIP(FD)

Gilberto Filé
Giuseppe Nardiello
Adriano Tirabosco[1]

ABSTRACT We consider a significant subset of the language CHIP, that we call CHIP(FD), containing atoms, delay declarations and constraints over finite domains handled by means of the arc-consistency and the sup-inf procedures.

At each point of the computation of a CHIP(FD) program several actions can be performed. Therefore, it is essential that the final result does not depend on which action is chosen (i.e., on the adopted computation rule). We show that this property holds in CHIP(FD), as long as the computation rule satisfies some reasonable conditions.

13.1 Introduction

During the last ten years there has been a growing interest for the extension of the Logic Programming (LP) paradigm. In particular, great attention has been devoted to the integration of constraints into logic programs. The theoretical foundation of this integration has been given in [17, 18], where it is shown that the nice features of logic programs hold also for constraint logic programs (CLP). In the CLP scheme the notion of unificability in the Herbrand Universe is replaced by that of constraint-solvability in some specified domains of application. A CLP(X) language, instance of the CLP scheme, is a many-sorted (a sort for each domain of application) first-order language. The intended meaning of some predicate symbols, function symbols, and constant symbols over the domain of computation X is specified by an algebraic structure $\Re_X$. Atoms built only from these symbols are called *constraints*. In particular LP languages like Prolog can be seen as instances of the CLP scheme [17, 19, 20].

A central idea of the *pure* CLP scheme is the presence of a decision

---

[1]Dipartimento di Matematica Pura ed Applicata, Università di Padova, Via Belzoni 7, I-35131 Padova (Italy); e-mail: { `gilberto` | `giuseppe` | `adriano` } `@hilbert.math.unipd.it`

procedure, called *constraint-solver*, that checks the satisfability of a given set of constraints with respect to $\Re_X$. Therefore, in any moment of the computation the current set of constraints is satisfiable. *Real* CLP(X) languages, like Prolog III [5], CLP(R) [21], may diverge a little from the CLP scheme for reasons of efficiency. Indeed, they can be provided with (explicit or implicit) mechanisms that delay constraints from being passed to the constraint-handler until some conditions on them are satisfied. For example, a way of dealing with non-linear equations is to delay them until they get linearized [21]. Therefore, the computation may proceed with an inconsistent set of constraints. The operational features of these languages can be accounted in the *Ask&Tell* framework introduced by [29] in the context of *concurrent* constraint programming (see [33]). This framework generalizes the CLP framework by adding the concept of *constraint entailment* (i.e. **asking** a constraint) to the concept of constraint-solving (i.e. **telling** a constraint). Despite the presence of these synchronization mechanisms, languages of the *Ask&Tell* family have a complete constraint-solver: when constraints, after being delayed, are finally passed to the constraint-solver they are checked for satisfiability. On the contrary, there are constraint logic languages which – for efficiency reasons – are provided with an *incomplete* constraint-solver [33, 34]. This is the case of the language CHIP [32].

CHIP(FD)

The language CHIP has been defined in '88 [32, 12] and, since then, it has been shown to be useful for specifying and efficiently solving real life problems (see [9, 10, 7, 8, 11, 13, 2]). CHIP integrates the logic paradigm with constraints over three domains of computation: booleans, rationals and finite sets of naturals (called *finite domains*) [4].

In this paper we focus our attention on the domain of finite domains (FD). We study a significant subset of CHIP, that we call CHIP(FD), including delay declarations, atoms and constraints over finite domains of naturals.

In CHIP(FD) constraints are handled by means of particular *local consistency* methods, developed in AI for solving particular combinatorial problems called Constraint Satisfaction Problems (CSPs) [22, 30]. A CSP is defined as a set of *variables* ranging over given *finite domains* of values and a finite set of *constraints* specifying the allowed assignment of values to subsets of the problem variables. Solving the problem means finding all the assignments of values to the problem variables that satisfy all constraints. Local consistency methods work by considering a subset of the problem constraints and removing from the domains values which are inconsistencies with respect these constraints (*domain refinement*).

More precisely, CHIP(FD) uses two different local consistency methods [32]: the *arc-consistency* procedure and the *iterated sup-inf* procedure. When applied to a constraint, the first method removes from the domains all its (locally) inconsistent values. The second method consists in applying (iteratively) an interval reasoning method that refines domains by restricting their lower and upper bounds; in this case not all the locally inconsistent values are necessarily removed. Both these methods do not guarantee that all (globally) inconsistent values are removed from the domains. Therefore, they do not ensure that in any moment of the computation the current set of (already handled) constraints is satisfied. As a consequence, in CHIP(FD) the constraint-handling procedure is not *complete (global)* as in other CLP languages [32, 34].

Despite the incompleteness of the resulting constraint-handling procedure, these methods are useful when integrated in the backtracking procedure to improve the efficiency of this search procedure [16, 22]. Intuitively, what happens is the following: when a constraint is handled, inconsistent values for variables not yet instantiated are removed, so that an *a priori* reduction of the search space is achieved. This ("active" [32]) use of constraints avoids, or at least mitigates, the combinatorial explosion of the search space.

The constraint-handling procedure iteratively applies, according to a given scheduling strategy, the appropriate local consistency methods to each of the constraints until no more domain is refined (*constraint propagation*). This scheduling strategy is realized by means of *delaying* and *waking mechanisms* which dynamically control the computation rule: atoms and constraints are selected only if some conditions on their arguments are satisfied, otherwise they are "suspended", that is they are considered not selectable. In particular, constraints are handled only when they are sufficiently instantiated so that they can be efficiently handled. Because of this "data-driven" mechanism [32], at some time during the computation it could happen that every atom and constraint in the goal is delayed. Such *suspensions* in the computation can be avoided by using special atoms called *value generators* that cannot be delayed. They instantiate some variables ranging over a finite domain with one of its possible values (*partial enumeration*), until some delayed atoms and constraints are possibly woken up and, hence, the computation can proceed. Therefore, in CHIP(FD) computations the constraint handling, by means of domain refinement and constraint propagation, is interleaved with the tree-search, by means of clause selection and partial enumeration [33].

Motivations and results

The soundness with respect to the model-theoretic semantics of the integration of constraints over finite domains in the logic paradigm has been studied and shown in [32]. Subsequently, in [34] the semantics of CHIP(FD) has been described by extending the *Ask & Tell*. However, we contend that there are quite fundamental properties of the language that have been disregarded in these studies. In particular, to our knowledge, it has not yet been shown that CHIP(FD) has the property of being independent from the computation rule, i.e. that the result of a CHIP(FD) program is independent of the adopted computation rule. This property, in addition to being important for the language itself, is essential for proving the soundness of any optimization technique affecting the computation rule. Therefore, the lack of this property is especially serious in a language like CHIP(FD) whose efficiency depends heavily on "clever" computation rules.

The main result presented in the paper is the proof that CHIP(FD) is independent from the computation rule adopted, as long as the rule is "acceptable", i.e. satisfying some reasonable conditions. The independence result relies on the proof of the monotonicity of all the basic operations of the language, i.e. (extended) unification, arc-consistency and sup-inf procedure. While the monotonicity for unification and arc-consistency are easy to show, the proof becomes quite tricky for the sup-inf procedure. The reason is that the sup-inf is a complex operation and that, interleaving it with unifications, may cause unexpected situations. The following simple example illustrates some of the problems.

Example 1 Consider equation $3X + 2Y = 3W + 2Z$, where X, Y, Z and W range over finite domains (that are not relevant here). Assume now that a unification step produces the binding $\{W/X\}$ that, applied to the equation, gives $3X + 2Y = 3X + 2Z$. Now the questions are:

- Should one simplify the new equation or apply the sup-inf to it as it is (in order to obtain bigger domain refinements)?

- By simplifying it we obtain: $2Y = 2Z$. Thus X and W are both disappeared. Can the sup-inf procedure, applied to this new equation, still give the domain refinement that it would have given when applied to the original one?

Plan of the paper   The paper is organized as follows. In section 13.2 we provide some preliminary definitions. The following sections describe, mainly by means of examples, the language CHIP(FD). More precisely, in section 13.3 we present the basic operation for handling atoms and constraints, and in section 13.4 we discuss the control of CHIP(FD). Section 13.4 contains also the definition of acceptable computation rule. The above-mentioned results of monotonicity and independence are shown in section 13.5. Due to space limitations, the proofs of these results are only sketched. The complete proofs can be found in [15]. Finally, section 5 concludes the paper.

13.2   Preliminaries

CHIP(FD) has two computation domains: the set of generalized terms and that of natural numbers. Accordingly, the set V of variables is partitioned into V_G and V_{FD}. The first variables range over generalized terms and the second ones, called *fd-variables*, over the naturals $\mathbf{N}$. A generalized term is a normal term possibly containing also variables of V_{FD} and naturals.

A program in CHIP(FD) is a set of definite clauses of the form

$$H \leftarrow B_1, ..., B_n \ ; \ \textit{FDS}$$

where $n \geq 0$ and where the head H is an atom, each element B_i of the *body* of the clause can be an atom or a constraint and *FDS* is a set of special constraints X *in* D called *domain constraints* which specify the domain D associated to the fd-variable X. We say that *FDS* is an *fd-set* and we let $\textit{FDS}(X)$ denote the finite domain D. As usual, a *goal* G is a clause without head.

CHIP(FD) atoms are like standard atoms except that they are built by using *generalized terms*, i.e. containing also fd-variables and naturals. The pool of constraints is described in the next section 13.3 where also the unification and the constraint-handling algorithms are presented. As mentioned in the introduction, CHIP(FD) programs may also contains *delay* declarations specifying when atoms can be handled during the computations while constraints are delayed according to *implicit* delay conditions that will be presented in section 13.4.

Fd-substitutions

In order to be able to account for the refinement of the domains of the fd-variables during a computation, we introduce an order relation of fd-sets.

Definition 1 [order relation on fd-sets] Given two fd-sets $\textit{FDS}_1$ and $\textit{FDS}_2$, we say that $\textit{FDS}_1$ is *more or equally general* than $\textit{FDS}_2$, denoted $\textit{FDS}_1 \geq \textit{FDS}_2$, when the following holds:

- if $X \in var(\textit{FDS}_1)$ then $X \in var(\textit{FDS}_2)$ and $\textit{FDS}_2(X) \subseteq \textit{FDS}_1(X)$.

We say that $\textit{FDS}_1$ is *strictly more general* than $\textit{FDS}_2$, denoted $\textit{FDS}_1 > \textit{FDS}_2$, when the previous condition holds and also:

- $\exists X \in var(\textit{FDS}_1) \cap var(\textit{FDS}_2)$ such that $\textit{FDS}_2(X) \subset \textit{FDS}_1(X)$.

Notice that, since during the computation new atoms, and hence new fd-variables with their domains, may be introduced, the comparison between the domains after and before a computation step is done only on the fd-variables that occurred before this step was performed.

CHIP(FD) programs compute generalized substitutions that we call *fd-substitutions* (similar to *d-substitutions* of [32]). This notion generalizes the standard notion of *substitution* [25].

Definition 2 [fd-substitutions] An *fd-substitution* φ is a pair (θ, FDS), where θ is a idempotent substitution and $FDS \in FD\text{-}Set$ such that the following conditions hold:

1. if $Z/t \in \theta$ and $Y \in var(t) \cap V_{FD}$ then $FDS(Y)$ is defined;

2. if $X/a \in \theta$, with $X \in V_{FD}$, then, if $FDS(X)$ is defined, it must be $\{a\} = FDS(X)$;

3. if $X/Y \in \theta$, with $X, Y \in V_{FD}$, then, if $FDS(X)$ is defined, it must be $FDS(Y) = FDS(X)$.

We let *FD-Subst* denote the set of all the fd-substitutions.

We also introduce the notion of *closed version* of fd-substitutions which is useful in order to define a partial order on fd-substitutions that generalizes the usual "being more general" order on substitutions. This notion is illustrated by the following example.

Example 2 Consider the fd-substitution $\varphi = (\theta, FDS) = (\{X/Y, Z/2\}, \{Y \text{ in } \{1,2\}, W \text{ in } \{4,5\}, Z \text{ in } \{2\}, V \text{ in } \{3\}\})$. We say that the fd-substitution $\varphi' = (\theta', FDS') = (\{X/Y, Z/2, V/3\}\ ,\ \{X \text{ in } \{1,2\}, Y \text{ in } \{1,2\}, W \text{ in } \{4,5\}, Z \text{ in } \{2\}, V \text{ in } \{3\}\})$ is the *closed version* of φ, denoted $\varphi' = close(\varphi)$, because θ' and FDS' contain explicitly *all* the bindings and domain constraints that are implied by φ. For instance, θ' contains $V/3$ that is implicit in FDS and FDS' contains $X \text{ in } \{1,2\}$ that is implicit in φ through $X/Y \in \theta$ and $(Y \text{ in } \{1,2\}) \in FDS$.

Definition 3 [order relation of fd-substitutions] Given two fd-substitutions $\varphi_1 = (\theta_1, FDS_1)$ and $\varphi_2 = (\theta_2, FDS_2)$, we say that φ_1 is *more or equally general* than φ_2, denoted $\varphi_1 \trianglerighteq \varphi_2$, when the following holds: let $close(\varphi_1) = (\theta'_1, FDS'_1)$ and $close(\varphi_2) = (\theta'_2, FDS'_2)$, then

1. $\theta'_1 \geq \theta'_2$ (where $\geq$ is the usual pre-order over the substitutions);

2. $FDS'_1 \geq FDS'_2$.

We say that φ_1 is *strictly more general* than φ_2, denoted $\varphi_1 \triangleright \varphi_2$ when both points (1) and (2) hold and either in point (1) $\theta'_1 > \theta'_2$ or in point (2) $FDS'_1 > FDS'_2$.

We say that φ_1 is *equivalent* to φ_2, denoted $\varphi_1 \simeq \varphi_2$, when $\varphi_1 \trianglerighteq \varphi_2$ and $\varphi_2 \trianglerighteq \varphi_1$.

For simplicity sake, in the following, unless explicitly stated, we will consider always closed versions of fd-substitutions.

Analogously to substitutions, also the notions of (solution of) set of equations, unifier and most general unifier can be generalized to take into account the finite domains of CHIP(FD).

Definition 4 [sets of fd-equations] A *set of fd-equations* $\mathcal{E}$ is a pair (E, FDS_E), where E is a set of equations of the form $s = t$, s and t being generalized terms, and FDS_E is an fd-set such that $var(E) \cap V_{FD} \subseteq var(FDS_E)$.

We let *FD-Eq* denote the set of all the sets of fd-equations.

We say that an fd-substitution $\varphi = (\theta, FDS)$ is *applicable* to a set of fd-equations $\mathcal{E} = (E, FDS_E)$, and we write $\mathcal{E}\varphi$, if $FDS_E \geq FDS$.

Example 3 Consider $\mathcal{E}_1 = (\{X = Z, Z = 1, W = f(X)\}, \{X \ in \ \{1, 3, 5\},$ $Z \ in \ \{1, 2\}\})$. The fd-substitution $\varphi_1 \equiv (\{X/Y\}, \{Y \ in \ \{1, 3\}\})$ is applicable to $\mathcal{E}_1$ while $\varphi_2 \equiv (\{X/Y\}, \{Y \ in \ \{1, 3, 7\}\})$ is not.

Definition 5 [fd-unifiers] Given $\mathcal{E} = (E, FDS_E) \in FD\text{-}Eq$, an fd-substitution $\varphi = (\theta, FDS)$ is an *fd-unifier* of $\mathcal{E}$ if it satisfies the following two conditions:

1. $\forall (s = t) \in E . (s\theta' = t\theta')$;

2. $FDS_E \geq FDS'$.

Condition 1 above is self-explanatory and condition 2 is the applicability of the fd-unifier to the set of fd-equations.

The notion of *most general fd-unifier* is defined as usual [23].

Definition 6 [fd-mgu's] An fd-unifier φ of $\mathcal{E} \in FD\text{-}Eq$ is a *most general fd-unifier* (or, simply, an *fd-mgu*) of $\mathcal{E}$ if φ is the maximal fd-unifier wrt to $\trianglelefteq$.

Example 4 Consider the set of fd-equations $\mathcal{E}_2 \equiv (\{X = Z, Y = Z, W = f(1)\}, \{X \ in \ \{1, 2, 3\}, Y \ in \ \{1, 3\}, Z \ in \ \{1\}\})$. The fd-substitution $\varphi_3 \equiv (\{X/V, Y/V, Z/V, W/f(1)\}, \{V \ in \ \{1\}\})$, where $X, Y, V \in V_{FD}$, is an fd-unifier for $\mathcal{E}_2$ while $\varphi_4 \equiv (\{X/Z, Y/Z, W/f(1)\}, \{Z \ in \ \{1\}\})$ is an fd-mgu for $\mathcal{E}_2$.

All the standard results proved for substitutions [25, 23] can be generalized to fd-substitutions (see [15]).

13.3   Atom and constraint handling in CHIP(FD)

As said, each computation step of a CHIP(FD) program consists either in handling an atom or a constraint. Handling an atom B consists in performing an (extended) unification between B and the head H of a program clause $H \leftarrow Body$. Handling a constraint B consists in applying to it the appropriate local consistency procedure to refine the domains of its fd-variables. Below we describe these basic operations.

Handling atoms

Since in handling atoms in CHIP(FD) generalized terms must be unified, the classical unification algorithm is appropriately extended. The *extended unification* algorithm [15, 32] is described in the following figure. It computes an fd-mgu of the set of fd-equations given as input.

1. $f(t_1, \ldots, t_n) = f(s_1, \ldots, s_n) \Rightarrow$ replace in E the equation with the equations $(t_1 = s_1), \ldots, (t_n = s_n)$;

2. $f(t_1, \ldots, t_n) = g(s_1, \ldots, s_m) \Rightarrow$ stop with failure;

3. $X = X \Rightarrow$ remove the equation from E;

4. $t = X$, where $(t \notin V) \vee ((X \in V_G) \wedge (t \in V_{FD})) \Rightarrow$ replace in E the equation with $(X = t)$;

5. $X = t$, where $(X \not\equiv t) \wedge (X \in V_G) \wedge (X$ has another occurrence in $E)$

$$\Rightarrow \begin{cases} \text{if } X \text{ occurs in } t & \text{then stop with failure} \\ \text{otherwise} & \text{replace } X \text{ with } t \text{ in every other equation of } E \end{cases}$$

6. $X = a$, where $(a \in \mathbf{N}) \wedge (X \in V_{FD}) \wedge ((FDS(X) \neq \{a\}) \vee (X$ has another occurrence in $E))$

$$\Rightarrow \begin{cases} \text{if } a \notin FDS(X) & \text{stop with failure} \\ \text{otherwise} & \text{replace } X \text{ with } a \text{ in every other equation of } E \\ & \text{and } FDS(X) \text{ with } \{a\} \text{ in } FDS \end{cases}$$

7. $X = Y$, where $(X, Y \in V_{FD}) \wedge (X \not\equiv Y) \wedge ((FDS(X) \neq FDS(Y)) \vee (X$ has another occurrence in $E) \vee (FDS(X) = FDS(Y) = \{a\}))$

$$\Rightarrow \begin{cases} \text{if } d = FDS(X) \cap FDS(Y) = \emptyset & \text{stop with failure} \\ \\ \text{otherwise} \begin{cases} \text{if } d = \{a\} & \text{replace the equation with the} \\ & \text{equations } X = a \text{ and } Y = a \text{ in } E, \\ & \text{every other occurrence of } X \text{ and } Y \\ & \text{in } E \text{ with } a, \text{ and the fd-sets } FDS(X) \\ & \text{and } FDS(Y) \text{ with } \{a\} \text{ in } FDS \\ \text{otherwise} & \text{replace every other occurrence of } X \\ & \text{in } E \text{ with } Y, \text{ and the fd-sets } FDS(X) \\ & \text{and } FDS(Y) \text{ with } d \text{ in } FDS \end{cases} \end{cases}$$

8. $X = t$, where $(X \not\equiv t) \wedge (X \in V_{FD}) \wedge (t \notin \{V \cup \mathbf{N}\}) \Rightarrow$ stop with failure.

FIGURE 13.1. The extended unification algorithm

Example 5 Consider the fd-equation $\mathcal{E} \equiv (\{p(X, Y, W) = p(Z, Z, f(1))\}, \{X \text{ in } \{1, 2, 3\}, Y \text{ in } \{1, 3\}, Z \text{ in } \{1, 3\}\})$. The fd-substitution $\varphi_2 \equiv (\{X/Z, Y/Z, W/f(1)\}, \{Z \text{ in } \{1\}\})$ is an fd-unifier of $\mathcal{E}$. The result of the extended unification algorithm applied to $\mathcal{E}$ is $\varphi_3 \equiv (\{X/Z, Y/Z, W/f(1)\}, \{Z \; in \; \{1,3\}\})$, that is an fd-mgu of $\mathcal{E}$.

Handling constraints

The CHIP(FD) constraints are presented hereafter, together with their meaning (that should be formally specified by some algebraic structure):

- *domain constraints*: $X \; in \; D$, where $X \in V_{FD}$ and $D \in \wp(\mathbf{N})$ is a finite domain of naturals, denoted by $\{a_1, ..., a_m\}$.

- *arithmetic constraints* are of two types:

  - *linear (dis)equations* $t_1 \bowtie t_2$, where $\bowtie$ is a predicate symbol in $\{=, <, \leq, >, \geq\}$ and where t_1 and t_2 are linear terms constructed over $(V_{FD} \cup \mathbf{N})$. *Linear terms* are recursively defined as follows [32]: i) X, where $X \in V_{FD}$, is a linear term; ii) c, where $c \in \mathbf{N}$, is a linear term; iii) $X * c$, where $X \in V_{FD}$ and $c \in \mathbf{N}$, is a linear term; iv) $s + t$, where s and t are linear terms, is a linear term.

  - *disequalities* $t_1 \neq t_2 + c$, where $c \in \mathbf{N}$ and $t_1, t_2 \in (V_{FD} \cup \mathbf{N})$.

- *symbolic constraints*: $element(I, L, X)$, where $I, X \in V_{FD} \cup \mathbf{N}$ and L is a list of natural numbers; it is true when X is the I-th element of L [32, 4].

- *value generators*: $indomain(X)$, where X is an fd-variable; this constraint has a non-deterministic behaviour: it instantiates X to a natural number belonging to its domain.

In the following, we will refer to disequalities and symbolic constraints as *constraints of class I* and to linear (dis)equations as *constraints of class II*. We refer to these constraints as *Constraints* while we let *Atoms* denote the set of all the atoms.

Class I constraints are handled by the (*full*) arc-consistency method [26, 30] which removes all inconsistent values from the domains. This method is illustrated by the following example.

Example 6 By applying the arc-consistency procedure to the constraint $(element(I, [3, 2, 5], X), \{I \; in \; \{1,3\}, X \; in \; \{1,2,3\}\})$ we obtain the fd-substitution $(\{I/1, X/3\}, \emptyset)$. All the other values for I and X are inconsistent. A *failure* occurs if at least one of the fd-variables gets its domain refined to the empty set (i.e. no values are locally, and hence globally, consistent with the constraint).

Notice that if the arc-consistency algorithm would be applied to the disequality $X \neq Y$ wrt an fd-set *FDS*, such that $\sharp FDS(X) > 1$ and $\sharp FDS(Y) >$

1, then no domain refinement would be obtained. Because of this, disequalities are implicitly delayed until they have at most *one* non-ground
fd-variable (see section 13.4).

Class II constraints are handled by the iterated sup-inf refinement algorithm that applies iteratively an interval reasoning method called *sup-inf
method* [1, 28, 24, 6, 32]. As explained in the introduction, this method does
not remove all the inconsistencies from the finite domains (it is a *partial*
arc-consistency procedure).

The basic sup-inf procedure is defined as follows. Let B be a linear
(dis)equation in *normal form*[2]:

$$B \equiv \sum_{i \in I_1} a_i X_i \bowtie \sum_{i \in I_2} a_i X_i + b$$

and let $FDS \in FD\text{-}Set$ such that $var(FDS) \supseteq \{X_i \mid i \in I_1 \cup I_2\}$. Letting

$$l_i = min(FDS(X_i)) \quad \text{and} \quad u_i = max(FDS(X_i)) \quad (i \in I_1 \cup I_2)$$

we have that the left-hand side of the equation ranges over the interval

$$[\sum_{i \in I_1} a_i l_i \ , \ \sum_{i \in I_1} a_i u_i] \equiv [L_1, U_1]$$

while the right-hand side of the equation ranges over

$$[\sum_{i \in I_2} a_i l_i + b \ , \ \sum_{i \in I_2} a_i u_i + b] \equiv [L_2, U_2]$$

For each variable we refine its domain as follows. We resolve the equation
wrt the given variable X_k (suppose $k \in I_1$)

$$a_k X_k = (\sum_{i \in I_2} a_i X_i + b) - \sum_{i \in I_1 \setminus \{k\}} a_i X_i$$

and maximizing and minimizing the right-hand side we derive the following
constraints on the lower and upper bounds of the domain of X_k:

$$a_k X_k \geq (L_2 - \sum_{i \in I_1 \setminus \{k\}} a_i u_i) \quad \text{(lb)}$$

$$a_k X_k \leq (U_2 - \sum_{i \in I_1 \setminus \{k\}} a_i l_i) \quad \text{(ub)}$$

---

[2] A (dis)equation B is said to be in normal form where each of its fd-variables
occurs only once in B, i.e. when $I_1 \cap I_2 = \emptyset$.

All the values $FDS(X_k)$ that do not satisfy these constraints have to be removed. If there are no values in $FDS(X_k)$ satifying them (for at least one fd-variable X_k) then a *failure* occurs. Otherwise, the following values

$$(L_2 - \sum_{i \in I_1 \backslash \{k\}} a_i u_i) \quad \text{and} \quad (U_2 - \sum_{i \in I_1 \backslash \{k\}} a_i l_i)$$

will be respectively the lower and upper bound of the refined domain of $X_k{}^3$. In this way, we derive a new fd-set for the fd-variables of B.

Since the sup-inf method is not idempotent it needs to be iterated until quiescience is reached. This not well recognized fact is illustrated by the following example.

Example 7 The sup-inf method applied to $(X + Y = 4, \{X \; in \; \{2, 6\},$ $Y \; in \; \{1, 2, 3\}\}$ operates the following domain refinements $X \leq 4 - 1 = 3$ and $Y \leq 4 - 2 = 2$ thus returing the fd-substitution $(\{X/2\}, \{Y \; in \; \{1, 2\}\})$. By re-applying the method wrt the refined domains $X \; in \; \{2\}$ and $Y \; in \; \{1, 2\}$ the following further domain refinement $Y \geq 4 - 2 = 2$ is obtained and so the final result is $(\{X/2, Y/2\}, \emptyset)$.

We introduce the following *refine* function summarizing the treatment of both atoms and constraints.

Definition 7 [**refine function**] Let A, H be atoms, B a constraint and $\varphi = (\theta, FDS)$ a fd-substitution. We define the function

$$refine \; : \; (Constraints \cup (Atoms \times Atoms)) \times FD\text{-}Subst \rightarrow (FD\text{-}Subst \cup \{fail\})$$

as follows:

$$refine(\Upsilon, \varphi) = (\theta\theta', FDS')$$

if

- either Υ is the pair of atoms (A, H) and (θ', FDS') is an fd-mgu of $(A\theta = H\theta, FDS)$;

- or Υ is the constraint B and (θ', FDS') is the result of the application of the appropriate domain-refinement algorithm to $(B\theta, FDS)$;

otherwise,

$$refine(\Upsilon, \varphi) = fail$$

if the corresponding basic operation produces a failure.

---

[3] Formulas (lb) and (ub) can also be derived from basic formulas of the Interval Arithmetic [27, 3].

13.4   Control in CHIP(FD): the computation rule

Using the notions introduced in the previous sections it is possible to define an operational semantics for CHIP(FD) as a transition system [14, 15].

Definition 8 [states] A *state* S is a pair $(G\theta, FDS)$ where $G\theta$ is the current goal and (θ, FDS) is the current fd-substitution.

We let *States* denote the set of all the states.

As discussed in the introduction, atoms and constraints are scheduled according to a *computation rule* which must take into account also delay conditions. Moreover, as we will see below, it seems reasonable to impose some other conditions on "acceptable" computation rules. For the time being we consider a very general notion of computation rule.

Definition 9 [computation rule] A computation rule is a function

$$\mathcal{R} : States \rightarrow \mathbf{N} \cup \{Suspend\}$$

that given a state returns either the index of the atom/constraint to select next in the current goal or suspends the computation.

On the basis of the *refine* function introduced in section 13.3 it is easy to define the notion of *transition* from a state S_1 to another state S_2 (via a computation rule $\mathcal{R}$), denoted $S_1 \underset{\mathcal{R}}{\rightarrow} S_2$. The notion of *derivation* is then defined as usual.

Definition 10 [derivations] Let $\mathcal{R}$ be a computation rule, P a program and G the goal $\leftarrow Body$; FDS. A *derivation* $\mathcal{D}$ for $P \cup \{G\}$ (via $\mathcal{R}$) is a (possibly infinite) sequence of states $S_0 \underset{\mathcal{R}}{\rightarrow} S_1 \underset{\mathcal{R}}{\rightarrow} \ldots S_n \underset{\mathcal{R}}{\rightarrow} \ldots$, where S_0 is the *initial state* $(Body, FDS)$, and for each $i \geq 0$ either S_i is the last state in the derivation or there is a transition from S_i to S_{i+1} (via $\mathcal{R}$).

Derivations may be finite or infinite. A *finite* derivation from S_0 to S_n is denoted $S_0 \overset{*}{\underset{\mathcal{R}}{\rightarrow}} S_2$. Finite derivations may be either successful, or failing or suspending derivation. A successful (resp. failing, suspending) derivation is one whose final state is a success (resp. failure, suspension) state:

- a state S such that $\mathcal{R}(S) = Suspend$ is said to be a *suspension state*;

- a *success state* is a state having its first component (the current goal) empty; in this case, the current substitution is the result of the derivation (the *computed answer* fd-substitution);

- a *failure state* is a state S such that if $\mathcal{R}(S)$ is an atom then it does not unify with the head of any clause of P, or, otherwise, the constraint-handling procedure applied to it fails.

Now we are in the condition to discuss the control in CHIP(FD). In order to take into account the delay conditions in the CHIP(FD) control rule, we introduce the notion of *availability* of atoms and constraints.

As said, CHIP(FD) programs may contain *delay declarations*. Let p be an n-ary predicate, denoted, as usual, as p/n. A delay declaration for p/n has the form *delay* $p(b_1, \ldots, b_n)$ where $b_i \in \{nonvar, any, ground\}$ ($i \in \{1, \ldots, n\}$) [4]. The effect of such a declaration is that all the atoms of the form $p(t_1, \ldots, t_n)$ present in the goal are not expanded until their instantiation state is such that each t_i satisfies the corresponding declaration a_i in the obvious sense. Atoms whose predicate is not subject to delay conditions are never delayed.

Constraints of class I are delayed according to fixed, implicit delay conditions. More precisely, $element(I, L, X)$ is handled only when L is instantiated to a list of naturals and disequalities are handled only when they contain at most one non-ground fd-variable. The reason for these conditions is obvious: there is no use in treating them if these conditions are not satisfied: the arc-consistency procedure would produce no refinement. Constraints of class II are not subject to delays[4]. As said, also *value generators* are not delayed.

Definition 11 [availability] Let P be a program and $S = (G\theta, FDS)$ be a state. An atom or constraint B belonging to G is said to be *available* in S (or, wrt to (θ, FDS)), denoted $available_P(B\theta, FDS) = true$, when $B\theta$ satisfies (wrt FDS) the delay condition.

Because of the form of the delay conditions, it is easy to see that the availability notion is monotonic wrt instantiation, as the following proposition affirms.

Proposition 1 Let P be a program, $B \in (Atoms \cup Constraints)$ and (θ_1, FDS_1) be an fd-substitution. Then, for each $(\theta_2, FDS_2) \in FD\text{-}Subst$ it holds

$$(\theta_2, FDS_2) \trianglelefteq (\theta_1, FDS_1)$$

$$\Downarrow$$

$$available_P(B\theta_1, FDS_1) = true \Rightarrow available_P(B\theta_2, FDS_2) = true$$

As already explained in section 13.1, the constraint-handling procedures of CHIP(FD) do not provide a *complete* constraint-solver. Because of this, constraints behave differently than atoms during computation in CHIP(FD).

---

[4]But remember that they have to be in normal form to be handled. This point is directly related to the questions raised in section 13.1 (example 1) and will be clarified in section 13.5 after the proof of the Lemma 1 on the monotonicity of the *refine* function.

While an atom once selected and expanded disappears (as usual) from the goal, a constraint, after being handled, must generally be kept in the goal because it may bring further refinements in a later stage of the computation. A constraint can be removed from the goal only when it contains at most one free variable. The following example shows this point.

Example 8 Consider the constraint $2X + 2Y = 3Z$ and the finite domains $\{X \ in \ \{1, 2\}, Y \ in \ \{1, 2\}, Z \ in \ \{1, 2\}\}$. The application of the sup-inf procedure does not refine the domains (see examples 7 and 9). However, the constraint has to be kept in the goal because it can lead to a domain refinement subsequently. For instance, if, in a later stage of the computation, the variable X gets instantiated to the value 2, then the iterated sup-inf procedure applied to it leads to the instantiation of Y to 1 and of Z to 2.

Since the constraint handling procedures of CHIP(FD) are idempotent (see next section), an acceptable computation rule should avoid to select a constraint just after it has been treated. For example, the simple left-most rule of Prolog does not satisfy this condition. More in general, a computation rule could continue to select useless constraints, completely neglecting others that would lead to domain refinements if selected. Such computation rules should be ruled out. In order to give a precise definition of the concept of acceptable computation rule, we define the following notion of *productivity* for constraints (and atoms). Notice that this is a stronger condition than availability for constraints.

Definition 12 [productivity of constraints] Let $S = (G\theta, FDS)$ be a state. We say that a constraint B is *productive* in S if it would lead to some domain refinement when handled (by means of the appropriate procedure) in S. An atom B in S is productive if it is available.

Making use of the notions of availability and productivity we can characterize the class of *acceptable* computation rules, that meets the requirements explained above.

Definition 13 [acceptable computation rule] We say that a computation rule $\mathcal{R}$ is *acceptable* when it respects the following three conditions:

I $\mathcal{R}$ selects an atom or constraint only if it is available wrt the current fd-substitution.

II $\mathcal{R}$ cannot select only *non*-productive constraints indefinitely.

III $\mathcal{R}$ cannot be such that a derivation suspends with a productive atom or constraint in its current goal.

Observe that conditions **I** and **II** imply that a computation using an acceptable computation rule suspends when it reaches a goal in which all atoms and constraints are non-productive. Notice also that **II** is weaker than a general property of fairness involving only atoms.

As we will see in section 13.5 these three conditions are somehow the minimal ones which are necessary to guarantee that the nice semantical properties we want to prove are satisfied.

13.5   Main results

An important property of the basic operations in CHIP(FD) is the monotonicity wrt the order relation $\trianglerighteq$ between fd-substitutions.

Lemma 1 [monotonicity of the *refine* function] Let Υ be either a couple of atoms (A, H) or a constraint B. Let $\varphi_1 \equiv (\theta_1, FDS_1)$ and $\varphi_2 \equiv (\theta_2, FDS_2)$ be two fd-substitutions such that B is available wrt to φ_2 and $\varphi_2 \trianglelefteq \varphi_1$. The following two points hold:

- if $refine(\Upsilon, \varphi_1) = \overline{\varphi}_1$ and $refine(\Upsilon, \varphi_2) = \overline{\varphi}_2$ then $\overline{\varphi}_2 \trianglelefteq \overline{\varphi}_1$

- if $refine(\Upsilon, \varphi_1) = fail$ then $refine(\Upsilon, \varphi_2) = fail$

Proof The monotonicity of the extended unification is proved by extending the classical results on substitutions [23] to fd-substitutions. The monotonicity of the arc-consistency procedure used for the class I constraints is also easy to show. On the contrary, the proof for class II constraints becomes quite tricky due to the interaction between the unification and the iterated sup-inf procedure. Only a sketch of this proof is given below. The interested reader is referred to [15] for the complete proof.

Assume that $B\theta_1$ is a linear equation in normal form

$$B\theta_1 \equiv \left(\sum_{i \in I_1} a_i X_i = \sum_{i \in I_2} a_i X_i + b \right)$$

Here we want to compare $refine(B, \varphi_1)$ and $refine(B, \varphi_2)$ in the case B is a linear equation (disequations constitute a specialization of this case) and $\varphi_2 \trianglelefteq \varphi_1$. The result of these two applications of $refine$ are obtained by iteratively applying the sup-inf procedure till the values become stable. Say that n_1 iterations are necessary for $refine(B, \varphi_1)$ and n_2 for $refine(B, \varphi_2)$. Let $n = max(n_1, n_2)$. Obviously, if both iterations continue n times the final results are not modified. Using this simple observation, it is easy to see that in order to prove the desired result, it suffices to show that the values computed after each iteration bear the desired relationship. We outline only the proof of this fact for the first iteration. The successive iterations are handled in the same way. Let $one(B, \varphi_i)$ $(i \in \{1, 2\})$, be the result of applying the non-iterated sup-inf procedure to B and φ_i. We want to show that $one(B, \varphi_1) \trianglelefteq one(B, \varphi_2)$. Recall that $\varphi_1 \equiv (\theta_1, FDS_1)$ and $\varphi_2 \equiv (\theta_2, FDS_2)$. In what follows we assume that φ_2 and φ_1 are equal to their maximal versions. Since $\varphi_2 \trianglelefteq \varphi_1$, it is the case that $\theta_2 \leq \theta_1$ and thus, there is a substitution σ such that $\theta_2 = \theta_1\sigma$. The set $var(\sigma)$ is partitioned according to the effect of σ on the variables in $var(B\theta_1)$. Let $U_1, \ldots, U_k$ be the maximal non-singleton subsets of $var(B\theta_1)$ such that

- all U_i's are disjoint

- $\forall\, i \in [1, k]$ *and* $X, Y \in U_i$ $X\sigma = Y\sigma$ and $\forall\, j \in [1, k]$, $j \neq i, Z \in U_j$
  implies that $X\sigma \neq Z\sigma$

Let $U = \bigcup_{i=1}^{k} U_i$, let also $\overline{U} = var(\sigma)/U$. Notice that σ either bounds the variables in $\overline{U} \cap var(B\theta_1)$ to ground terms or leaves them free and renamed apart from all other variables of $var(B\theta_1)$. The sets $\overline{U}, U_1, \ldots, U_k$ allow us to "slice" σ and thus also the proof as follows. Let $\delta_0 = \sigma|_{\overline{U}}$ and $\delta_i = \sigma|_{U_i}$ for $i \in [1, k]$. Obviously, $\sigma = \delta_0\delta_1 \ldots \delta_k$. The proof is organized in 2 steps as follows.

- In <u>step 1</u> we show that

$$one(B, \varphi_1) \trianglerighteq one(B, (\theta_1\delta_0, FDS_2))$$

- <u>Step 2</u> is repeated k times, one for each set $U_1, \ldots, U_k$. For each $i \in [1, k]$ we show that

$$one(B, (\theta_1\delta_0 \ldots \delta_{i-1}, FDS_2)) \trianglerighteq one(B, (\theta_1\delta_0 \ldots \delta_i, FDS_2))$$

This result is shown in 2 substeps:

- First, the sup-inf procedure is applied to $B\theta_1\delta_0 \ldots \delta_i$ as it is, i.e. without putting in normal form. Let ψ the result of this application. In this substep it is shown that

$$one(B, (\theta_1\delta_0 \ldots \delta_{i-1}, FDS_2)) \trianglerighteq \psi$$

- Then the equation $B\theta_1\delta_0 \ldots \delta_i$ is now put in normal form. We show that

$$\psi \trianglerighteq one(B, (\theta_1\delta_0 \ldots \delta_i, FDS_2))$$

□

The proof of the monotonicity of *refine* allows us to answer the questions raised in the introduction (cf. example 1). Indeed, this proof shows that:

- the sup-inf procedure obtains the largest possible domain refinement when it is applied to a linear (dis)equation *in normal form*, and

- the domains of the fd-variables that disappear, when putting a linear (dis)equation e in normal form, would not be refined applying the sup-inf procedure directly to e.

The following example illustrates these facts:

Example 9 Consider the linear equation of example 1: $3X + 2Y = 3X + 2Z$. Let $X \in \{1, 2, 3\}$, $Y \in \{2, 3\}$, $Z \in \{1, 2\}$ be the domains for its fd-variables. By applying the sup-inf method no domain gets refined. On the contrary, by simplifying the equation in normal form $2Y = 2Z$, and applying the iterated sup-inf, both the fd-variables Y and Z get instantiated to the value 2.

The motonicity wrt instantiation of the *availability* notion and the monotonicity of the *refine* function are essential to prove the following results on CHIP(FD) computations. Here we only give a sketch of the complete proofs that are contained in [15].

Lemma 2 Let $\overline{\mathcal{R}}$ be an acceptable computation rule. Let P be a program, G a goal and $\overline{\mathcal{D}}$ be a finite non-failing derivation for $P \cup G$ via $\overline{\mathcal{R}}$, denoted $S_0 \equiv S(G) \overset{*}{\underset{\mathcal{R}}{\Rightarrow}} \overline{S}_1 \overset{*}{\underset{\mathcal{R}}{\Rightarrow}} \overline{S}_n$, with computed answer fd-substitution $\overline{\varphi}_n$. Then, for any acceptable computation rule $\mathcal{R}$ there is a finite derivation $\mathcal{D}$ for $P \cup G$ via $\mathcal{R}$, denoted $S_0 \equiv S(G) \overset{*}{\underset{\mathcal{R}}{\Rightarrow}} S_1 \overset{*}{\underset{\mathcal{R}}{\Rightarrow}} S_m$, such that:

i) for each $i \in \{0, ..., m\}$ it holds that $\varphi_i \trianglerighteq \overline{\varphi}_n$, where φ_i is the computed fd-substitution of $S_0 \overset{*}{\underset{\mathcal{R}}{\Rightarrow}} S_i$;

ii) each atom selected by $\mathcal{R}$ in $S_0 \overset{*}{\underset{\mathcal{R}}{\Rightarrow}} S_i$ is unified with the same clause that is used for the corresponding atom in the derivation $\overline{\mathcal{D}}$ via $\overline{\mathcal{R}}$.

Proof The proof uses an induction on the lenght of $\mathcal{D}$. Obviously, $\varphi_0 \trianglerighteq \overline{\varphi}_n$. Lemma 1 shows that, if $\varphi_{i-1} \trianglerighteq \overline{\varphi}_n$ and in the i-th step of $\mathcal{D}$ is handled a unification/constraint that is also handled in $\overline{\mathcal{D}}$, then $\varphi_i \trianglerighteq \overline{\varphi}_n$. In order to be able to show that all steps of $\mathcal{D}$ are also executed in $\overline{\mathcal{D}}$, it suffices to show that ii) holds. This implies, in fact, that all constraints in $\mathcal{D}$ are also in $\overline{\mathcal{D}}$. Assume, then, that the i-th step of $\mathcal{D}$ unifies some atom A. This means that A is available wrt φ_{i-1} and thus, by the monotonicity of delays, A is also available wrt $\overline{\varphi}_n$. Since $\overline{\mathcal{R}}$ is acceptable, it satisfies condition **III** and hence A is selected in $\overline{\mathcal{D}}$ too. Since the unification involving A in $\overline{\mathcal{D}}$ agrees with $\overline{\varphi}_n \trianglelefteq \varphi_{i-1}$, then by Lemma 1 the same unification succeeds in the i-th step of $\mathcal{D}$. Since $\mathcal{R}$ satisfies condition **II** and $\overline{\mathcal{D}}$ is finite, $\mathcal{D}$ is also finite. $\qquad\Box$

Lemma 3 Let $\overline{\mathcal{D}}$ and $\overline{\varphi}_n$ be as in Lemma 3. For any acceptanle computation rule $\mathcal{R}$ and for any (partial) derivation $\mathcal{D}$ for $P \cup G_0$ via $\mathcal{R}$, denoted $S_0 \equiv S(G) \overset{*}{\underset{\mathcal{R}}{\Rightarrow}} S_1 \overset{*}{\underset{\mathcal{R}}{\Rightarrow}} S_m$, such that each atom selected in $\mathcal{D}$ is unified with the same clause that is used for the corresponding atom in the derivation $\overline{\mathcal{D}}$, it holds that

$$\varphi_i \trianglerighteq \overline{\varphi}_n$$

where φ_i is the fd-substitution computed in the derivation $S_0 \overset{*}{\underset{\mathcal{R}}{\Rightarrow}} S_i$.

Proof The proof follows immediately from Lemma 2.   □

Using Lemma 2 and Lemma 3 we can now show the main result of the paper.

Theorem 1 [independence of the computation rule] Let $\mathcal{R}$ be an acceptable computation rule. Let $\mathcal{D}$ be a finite non-failing derivation for $P \cup G_0$ via $\mathcal{R}$, denoted $S_0 \equiv S(G) \xrightarrow[\mathcal{R}]{*} S_n$, with computed answer fd-substitution φ_n. For any acceptable computation rule $\mathcal{R}'$ there is a finite non-failing derivation $\mathcal{D}'$ for $P \cup G$ via $\mathcal{R}'$, denoted $S_0 \equiv S(G) \xrightarrow[\mathcal{R}]{*} S'_m$ with computed answer fd-substitution φ'_m, such that $\varphi_n \simeq \varphi'_m$. Moreover, $\mathcal{D}$ is suspended iff $\mathcal{D}'$ is suspended and, if this is the case, then G_n and G'_m contain the same atoms and constraints.

Proof From Lemma 2 it follows that there exists a derivation $\mathcal{D}'$ finite and such that $\varphi'_m \unrhd \varphi_n$ and that each atom selected by $\mathcal{R}'$ in $\mathcal{D}'$ is unified with the same clause that is used for the corresponding atom in $\mathcal{D}$. It suffices now to show that $\mathcal{D}'$ does not suspend before having made *all* the unification steps of $\mathcal{D}$. In fact, if this is true, we can show that $\varphi'_m \unlhd \varphi_n$ by switching around the roles of $\mathcal{D}$ and $\mathcal{D}'$ and using Lemma 3. Let us then assume that in $\mathcal{D}$ there are steps selecting atoms not selected in $\mathcal{D}'$. Assume that the first step of $\mathcal{D}$ in which this happens is the j-th step and that A is the atom selected. Let us apply Lemma 3 to the two derivations $\mathcal{D}'$ (that plays the role of $\overline{\mathcal{D}}$ in the statement of the Lemma) and $S_0 \xrightarrow[\mathcal{R}]{*} S_j$. By Lemma 3, it follows that $\varphi_j \unrhd \varphi'_m$. It suffices now to observe that (an instance of) A is present in G'_m (recall that A is the *first* atom selected in $\mathcal{D}$ and not in $\mathcal{D}'$). Since A is available wrt φ_j, it is also available wrt φ'_m and thus, since $\mathcal{R}'$ is acceptable and $\mathcal{D}'$ is finite, A must be selected also in $\mathcal{D}'$ (condition **III**).   □

It is important to observe that this Theorem does not say anything for the cases of failing and not terminating computations. Thus, it is possible that a computation using a given acceptable computation rule may fail whereas using another acceptable computation rule it may not terminate. In order to obtain a uniform behaviour also in these cases, it would suffice to turn condition **II** of acceptability into the following fairness condition: every productive constraint and every available atom must be selected after a finite number of steps.

13.6   Conclusions

This paper is a contribution to a rigorous formalization of the part of the CHIP language that we have called CHIP(FD). A formal framework, that completes that described by Van Hentenryck [32], is presented in which some important properties of the constraint handling and of the computations of CHIP(FD) are shown. The main fact proved is that, as long as acceptable rules are adopted, the result of a computation of CHIP(FD) is independent from the particular computation rule used. The proof of this property has required the analysis of the integration of the constraint-handling procedures used, in particular of the *sup-inf* method, with the extended unification procedure. In order to achieve this result, we proved the monotonicity of the domain-refinement procedures.

13.7 REFERENCES

[1] W.W. Bledsoe. The Sup-Inf Method in Presburger Arithmetic. Technical Report Memo ATP-18, University of Texas at Austin, Texas, December (1974).

[2] P. Boizumault, Y. Delon, L. Péridy. Solving a Real-life Planning Exams Problem using Constraint Logic Programming. In *Constraint Processing – Proc. of the Int. WS at CSAM'93* (M. Meyer ed.), DFKI Research Report 93-39, pp.106-112, August (1993).

[3] A. Bundy. A Generalized Interval Package and Its Use for Semantic Checking. ACM Trans. on Math. Software, 10(4), pp. 397-409, (1984).

[4] CHIP User's Guide. Version 4.0. COSYTEC SA, June, France (1993).

[5] A. Colmerauer. An Introduction to Prolog III. ACM Comm., 33(7), pp. 70-90, July (1990).

[6] E. Davis. Constraint propagation with interval labels. *Artificial Intelligence*, 32(3):281–331, July (1987).

[7] M. Dincbas, H. Simonis, and P. Van Hentenryck. Solving large scheduling problems in logic programming. In *EURO-TIMS Joint International Conference on Operations Research and Management Science*, Paris, July (1988).

[8] M. Dincbas, H. Simonis, and P. van Hentenryck. Solving a Cutting-Stock Problem in Constraint Logic Programming. In (Robert A. Kowalski and Kenneth A. Bowen, editors), *Fifth International Conference on Logic Programming*, pages 42–58, Seattle, WA, MIT Press, August (1988).

[9] M. Dincbas, H. Simonis, and P. van Hentenryck. An Extension of PROLOG to Solve Combinatorial Problems. In *Actes de la Journee Combinatoire de l'AFCET*, Paris, France, CNAM, June (1987).

[10] M. Dincbas, H. Simonis, and P. van Hentenryck. A Logic Programming Language to Solve Discrete OR Problems. In *12th Symposium on Operations Research*, Passau, Germany, September (1987).

[11] M. Dincbas, P. Van Hentenryck, H. Simonis, A. Aggoun, and T. Graf. Applications of CHIP to industrial and engineering problems. In *First International Conference on Industrial and Engineering Applications of Artificial Intelligence and Expert Systems*, Tullahoma, Tennessee, June (1988).

[12] M. Dincbas, P. Van Hentenryck, M. Simonis, A. Aggoun, T. Graf, F. Berthier. The Constraint Logic Programming Language CHIP. In Proc. Int. Conf. on Fifth Generation Computer System (FGCS'88), Tokyo, Japan, December, pp. 693-702 (1988).

[13] M. Dincbas, M. Simonis, and P. Van Hentenryck. Solving Large Combinatorial Problems in Constraint Logic Programming. Journal of Logic Programming, 8(1-2), pp. 75-93, (1990).

[14] G. Filé, G. Nardiello and A. Tirabosco. An Operational Semantics for CHIP. In Proc. of the Eighth Conf. on Logic Programming GULP'93, Gizzeria Lido, Italy, June, pp. 633-647 (1993).

[15] G. Filé, G. Nardiello and A. Tirabosco. Semantic properties of CHIP(FD): the independence of the computation rule. *draft*, Università di Padova, Italy (1994).

[16] R.M. Haralick and G.L. Elliott. Increasing Tree Search Efficiency for Constraint Satisfaction Problems. Art. Int. 14, pp. 263-313, (1980).

[17] J. Jaffar and J.-L. Lassez. Constraint Logic Programming. Tech. Rep. 86/73, Monash University, Victoria, Australia, June (1986).

[18] J. Jaffar and J.-L. Lassez. Constraint Logic Programming. In Proc. 14th ACM Conf. on Priciples of Programming Languages (POPL'87), Munich, January, pp. 111-119 (1987).

[19] J. Jaffar and J.-L. Lassez. ¿From Unification to Constraint. In Proc. 6th Japanise Logic Programming Conf., Tokyo, Japan, June, (1987). Lecture Notes in Computer Science No. 315, Springer-Verlag, Berlin, pp. 12-24 (1987).

[20] J. Jaffar and M.J. Maher. Constraint Logic Programming: A Survey. J. Logic Programming 19/20 (May/July), pp. 503-581 (1994).

[21] J. Jaffar, S. Michaylov, P.J. Stuckey and R.H.C. Yap. The CLP($\mathcal{R}$) Language and System. ACM Trans. on Prog. Lang. and Systems, vol. 14(3), pp. 339-395, (1992).

[22] V. Kumar. Algorithms for Constraint-Satisfaction Problems: A Survey. AI Magazine, pp. 32-44, Spring (1992).

[23] J.-L. Lassez, M. Maher and K. Marriott. Unification Revisited. In (Minker ed.) *Foundation of Deductive Databases and Logic programming*, Morgan Kaufmann, Los Altos, CA, (1988).

[24] J.-L. Lauriere. A Language and a program for Stating and Solving Combinatorial Problems. Artificial Intelligence, 10(1), pp. 29-127, (1978).

[25] J.W. Lloyd. *Foundations of Logic programming*. 2nd edition, Springer-Verlag, (1987).

[26] A.K. Mackworth. Consistency in Network of Relations. AI Journal, 8(1), pp.99-118, (1977).

[27] R. Moore. *Interval Arithmetic.* Prentice-Hall, Englewood Cliffs, NJ, (1966).

[28] R. E. Shostak. A practical decision procedure for arithmetic with function symbols. *Journal of the ACM*, 26(2):351–360, April (1979).

[29] V.A. Saraswat. Concurent Constraint Programming Languages. PhD thesis, Carnegie-Mellon University, (to appear by MIT Press), (1989).

[30] E. Tsang. *Foundations of Constraint Satisfaction.* Academic Press, (1993).

[31] P. Van Hentenryck. A Theoretical Framework for Consistency Techniques in Logic Programming. In Proc. of Int Joint Conf. on Artificial Intelligence (IJCAI-87), pp. 2-8, Milan, Italy, August (1987).

[32] P. Van Hentenryck. *Constraint Satisfaction in Logic Programming.* MIT Press, (1989).

[33] P. Van Hentenryck. *Constraint Logic Programming.* Tech. Rept., Brown Univ., Providence, RI, January (1991).

[34] P. Van Hentenryck and Y. Deville. Operational Semantics for Constraint Logic Programming over Finite Domains. In Proc. of PLILP'91, Passau, Germany, August, LNCS 528, Springer-Verlag, pp. 395-406 (1991).

[35] P. Van Hentenryck, H. Simonis and M. Dincbas. Constraint Satisfaction using Constraint Logic Programming. Artificial Intelligence 58(1-3), December (1992).

14

Combining Hill Climbing and Forward Checking for Handling Disjunctive Constraints

Dan R. Vlasie[1]

ABSTRACT The paper describes a simple search method which ameliorates the standard forward checking by a preliminary hillclimbing step. We apply this method to solve a combinatorial search problem: checking the consistency of disjunctive constraint sets.

In the second part we give a qualitative model allowing us to predict the usefulness of the combined method on the average case, comparing it with forward checking.

14.1 Introduction

The combinatorial explosion implied by the resolution of the NP-complete problems is a permanent challenge in designing new and more appropriate search procedures.

Our aim in this article is to explore the possibility of combining two well known search methods: *hillclimbing* and *forward checking*. With this combined method we hope to benefit from both the speed of hillclimbing and the pruning power of forward checking. The intuitive idea behind the method is based on the typical repartition of the algorithmic effort during the forward checking search, that we established both experimentally and theoretically.

We choose to study the behavior of our method on problems involving disjunctive constraints. Such problems arise in such domains of practical interest as scheduling, transportation, circuit design and so on. As a representative application, we apply the method to graph coloring, which is known to be an NP-complete problem.

Processing disjunctive constraints gives us also the occasion to show how

---

[1]I3S Laboratory, University of Nice, Bât. ESSI, Route des Colles, BP 145, 06903 Sophia Antipolis, France; e-mail: `vlasier@essi.fr`

a basic constraint solver can be reused in implementing the search. The key idea is to use a basic solver able to handle *constraint hierarchies* and which incrementally maintain consistency after adding or removing constraints.

The second part of the paper covers an analysis explaining the experimental results obtained on graph coloring problems. This is a qualitative analysis intended to compare the combined method with the standard forward checking. For this purpose we use a statistical model called *deep structure model*([8]), that was previously used for CSPs[2] and TMSs[3]. Now we show that the same model can be useful to better understand the structure of problems involving disjunctive constraints.

14.2   Solving Disjunctive Constraints

Informally, a disjunctive constraint D can be viewed as a construction of the form $D = c_1$ or $\ldots$ or c_M, where c_i are constraints belonging to a certain *basic constraint class*. We write $c \in D$ to show that c is a constraint of the disjunction D.

We are interested in checking the consistency of a disjunctive constraint set $\{D_1, \ldots, D_N\}$ of N disjunctions. This means solving the following problem:

Problem 1 (CCDC) Take from each disjunction one constraint such that the corresponding union of the picked constraints forms a consistent set (according to the consistency definition in the basic constraint class).

This is an interesting problem since an eventual solution of the selected consistent constraint set satisfies also the disjunction set. Please note that CCDC problems does not relate to assignments of values to variables, but to assignments of constraints to disjunctions.

Example 2 (Graph Coloring) Let us consider the simple problem to color the graph from Figure 14.1, using three colors. The problem can be expressed as a CCDC problem where the variables representing the nodes can take integer values between 0 and 2. Each edge between the nodes x_i, x_j , representing the constraint $x_i \neq x_j$, is translated into the disjunction $x_i \leq x_j - 1$ or $x_j \leq x_i - 1$. This leads to the following eight disjunctions:

$$D_1 = x_1 \leq x_2 - 1 \text{ or } x_2 \leq x_1 - 1$$
$$\ldots$$
$$D_8 = x_5 \leq x_4 - 1 \text{ or } x_4 \leq x_5 - 1$$

---

[2] Constraint Satisfaction Problems.
[3] Truth Maintenance Systems.

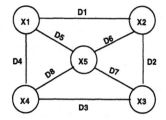

FIGURE 14.1. A simple graph to color, using 3 colors

A solution of this $CCDC$ problem is done, for instance, by the following constraint per disjunction selection:

$sol = \{D_1 : x_1 \leq x_2 - 1,\ D_2 : x_3 \leq x_2 - 1,\ D_3 : x_3 \leq x_4 - 1,\ D_4 : x_1 \leq x_4 - 1,\ D_5 : x_1 \leq x_5 - 1,\ D_6 : x_2 \leq x_5 - 1,\ D_7 : x_3 \leq x_5 - 1,\ D_8 : x_4 \leq x_5 - 1\}$

A solution of this consistent constraint set is a good coloring for our graph; for example:
$\{x_1 = 0,\ x_2 = 1,\ x_3 = 0,\ x_4 = 1,\ x_5 = 2\}$

14.3   Searching for Solutions

In order to solve CCDC problems, it can be useful to take a closer look at the similarities between these and CSPs on finite domains. Indeed, constraint disjunctions can be viewed as variables of a CSP, the basic constraints corresponding to variable values.

A more subtle point is to find at what corresponds in the CCDC frame the notion of constraint in the CSP sense. We can consider in fact that there is a *metaconstraint* between a group of disjunctions whenever there is at least one possibility to pick an inconsistent set of basic constraints from the involved disjunctions. Furthermore, one can consider only the groups of disjunctions that cannot be entailed from any included subgroup.

This parallel might give hints to apply CSP methods for solving CCDC problems also. In this article we focus on *hill climbing* (HC) and *forward checking* (FC).

14.3.1   THE SEARCH SPACE

It is evident that in the general case, a CCDC problem needs combinatorial search. The states explored by a search algorithm for CCDC problems will be conjunctions of assumptions of the form "choose the constraint c from the disjunction D". We denote such an assumption by "$D : c$", calling it a *disjunction assignment*. Then a search state is a set of disjunction assignments such that no disjunction has two constraints assigned to it. Sometimes we note by $A(w)$ the set formed by the constraints selected in the state w. We immediately classify the search states in *consistent states* and *inconsistent* ones, following the consistency of the selected constraint set. A *solution state* is a consistent state assigning all the N disjunctions.

14.3.2 SEARCHES

In the followings we will describe how HC and FC searches are adapted for CCDC problems, and we characterize the specific states explored by these algorithms.

The HC algorithm navigate through a particular kind of search states, called HC-*states*. A HC-state assigning some disjunctions is defined by the fact that it is a consistent state and there is no possibility to consistently extend it with an assignment of any remained disjunction.

Example 3 Considering the previous graph coloring problem, a HC-state is:
$w0 = \{D_1 : x_1 \leq x_2 - 1, D_3 : x_4 \leq x_3 - 1, D_5 : x_1 \leq x_5 - 1, D_6 : x_2 \leq x_5 - 1, D_7 : x_3 \leq x_5 - 1, D_8 : x_4 \leq x_5 - 1\}$
In this state, no assignment for D_2 or D_4 can be joined to $w0$, because the consistency is not preserved.

At each step the HC method tries to reach a HC-state having a size greater than the previous explored state. We will see in the implementation section how this work is done by looking at the neighbors of the current state.

The typical pathology of this kind of search is that it can get stuck into local maxima ([3],[5]).

As opposite to HC, the FC algorithm ([4], [7]) does a systematic search among the consistent states. A FC-state is a consistent search state such that for each not yet assigned disjunction there is at least one possibility to assign it consistently with the already assigned disjunctions.

Example 4 The following state is a FC-state:
$w1 = \{D_1 : x_1 \leq x_2 - 1, D_5 : x_1 \leq x_5 - 1, D_6 : x_2 \leq x_5 - 1, D_7 : x_3 \leq x_7 - 1, D_8 : x_4 \leq x_5 - 1\}$
because each disjunction D_2, D_3, D_4 contains at least one constraint which can be joined to the selected constraint set $A(w1)$, such that the consistency is preserved. This is easy to verify: the selected constraint set is
$A(w1) = \{x_1 \leq x_2 - 1, x_1 \leq x_5 - 1, x_2 \leq x_5 - 1, x_3 \leq x_5 - 1, x_4 \leq x_5 - 1\}$,
and

- taking $c = x_3 \leq x_2 - 1$ from D_2, we have that $\{D_2 : c\} \cup w1$ is consistent;

- taking from D_3 either $c = x_3 \leq x_4 - 1$ or $c = x_4 \leq x_3 - 1$ we have that $\{D_3 : c\} \cup w1$ is consistent;

- taking $c = x_1 \leq x_4 - 1$ from D_4 we have that $\{D_4 : c\} \cup w1$ is consistent.

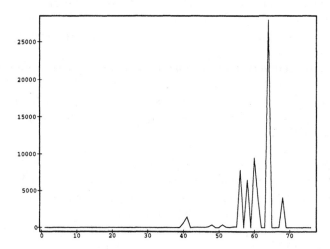

FIGURE 14.2. The average experimental behavior of the FC search. We see that the essential of the search effort is concentrated in a narrow region where more than 3/4 of disjunctions are assigned.

Let us remark that the difference between $w1$ and $w0$ is the fact that the HC-state assigns D_3 whereas the FC-state does not.

At each step the FC algorithm constructs a FC-state extending a previous one with a new disjunction assignment. If there is no possibility to pass into a new FC-state, then the last choice is reconsidered by backtracking. As pathology for the FC-search we note the *thrashing*, manifested by a dramatic increase in the number of reconsidered choice points when constructing FC-states of some intermediate size.

14.4   The Combined Method

Let us make an empirical study concerning the repartition of the algorithmic effort during the FC search. For that we counted for each state size n the number of search states expanded so far in order to reach the first FC-state of size n, considering that the search stopped when the first solution was found. If we note by $C_n, n = 1 \ldots N$ the corresponding obtained amounts, then the difference $C_{n+1} - C_n$ enlighten us about the repartition of the search effort following the state sizes.

Figure 14.2 plots the behavior of the difference $C_{n+1} - C_n$ averaged over about 10 samples of a 3-coloring problem involving 75 disjunctions and

37 variables. We see that at the beginning of the search, the algorithm does not encounter any difficulty until about 3/4 of the disjunctions are assigned. Then there is a narrow region concentrating the essential of the search effort . We see also that once this difficult region is overstepped, the search reaches the solution level very quickly.

These empirical observations lead us to the following idea: *if we are able to construct a* FC*-state with the size overstepping the difficult region, perhaps continuing the* FC *search from this state is more efficient*[4]. Of course, constructing this FC-state must be less expensive than reaching a state of the same size by FC .

In order to construct a starting FC-state with a large size, we firstly use the HC method, since it reaches large consistent states very quickly. After reaching a large HC-state, it is possible to obtain a FC-state by simply unassigning some disjunctions (see section 14.4.1 below), hoping that the size of this FC-state oversteps the difficult region.

To summarize, we propose a method -that we call HCFC- combining the HC and the FC, which consists in the following steps:

hillclimbing : a local maximal HC-state is reached using a HC method;

transforming phase: the HC-state is transformed into a FC-state;

forward checking: the search proceeds from the FC-state by FC.

This combined method can be viewed as a FC algorithm ameliorated by a preprocessing phase which try to construct a state from which the search can proceeds with potentially more success.

14.4.1 THE TRANSFORMING PHASE

This phase transforms a HC-state into a FC-state and is based on the following considerations.

Let us consider a consistent constraint set A and a constraint c such that $A \cup \{c\}$ is not consistent. We will note the smallest subsets which should be eliminated from A in order to preserve the consistency when adding c, by:

$$\alpha_A(c) = \{u \subseteq A, u \text{ minimal} \mid A \cup \{c\} \setminus u \text{ is consistent } \} \qquad (14.1)$$

Let us now consider a HC-state w, $A(w)$ the set of the constraints selected by w, and let $\{F_1, \ldots, F_j\}$ be the list of disjunctions not assigned by w. For each not assigned disjunction F_i, we note

$$\alpha_{A(w)}(F_i) = \bigcup_{c \in F_i} \alpha_{A(w)}(c) .$$

---

[4]We suppose that between two FC-states of the same size, no one can be apriorically considered worse than other for the future of the search.

With these notations, the following theorem gives a sufficient condition to obtain **FC**-states by removing assignments from w:

Theorem 5 *Let $R \subseteq A(w)$ be such that $\forall F_i, i = 1 \ldots j$, we have that $\mathcal{P}(R) \cap \alpha_{A(w)}(F_i) \neq \emptyset$. Then the state v selecting the constraint set $A(v) = A(w) \setminus R$ is a **FC**-state.*

We remember that $\mathcal{P}(R)$ denote the set of all the subsets of R.

Please note that the above theorem does not provide any particular method to compute the set $R \subseteq A(w)$. However, it suggests a direct method as follows:

(i)   randomly take one constraint c_i from each disjunction $F_1, \ldots, F_j$;

(ii)   randomly take one set u_i from each $\alpha_A(c_i)$, $i = 1 \ldots j$, where $\alpha_A(c_i)$ is given by (14.1).

(iii)   put

$$R = \bigcup_{i=1}^{j} u_i .$$

Example 6 Let us recall the previous Example 3 where $w0$ is a **HC**-state. The list of non-assigned disjunctions in $w0$ is $\{D_2, D_4\}$. We remember that $D_2 = \{x_2 \leq x_3 - 1, x_3 \leq x_2 - 1\}$, $D_4 = \{x_1 \leq x_4 - 1, x_1 \leq x_4 - 1\}$, and that $A(w0) = \{x_1 \leq x_2 - 1, x_4 \leq x_3 - 1, x_1 \leq x_5 - 1, x_2 \leq x_5 - 1, x_3 \leq x_5 - 1, x_4 \leq x_5 - 1\}$

Applying the above method, we can choose:

(i) $c_1 \in D_2, c_1 = x_2 \leq x_3 - 1$ and $c_2 \in D_4, c_2 = x_1 \leq x_4 - 1$

(ii) $u_1 = \{x_4 \leq x_3 - 1\}$ and $u_2 = \{x_4 \leq x_3 - 1\}$; that is, $A(w0) \setminus u_i \cup \{c_i\}$ is consistent, $i = 1 \ldots 2$.

(iii) $R = u_1 \cup u_2 = \{x_4 \leq x_3 - 1\}$

Since $A(w0) \setminus R = A(w1)$, it follows that $w0$ has been transformed into $w1$ and we have seen that $w1$ is a FC-state.

14.5   Implementation

We have implemented our method for disjunctions over the basic constraint class formed by the *precedence constraints*, i.e. binary constraints of the form $X \leq Y + Const$, with the variables taking values in integer finite intervals.

The constraints are labeled with *strengths*, defining a *constraint hierarchy* ([1]) over the current state of the search.

The basic solver works by incrementally maintaining a dependency graph (constraint net) between the *min, max* bounds of the variables.

14.5.1 BASIC SOLVER PRIMITIVES

The main primitive of the solver is called **add_making_place** and allows the addition of a new constraint to the consistent constraint set which defines the current state of the search. This primitive implements the computation of an element from the set given by the formula (14.1).

The result of this operation is a set containing the constraints that was removed from the current state in order to allow the insertion of the new constraint. Of course the result of the operation is not uniquely defined, but the strengths associated to the constraints are used to impose the choices.

To clarify the semantics of the **add_making_place** primitive, we give below the preconditions and the postconditions of the operation $R = S.\text{add\_making\_place}(c)$, where S is the current state, c is the constraint to add, S' is the new state and R is the set of removed constraints.

precondition:

- S is a consistent constraint set;

postconditions:

- $S' = \{c\} \cup S \setminus R$,
- S' is a consistent constraint set,
- for all removed constraint $r \in R$ it follows that $S' \cup \{r\}$ is not consistent,
- R is better than any other constraint set Q verifying the above conditions, in the sense that

$$\max_{r \in R} r.strength \leq \max_{q \in Q} q.strength$$

We notice that this relation defines a *local comparator* between the solutions of the constraint set $S \cup \{c\}$, in the sense of the definition done in [1].

Let X and Y be the variables involved in the constraint c that must be added. The implementation of the primitive **add_making_place**(c) consists in successively removing the weakest constraint implied in the computation of the bounds of X and Y. This removing process is done until the consistency is achieved, then the removed constraints are collected in the set R.

As it was already suggested, another important primitive is **remove**, which allows the elimination of a constraint from the current consistent set. The result of **remove** is an appropriate incremental modification of the constraint net, implying the modification of some *min*, *max* bounds. If S is a consistent constraint set, let us denote by $Bounds(S)$ the set formed by taking the bound values *min*, *max* of all variables involved in S. Then the remove operation verifies the following identity:

$$Bounds(S.remove(c)) = Bounds(S \setminus \{c\})$$

14.5.2 Implementing the Hill Climbing

Let us denote by T the (multi)set of all the basic constraints involved in the problem, obtained by putting together all disjunction members. Each step of the HC search consists in partitioning the set T in two disjoint sets: $T = P \cup N$, such that the search state w with $A(w) = P$, is a HC-state, as defined in the section 14.3.2. That is, P is a consistent constraint set and for any constraint c from N, we have that $P \cup \{c\}$ is not consistent.

We associate at each such HC-state the objective function which simply counts the number of disjunctions having a member in the set P (that is, the number of satisfied disjunctions). A step of the method consists in passing from the current partition $T = P \cup N$ to a new one, say $T = P1 \cup N1$, such that the objective function reaches a greater value. This is done by choosing between some *local moves*.

A local move consists in selecting a constraint $c \in N$, and inserting it in the consistent set P using P.add_making_place(c). We have seen that the primitive add_making_place has as a side effect to remove some constraints from P. It follows that there are constraints from N which now can be added to P in order to construct a new HC-state $P1$.

In order to avoid the exploration of the same state, the strengths of the constraints are updated at each step according to the following principles:

- constraints that are recently arrived in the set P get higher strengths;

- constraints that are recently arrived in the set N get lower strengths;

- constraint strengths are modified during the search, according to the constraint membership in the set P or in the set N: for the constraints in P the strengths decrease in time, while for the constraints in N the strengths increase.

According to these principles the constraint strengths keep track of the history of the search, allowing the move selection on the basis of *recency* and *frequency* criteria ([3]).

14.5.3 Implementing the Transforming Phase

Transforming a reached HC-state into a FC-one, according to the direct method described in section 14.4.1, is simply done by repeated calls of the primitive add_making_place. The successive arguments of the calls are constraints randomly choiced between the components of the not yet assigned disjunctions. After each call the constraint used as argument for add_making_place is removed from the constraint set. At the end, the resulted consistent constraint set forms a FC-state, as stipulated by the Theorem 5.

14.6   Experimental Results

We made a series of experiments in order to empirically conclude on the effectiveness of our combined method. We compared the algorithmic time spent by the HCFC with the one needed by the FC alone on the same problem instances. The searches stopped when a first solution was found, or when they discovered that there is no solution.

As a measure for the algorithmic time we used the number of FC-states expanded during the search. We did not count the effort made by the HC phase, since it does not involve any kind of backtracking: the HC phase stops when the first local maximum is encountered, thus the number of explored HC-states is subquadratically related to the problem size. We ignored also the effort needed by the transforming phase, which is expressed by the number of calls at the **add_making_place** and **remove** primitives, multiplied by N minus the size of the reached maximal HC-state. Since there is no backtracking involved in this phase[5], its influence on the total cost is lower.

We checked both methods on random graph coloring instances belonging on various classes defined by the rapport (i.e. density) between the number of disjunctions (i.e. edges) and the number of variables (i.e. nodes). The obtained results are showed in the table below. The last two columns contain the average size of the maximal state reached after the HC phase, and respectively the average size of the state obtained after the transforming phase.

TABLE 14.1. Experimental Results

soluble instances? (y/n)	problem density (ρ)	average effort		size of the maximal HC-state	size of the constructed FC-state
		FC	HCFC		
	1.75	23250	4200	73.5	71
yes	2.0	62800	8300	72	68
	2.3	19300	9800	72	66
	2.3	300500	250000	71	55
no	3.0	6900	8100	67.5	49
	3.75	1100	1000	63	36

Averaged over about 10 samples per case, for problems with 75 disjunctions.

These experiments show that in the case of instances having solutions the difference in average effort is about a magnitude order in the favor of the combined method. For instant, we see that for the density $\rho = 1.75$ the size of the maximal HC-state is very close, on average, to the problem size; in fact there were instances directly solved by HC, thus needing a null

---

[5]The transforming phase is done by the "random choice" method exposed in the section 14.4.

HCFC effort. As opposite, the simple FC algorithm will spent some significant effort, suggesting that the systematic search is too expensive for these easy problems.

Another experimental conclusion is that for instances not having solution both methods have comparable efficiencies.

14.7   Analysis

In this section we try to theoretically estimate the usefulness of our method. The idea is to deduce and to compare the average search costs of FC and HCFC. Next, we look at how the deduced theoretical behavior fits with the experimental results.

14.7.1   THE "DEEP STRUCTURE" MODEL

For our purpose we will consider a simple model to describe CCDC problems, called the *deep structure* model. This model was defined in [8] in order to analyze the intrinsic complexity of CSPs. Previously, some similar considerations were made in [6], related to the complexity of scene analysis with TMSs. Now we consider that the same model can help understanding the structure of CCDC problems.

We begin by observing that the search space of a CCDC problem, defined as in section 14.3.1, can be structured into a lattice with N levels, regarding the operation of set inclusion. A level groups the states with the same size.

Since any constraint set containing an inconsistent constraint set is inconsistent, we can classify the inconsistent nodes of the lattice in: *minimal nogoods*, i.e. inconsistent nodes do not containing inconsistent subsets, and *nogoods*, i.e. nodes which are supersets of inconsistent nodes.

In this model a given CCDC problem is completely defined by four numbers: N -the number of disjunctions, M -the number of constraints per disjunction, k -the average size of minimal nogoods, and m -the number of minimal *independent* nogoods.

Example 7 (3-Coloring Problems) Graph coloring problems for random graphs are simply modelised by taking N equal to the number of edges, and $M = 2$, since there are two constraints per edge, as showed in Example 2. Let us consider that the number of colors is equal to three. In this case, any path of 3 edges (called 3-path) introduces 2 minimal nogoods. Figure 14.3 details two such minimal nogoods generated by an open 3-path and a triangle. It follows that the size of minimal nogoods is $k = 3$.

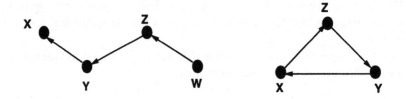

FIGURE   14.3.   Any 3-path in the graph introduces two minimal nogoods.
The figure depicts two such generated minimal nogoods:
$\{X \leq Y - 1, Y \leq Z - 1, Z \leq W - 1\}$ and $\{X \leq Y - 1, Y \leq Z - 1, Z \leq X - 1\}$.

14.7.2   INSIDE THE SEARCH SPACE

It is easy to see that each level of the search lattice contains $\binom{N}{n} M^n$ nodes.
The deep structure model allows us to compute the probability that a node
at level n in the lattice represents a consistent state. Let us note by q_n this
probability. As showed in [8], in the hypothesis that the m minimal nogoods
are *independent*, the consistency probability at level n is [6]:

$$q_n = \frac{\left(\begin{array}{c} \binom{N}{k} M^k - \binom{n}{k} \\ m \end{array} \right)}{\left(\begin{array}{c} \binom{N}{k} M^k \\ m \end{array} \right)} \tag{14.2}$$

In particular, the value of the expected number of solutions is done by

$$\langle Sols \rangle = q_N M^N. \tag{14.3}$$

Example 8 (3-Coloring Problems) In order to complete the parameter identification for graph coloring, we need m, the number of independent
minimal nogoods. Deducing this parameter could be complex, since it delicately relates to the graph topology. However, m is also related to another
problem parameter, the expected number of solutions $\langle Sols \rangle$. Applying a
Stirling approximation[7] in the expression of $\ln \langle Sols \rangle$ (see (14.2), (14.3)),
we obtain that:

$$m \approx \frac{\ln \langle Sols \rangle - N \ln 2}{\ln(1 - 1/2^3)}. \tag{14.4}$$

---

[6] This expression is easy to understand: a node at level n is above exactly $\binom{n}{k}$
nodes at level k, and it is consistent if and only if it is not a superset of any of the
m minimal nogoods at level k. The numerator in (14.2) gives the number of ways
of selecting m minimal nogoods such that a given node at level n is consistent;
the denominator gives the total number of ways of selecting m minimal nogoods
among the nodes at level k.

[7] i.e. $\ln \frac{\binom{x-y}{z}}{\binom{x}{z}} \approx z \ln(1 - \frac{y}{x})$, when $z << y$.

There is also a direct relation between the expected number of solutions and the expected number of good colorings of the graph (noted $\langle Cols \rangle$):

$$\langle Cols \rangle = f \langle Sols \rangle, \text{ with } 1 \leq f \leq 3. \tag{14.5}$$

In this equation the scaling factor f is almost 1 when the problem size grows. An independent way to compute $\langle Cols \rangle$ is given by the following expression[8]:

$$\langle Cols \rangle = K^\mu (1 - 1/K)^N, \tag{14.6}$$

where μ is the number of nodes in the graph and K is the number of colors (in our case we put $K = 3$).

Thus the system formed by the equations (14.4), (14.5) and (14.6) determines the value of the missing parameter m, the number of independent minimal nogoods.

Once the consistency probability computed, we can derive the probability that a consistent state is a FC-state one. Let us consider a consistent state s which assigns n disjunctions. We first compute the probability that s can be consistently extended with at least an assignment of a given new disjunction. The state s is one among the $Q_n = q_n M^n$ consistent states assigning the considered n disjunctions. There are $M Q_n$ possibilities to extend these states with a new assignment. Among these extensions, only $Q_{n+1} = q_{n+1} M^{n+1}$ are consistent. Since s can be extended in M different manners, it follows that the probability that no one of these extensions is consistent is given by $\binom{M Q_n - Q_{n+1}}{M} / \binom{M Q_n}{M}$. Subtracting this from 1 gives the probability that there is at least one possibility to extend s in a consistent manner with the assignment of a new disjunction. The state s is a FC-state when it can be consistently extended assigning any disjunction from the $N - n$ left ones. Applying the Stirling approximation[7] we obtain the following approximation for the probability that a consistent state is a FC-state:

$$f_n \approx [1 - (1 - q_{n+1}/q_n)^M]^{N-n} \tag{14.7}$$

A similar argumentation allows the computation of the HC-state probability:

$$h_n \approx [(1 - q_{n+1}/q_n)^M]^{N-n} \tag{14.8}$$

By convention, f_N and h_N are considered equal to one.

---

[8] The probability that a random assignment of colors to nodes is a good one for a given pair of connected nodes is $1 - \frac{K}{K^2}$, where K is the number of colors. Assuming that the edges in the graph are independent, we obtain (14.6) as expression for the expected number of good colorings.

14.7.3 EVALUATION

In order to assert the usefulness of the HCFC method we must evaluate if on the average case it actually performs better than the simple FC.

We begin by estimating the mean cost to first solution or to failure for the simple FC search. The FC proceeds by constructing a succession of FC-states with the size going from 1 to N if the problem has solution, or until some intermediate size F if there is no solution. We note by s_n the *first* FC-state of size n reached by the FC algorithm during the search, and let us associate at each FC-state s_n the algorithmic effort $C(s_n)$ made by the FC *so far*.

Mean Cost to First Solution or to Failure

We consider now the difference $C(s_n) - C(s_{n-1})$, which can be interpreted as being the effort to pass from a FC-state of size $n-1$ to a FC-state of size n. This local effort depends on the probability to find a FC-state at level n: the lower this probability is, the greater the difference $C(s_n) - C(s_{n-1})$ is.

Since we are primarily interested by qualitative aspects (comparing between two methods) rather than by quantitative evaluations, we will consider roughly the mean of the local effort as being[9]:

$$\langle C(s_n) - C(s_{n-1}) \rangle = \frac{1}{f_n},$$

where f_n is the FC-state probability given by (14.7). It follows that the mean cost for the FC search can be estimated by[10]:

$$\langle C(s_F) \rangle \approx \langle C(s_I) \rangle + \sum_{n=I+1}^{F} \frac{1}{f_n}, \qquad (14.9)$$

where F denotes either the size N if the problem has solution or the expected size of the maximal reached state after which the search fails if there is no solution. The size I can be any state size between $1 \ldots F$. Putting $I = 1$ gives the mean cost of the simple FC method.

In the case that the problem has no solution, the expected size F, after which the search fails, is simply the level in the search tree[11] at which the expected number of FC-states drops to zero. This can be stated by

---

[9] That is, if p is the favorable case probability, one must explore, on average, $\frac{1}{p}$ cases in order to obtain *one* favorable case.

[10] We implicitly use the mean-field approximation $\langle f(X_1, \ldots, X_n) \rangle \approx f(\langle X_1 \rangle, \ldots, \langle X_2 \rangle)$.

[11] The FC algorithm is supposed doing a simple search with no disjunction ordering heuristics. Thus the order in which the disjunctions are assigned is arbitrary but fixed.

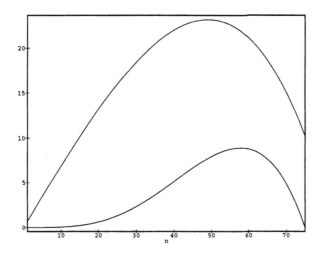

FIGURE 14.4. Logarithmic plot of the expected number of consistent states (upper curve) and of the local mean effort $1/f_n$ (lower curve), as functions of the level n. The model parameters are taken for 3-colorings with $N = 75$ and $\rho = 2$.

considering F as being the smallest n between $1 \ldots N$ which verifies the following inequation:

$$2^n q_n f_n < 1. \qquad (14.10)$$

If there is no solution for the above inequation in n, then the problem is expected to have solution and thus $F = N$.

For example, in Figure 14.4 we logarithmically plot the expected number of consistent states $2^n q_n$ (the upper curve) and the value of $1/f_n$ (the lower curve) for 3-coloring problems defined by 75 disjunctions and the density $\rho = 2$ (i.e. about 37 graph nodes). We see that the two curves does not intersect, thus there is no solution for the inequation (14.10) and then the problem is expected to have solutions. The mean cost is given by the area delimited by the exponential of the lower curve. The figure gives also a qualitative explanation about the behavior of the FC search. At the beginning of the search the FC algorithm spends little effort, until some intermediate levels around three quart of N are reached. At these intermediate levels the search spends the essential of the effort, after that it quickly reaches the solution level. This theoretical qualitative behavior fits very well with the experimental one, plotted in Figure 14.2.

We also plot the model predictions for 3-coloring problems defined by $N = 75$, $\rho = 3.75$. The intersection of the two curves from Figure 14.5 gives the value of the level F at which the search is expected to fail.

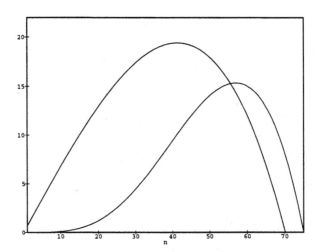

FIGURE 14.5. Logarithmic plot of the expected number of consistent states (upper curve) and of the local mean effort $1/f_n$ (lower curve), as functions of the level n. The model parameters are taken for 3-colorings with $N = 75$ and $\rho = 3.75$.

We turn now attention to estimate the mean cost of the HCFC method. This is easy to do by plugging into formula (14.9) the level I equal to the size of the constructed FC-state after the HC and the transforming phase. In this case the term $\langle C(s_I) \rangle$ in the sum (14.9) means the expected effort done by the HC and the transforming phase.

Comparison

Looking at the behavior of the $1/f_n$ as a function of state sizes, we remarked that there is a bulge situated at some intermediate levels. In fact, as the problem size grows, this peak becomes sharper, exponentially dominating all other terms in the sum (14.9), and thus imposing the value of the mean cost.

Let us consider that the problem has solutions and let us note by L the level at which the peak appears. It follows that *the mean cost of* HCFC *is better than the mean cost of* FC *if and only if the size I of the constructed* FC-state is greater than the level L.

We can now give the theoretical explanation of the experimental results regarding the soluble problems (see the table 14.6). Studying the maximum of the expression $1/f_n$ for various values of the density ρ we found that the peak appears at $L \approx 60$. Getting the corresponding values of I from the last column of the table, we see that $I > L$, so our analysis provide the explanation for the better performance of the combined method.

When the problem is expected to have no solution[12] there are two situations to consider: the expected level F is either beyond the peak location L, or before this[13].

In the first case $(F \geq L)$ the mean cost of FC, when the problem size grows, is given by the value $1/f_L$. The experimental results from the table 14.6 shows that the average size I of the constructed FC-state is lower than the peak location $L \approx 60$. This implies that the mean cost of HCFC is also given by the same expression $1/f_L$, confirming the experimental conclusion. In particular this is a disappointing result, because in this case the problems are expected to be hard, as being located near a "phase transition region" (see [2]). It follows that the combined method is unable to perform better on these hard problems, the reason being that *the bulge in the cost cannot be avoided*, at least using the direct random choice method in the transforming phase.

The second case $(F < L)$ implies that F is located in a region where $1/f_n$ is a monotonically increasing function of n. Then the mean cost of the FC, when the problem size grows, is given by the value of $1/f_F$, the maximal term of the sum (14.9). On the other side, the size I of the constructed FC-state is at most equal to F, since after this size the probability to found a FC-state is almost zero. It follows that the mean cost for HCFC is given by the same expression $1/f_F$ and then both methods have on average the same complexity, as experimentally observed.

14.8 Conclusion

In this article we described a search method combining hill climbing and forward checking. This method is inspired by some empirical evidence concerning the repartition of the algorithmic effort during the forward checking search. We applied this method to solve combinatorial search problems involving disjunctive constraints.

The implementation raises questions about the efficient handling of constraint disjunctions, that we overcome by using a basic constraint solver able to react incrementally at operations like adding or removing constraints. In particular, the hillclimbing procedure is implemented by driving the basic solver through modifications of constraint strengths.

Experimental results on graph coloring problems are reported. We also made a simple qualitative analysis which allows us to better understand

---

[12] Seeing for which values of 3-coloring parameters the inequation (14.10) has solution gives $\rho \geq 2.7$.

[13] The first situation is expected for 3-coloring problems having the density ρ between 2.7...3.4. The second one is expected for $\rho > 3.4$. These values are independent of the problem size.

the behavior of our method.

Following the experiments and the theoretical analysis we concluded that the combined method performs better on average than the simple forward checking on graph coloring problems having solutions. We concluded also that for graph coloring problems not having solutions the average efficiency of the combined method is the same as for the standard forward checking. This is in particular disappointing for problems located in a so called "phase transition region", where the bulge in the forward checking cost cannot be avoided by the random choice method that we used to construct the initial FC-state. This conclusion suggests that the performance of the method could be ameliorated by paying more attention to the transforming phase. Indeed, more sophisticated heuristics than the random choice could be imagined in order to maximize the size of the starting FC-state.

Acknowledgements: My thanks go to M. Rueher for his comments on preliminary versions of this work. I also thank the anonymous referees of *Constraint Processing Workshop at ECAI'94* that pointed out some omissions in a previous submitted version. J. Montaldi and P. Marti helped me with the English in this paper.

14.9 REFERENCES

[1] A. Borning, B. Freeman-Benson, and M. Wilson. *Constraint Hierarchies. Lisp and Symbolic Computation*, (5):223–270, 1992.

[2] P. Cheeseman, B. Kanefsky, and W.M. Taylor. *Where the Really Hard Problems Are.* In Morgan Kaufmann, editor, *Proceedings of IJCAI-91*, pages 331–337, 1991.

[3] F. Glover and M. Laguna. *Tabu Search.* A Chapter in *Modern Heuristic Techniques for Combinatorial Problems*, June 1992. University of Colorado at Boulder.

[4] R.M. Haralick and G.L. Elliot. *Increasing Tree Search Efficiency for Constraint Satisfaction Problems. Artificial Intelligence*, (14):263–313, 1980.

[5] S. Minton and al. *Minimizing conflicts: a heuristic repair method for constraint satisfaction and scheduling problems. Artificial Intelligence*, (58):161–205, 1992.

[6] G. Provan. *Efficiency Analysis of Multiple Contexts TMSs in Scene Representation.* In Morgan Kaufmann, editor, *Proceedings of AAAI-87*, pages 173–177, 1987.

[7] Pascal Van Hentenryck. *Constraint Satisfaction in Logic Programming.* The MIT Press, 1989.

[8] C. P. Williams and T. Hogg. *Using Deep Structure to Locate Hard Problems*. In *Proceedings of AAAI-92*, pages 472–477, 1992.

15

GA-easy and GA-hard Constraint Satisfaction Problems

Ágoston Eiben
Paul-Erik Raué
Zsófia Ruttkay[1]

ABSTRACT In this paper we discuss the possibilities of applying genetic algorithms (GA) for solving constraint satisfaction problems (CSP). We point out how the greediness of deterministic classical CSP solving techniques can be counterbalanced by the random mechanisms of GAs. We tested our ideas by running experiments on four different CSPs: N-queens, graph 3-colouring, the traffic lights and the Zebra problem. Three of the problems have proven to be GA-easy, and even for the GA-hard one the performance of the GA could be boosted by techniques familiar in classical methods. Thus GAs are promising tools for solving CSPs. In the discussion, we address the issues of non-solvable CSPs and the generation of all the solutions.

15.1 Introduction

In this paper we consider *genetic algorithms* (GA) for solving *constraint satisfaction problems* (CSP) with finite domains. The majority of CSP solving algorithms, which we will refer to as *classical* ones, are deterministic and constructive search algorithms. That is, solution – a member of the search space (being the direct product of the finite domains) – is constructed by step-by-step specifying a value for a still uninstantiated variable in such a way that all the constraints which can be evaluated, are satisfied. If there is no such value for the current variable to be instantiated, then previous instantiations are revised (backtracking). The selection of the variable to be instantiated and of the value to be assigned to it are done in a deterministic way, based either on the representation or on some evaluation of the uninstantiated variables and their possible values. The algorithms differ in

---

[1] Dept. of Mathematics and Computer Science, Vrije Universiteit Amsterdam, De Boelelaan 1081a, 1081HV Amsterdam, The Netherlands

the evaluations applied as the basis for heuristics for variable and value selection. For effective CSP solving algorithms with specific characteristics see [18, 19, 22, 30].

It is known that the general CSP is NP-complete [29], hence it is unlikely that a classical search algorithm exists which can find a solution for any CSP in an acceptable time. What makes constructive methods 'weak' in certain cases is just what makes them 'strong' for others: they restrict the scope of the search, based on some (explicit or implicit) heuristics. If the heuristics turns out to be misleading, it is often very tiresome to enlarge or shift the scope of the investigation using a series of backtrackings. This problem can be overcome by diversifying the search, for instance by:

1) maintaining several different candidate solutions in parallel,

2) counterbalancing the greediness of the heuristics by incorporating random elements into the construction mechanism of new candidates.

These two principles are essential for evolutionary algorithms, in particular for GAs. Hence, the basic idea of our research, to apply GAs to solve CSPs, is a natural response for the (both theoretical and practical) limitations of the classical CSP solving methods. Note that (2) allows many combinations of different heuristics and random components. Moreover, when creating new candidates it is possible to adopt some well-known heuristics from the classical constructive methods as well as to exploit information gained by statistical analysis of the present set of candidates.

Non-classical CSP solving methods have gained attention only recently. In [3] it is proved that an algorithm based on random selection performs better than depth-first search (which can be seen as a 'bad' heuristics) and thus should be used when no explicit heuristics for variable and/or value selection exist. Despite of this result the representation-based selection is rarely replaced by random selection (mostly for tie-breaking). There are a few practical applications where iterative and random mechanisms play an essential role. In [1] a stochastic network was used to solve a scheduling problem. Another direction in stochastic CSP solving methods is the application of simulated annealing [26]. In [33] a generate and repair method was used with min-conflict hill climbing heuristics to solve CSPs, inspired by ideas employed in the network reported in [1]. This technique could find a solution for the N-queens problem up to one million queens very quickly [33], just like another iterative method described in [38]. It is a common problem of non-exhausitve methods of possibly getting stuck in a local optimum. In [7] a neural network was presented to solve CSPs on the basis of iterative improvement, with learning feature to escape local minima, the GA in [11] maintaines breakout-points.

Some research into exploiting the benefits of evolutionary techniques has been done for discrete constrained optimisation problems [31, 37, 40]. Recently GAs have also been applied to the subset sum problem and the minimum tardy task [27], scheduling [41], graph partitioning [2, 28], set covering [25], satisfiability problems [21], timetable problem [36] as well as the N-queens problem [6, 10]. In [32] systems for constrained optimization problems with continous domains are discussed.

15.2   Genetic Algorithms

Genetic algorithms are generate-and-test methods with a philosophy and terminology taken from evolution theory [20, 8, 23, 32]. They operate on a search space where the quality of the candidate solutions is given by a so-called *fitness function*. The goal of the search is to find (one of) the fittest element(s) of the search space or at least to approximate it. In the genetic approach candidate solutions are perceived as *individuals* (often called *chromosomes*). A GA simultaneously processes a set of individuals, called the *population*. The population is changed by selecting individuals playing the role of *parents* and creating *children* from the parents by *genetic operators*. In classical GAs individuals are binary strings and the operators that create new candidates from old ones are called *mutation* and *crossover*. Mutation creates one child from one parent by altering one value; crossover applies to two parents and yields two children by applying a tail-exchange between the parent strings. Both operations have a random element, namely the selection of the position of the altered value for mutation and of the crossover point for crossover. The selection of parents, i.e. the individuals involved in the creation of new ones, is done stochastically with a probability that is proportional to the fitness of the individuals. Thus, a randomised *mating-of-the-fittest* principle is applied. In many GAs new-born individuals have to compete with old ones in order to be included in the next population. Selecting the survivors is again done using a fitness-based random mechanism, that is a *survival-of-the-fittest* principle is applied. The pseudo-code for a (generational) Genetic Algorithm is given in figure 15.1.

In general there is no guarantee that a GA will find (one of) the fittest individual(s). Therefore, the typical termination condition for a GA is given as a disjunction: stop if either an optimal candidate is found or the number of generations has reached a certain limit. In other cases the GA stops if the improvement of the fitness values in successive generations drops below a certain threshold or if genetic diversity has been lost.

15.2.1   GAs and Constrained Problems

One of the basic assumptions behind the classical GA is that values at different positions of an individual are independent; in other words there is no *epistasis*. For these problems GAs show a good performance in practice. The Schema Theorem [23, 20] establishes theoretically that individuals with highly fit gene patterns dominate the population on the long term.

```
procedure GA
begin
  t = 0
  initialize population P(t)
  evaluate fitness of individuals in P(t)
  while termination_condition = FALSE do
  begin
    t = t+1
    Parents = select_parents_from P(t-1)
    Children = generate_children_from Parents
    mutate Children
    evaluate Children
    Survivors = select_survivors_from Parents
                    and Children
    add Survivors to P(t)
  end
end
```

FIGURE 15.1. Pseudo-code for GA

Formally it states that the expected number of individuals exhibiting a gene pattern (schema) with above average fitness increases from generation to generation.

It is difficult to treat epistatic problems, such as CSPs, using a GA. If there are constraints on the values of different variables (positions), then not all individuals are allowed. The classical crossover might not respect this allowability, i.e. it is possible that a child created from allowed parents is not allowed. Traditionally, GA research has addressed constrained optimisation problems (COPs), i.e. constrained problems where an objective function is given, such as routing or scheduling. Many of these problems require sequencing, for which the most natural representation is a permutation (e.g. of city labels or job names). For this representation the standard crossover is not applicable. Therefore a number of *order-based crossovers* have been invented so that the children of permutations are permutations as well [17, 39].

We investigate the applicability of GAs for solving CSPs. Our basic idea is to divide the set of constraints given in a CSP into two subsets. One subset is represented directly in the so-called *allowability condition* and the GA is adapted by defining suitable genetic recombination operators that respect this condition. Hence, constraints in the allowability condition are satisfied by every individual. The other subset of the constraints is represented in the fitness function. For instance, one can define the fitness as the number of satisfied constraints in the second subset. In this case, candidates with maximal fitness satisfy all the constraints of the second subset. Thus, the (allowed) individuals with maximal fitness are solutions of the given CSP.

The fitness should thus measure to what extent the constraints are satisfied. This can be achieved in a number of ways. For technical reasons, we will assume that the fitness is defined in such a way that the fitness value is always positive, and the fittest element has 0 as fitness value. The most straightforward possibility is to consider the number of violated constraints. This measure, however, does not distinguish between difficult and easy constraints. A difference between constraints can be reflected by assigning weights to the constraints, e.g. on the basis of the measures used in classical CSP solving methods to evaluate the difficulty of constraints.

Another definition of fitness can be based on the evaluation of the incorrect positions, that is positions where the value violates at least one constraint. In the simplest form, the number of the positions with incorrect values is used. More sophisticated definitions can be given on the basis of the evaluations of the positions.

A third possibility is to consider the fitness as a kind of distance of the candidate from the set of solutions. In order to define the fitness as such a distance, first of all a distance measure (e.g. Euclidean, or Hamming) on the search space has to be given. Secondly, the set of solutions must not be empty. Since the solutions are not known in advance, the real distance can only be estimated. One such an estimation is based on the idea of using the distance of a candidate from the cylindrical sets represented by the constraints. Since the solutions are the elements of the intersection of all sets corresponding to the constraints, it is a natural idea to define the fitness of an individual as the total sum or the maximum of the distances of the individual in question from the cylindrical sets.

In all the cases that we investigated, except for a specific variable-order-based representation, the individuals considered by the GA correspond to complete instantiations of the variables. Hence, the GAs basically 'repair' complete instantiations until all the constraints are satisfied. However, it would also be possible to consider partial instantiations as individuals. A more in depth discussion of these issues can be found in [12].

15.2.2 Genetic Operators

We investigated three different types of genetic operators: classical order-based operators that apply to two parents, (heuristic) asexual operators that apply to one parent and multi-sexual operators applying to an arbitrary number of parents. The order-based operators are well-known in the GA literature, for details see [17, 39].

The *heuristic asexual operators* are based on the idea of improving an individual by changing some of its genes. An asexual operator selects a number of positions in the parent, then selects new values for these positions. The number of modified values, the criteria for identifying the position of the values to be modified and the criteria for defining the new values for the child are the defining parameters of the asexual operators. Therefore, an asexual operator will be denoted by the triple (n, p, g) where n indicates the number of modified values, and the values for p and g are chosen from the set $\{r, b\}$, where r indicates uniform random selection and b indicates some heuristic-based biased selection. We have restricted ourselves to asexual operators where n is either 1, 2 or #, # meaning that the number of values to be modified is chosen randomly but is at most 1/4 of all positions. When selecting the positions of the values to be modified some classical CSP solving measures on variables can be used, while for defining the new values for these positions some measure on values is needed. The most straightforward measure for position selection is the number of unsatisfied constraints referring to the appropriate variable, while for the new value selection it is the number of constraints which refer to the position and are satisfied, assuming the new value. We have used these measures in the case of asexual operators.

It is reasonable to define asexual operators which manipulate strongly constrained variables - given by a so-called mask - together. A specific case is when the variables are arranged into a matrix and the masks are the rows and/or columns of the matrix. Note that the matrix representation is a representation with two-dimensional individuals.

Multi-sexual operators, such as *scanning*, merge two or more individuals into a new, presumably better, individual. The use of more parents (selected on the basis of their fitness) may result in a (statistical) bias towards relatively good genes. This bias can be amplified in a number of ways, e.g. by considering the fitness of the parents or incorporating heuristics [14].

An operator should always create allowed children from allowed parent(s). Often, the basic mechanism of an operator (e.g. change the worst value) does not ensure this. Hence, it necessary to repair individuals after the basic mechanism has been applied to ensure that the newly generated candidate is allowed. This is illustrated for order-based representation and an asexual operator in figure 15.2.

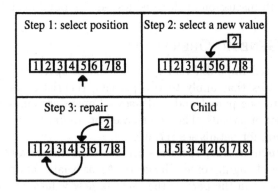

FIGURE 15.2. Repairing a child

15.3   The Test Problems

When testing different GAs, we were mainly interested in two questions:

1) What is the scope of applicability of a GA in solving CSPs?

2) How is the performance of GAs compared to classical methods?

In this paper we use these terms 'GA-easy problem' and 'GA-hard problem' in a pragmatic sense with respect to the performance of the GAs, as also proposed in [16]. We used two measures to evaluate the performance of GAs:

a) the percentage of all cases in which a solution was found, as a measure for effectivity;

b) the number of generations needed to find a solution, as a measure for efficiency.

If no solution was produced, the fitness of the best individual was used instead of (a).

We included different types of problems into our test-bench, difficult and easy ones, binary and non-binary ones, ones with and without tight constraints. To be able to compare our results to those obtained by classical methods, we chose problems which have been common test cases for classical CSP solving methods. In all of our experiments we ran (at least) 100 tests with each specific setting and took the average results. The figures and tables we present contain these average values.

15.3.1   N-QUEENS

We model the classical N-queens problem as a CSP with N variables, where the value of the i-th variable represents the row of the queen in the i-th column. The domain for each variable is the set $\{1,2,...,N\}$, and for all variables the following constraints must hold:

$v_i \neq v_j$ for $i \neq j$ (row constraint);

$| v_i - v_j | \neq | i - j |$ for $i \neq j$ (diagonal constraint).

The column constraints are always satisfied, due to the selected representation. The row constraints are maintained by allowing only permutations of $[1,2,...,N]$ as individuals. The fitness of an individual is defined as the total number of unsatisfied diagonal constraints. We investigated different problem sizes, up to N=10000.

All asexual operators were able to solve problems for N above 100, which is out of the scope of many of the traditional constructive methods. For all problem sizes, the best (with respect to the generation number as well as time) of the heuristic operators is $(\#, b, b)$. In general, one can say that improving more genes and more critical genes is better. For a detailed comparison of the different genetic operators, see [12, 13].

We also investigated the effect of the poolsize by running extensive tests on large problems for a cheap, but quite effective crossover, $(1, b, b)$. The most important conclusions of our experiments are:

1) Our heuristic crossovers performed much better than the crossovers applied in [6] for the same problem. But even with the best genetic operator, our GA did not outperform the best, repair-based method relying on similar heuristics [33]. However, it is remarkable that in the good performance of this repair method random tie-braking was essential [35].

2) The genetic diversity (the size of the population) played a limited role for the asexual operators: the performance of the GA did improve slightly as the poolsize was increased up to 30-40, but increasing the pool size further had almost no effect. This phenomenon was more pronounced for smaller problems than for larger ones.

These observations can be explained on the basis of the structure of the solution space of the N-queens problem. It has been shown analytically that N-queens is, after all, an easy problem: as N increases, the probability that from an arbitrary starting element a solution can be gained by consecutive local repairs approaches 1 [35].

15.3.2   GRAPH COLOURING

In the graph 3-colouring problem the nodes of a graph have to be coloured using three colours in such a way that nodes connected by an edge do not have the same colour. We only considered colourable graphs. We experimented with two representations for this problem. In the most straightforward representation, also used in [33], N variables (representing the colour of the N nodes) must have a value in the domain $\{1, 2, 3\}$ in such a way, that non-equality binary constraints are satisfied. We considered the number of violated constraints as the fitness function.

We experienced that the best operator was $(\#, r, b)$, which significantly outperformed the corresponding repair method [33]. It found a solution in 56% of all cases for difficult graphs with 50 nodes, in contrast to Minton's 18% [33]. Hence, the GA with the heuristic asexual operator $(\#, r, b)$ proved to be more effective than the appropriate min-conflict backtracking method. In accordance with this, we found that the size of the population did have a clear effect on the performance: There seems to be a stable linear correlation between the pool size and effectivity. As for efficiency, the increase of the poolsize resulted in an increase in the total number of generated elements needed to find a solution. However, as a solution was found in more cases, the run of the GA terminated after fewer generations on average than with a smaller poolsize. Namely, with a small poolsize the maximum number of generations (prescribed as the termination condition) was often reached. Thus the number of individuals actually generated did not increase significantly when increasing the poolsize.

We have also tested a more sophisticated order-based representation, suggested by [8] for a similar problem. Each of the nodes is identified by a number, and an individual is encoded as a permutation of these numbers. When a colouring has to be produced, we colour the nodes in the order in which they appear in the individual. A node is coloured using the fist colour not yet used for any of its neighbours. If there is no applicable colour, the node remains uncoloured. Hence, in this case the individuals may denote partially coloured graphs (i.e. partially instantiated candidates). Note that not all the solutions can be reproduced by this method. The fitness was the number of uncoloured nodes.

Using this representation, the superiority of the GAs was even bigger, see figure 15.3. The mutation rates applied for $(1, r, r)$, order2 and scanning are 1.0, 0.5 and 0.75, respectively (per individual, not per position), for N nodes we used $2 * N$ as the poolsize and $9 * N$ as the maximal number of generations. The graphs had 4 edges per node on average, corresponding to about 12% connectivity percentage.

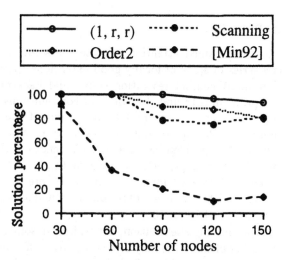

FIGURE 15.3. Effectivity of genetic operators vs. min-conflict backtrack on graph colouring

Using the order-based representation, we found that:

1) The best operator was the purely random (1,r,r), which was able to find a solution in more than 93% for all problem sizes we tested.

2) Several other, classical and scanning operators performed almost as

good as (1,r,r).

Finally, we also experienced the difference in difficulty for problems with different edge densities. For both representations the graphs with on average 5 edges per node (15% connectivity) turned out to be the most difficult, see fig. 4 for experimental results with graphs with 50 nodes and a pool size of 100. The same critical density was reported in [4], when using different methods.

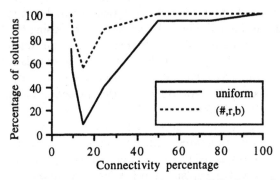

FIGURE 15.4. What are the most difficult graphs?

15.3.3 TRAFFIC LIGHTS

This test problem has gained attention because the solutions cannot be constructed as a series of steps of locally good extensions (providing local consistency), but many conflict resolution steps (and backtrackings) are needed [24]. The problem is to find the safe light combinations for 8 traffic lights in a simple crossing. There are 4 solutions out of the 212 locally consistent assignments. We found that this was a very easy problem for GAs. We represented the problem using a string of length 8, the first four positions having a domain of {1,...4}, the last 4 of {1,2}.

With the 1-point crossover we found a solution in more than 95% of all cases (for a pool-size of 100). In most of the runs we found a solution within 10 generations with a poolsize of 100.

The real task is not finding one solution, but finding all solutions. By running the GA a number of times (usually 20 or less) with different, randomly generated initial pools we were able to find all four solutions. However, since there is no guarantee that subsequent runs of the GA find different solutions, we improved our GA. Those solutions that have already been found are penalised by increasing the fitness of individuals approaching this solution. Upon running tests, we found that the average number of experiments needed to find all four solutions was 5.24 when using this penalty fitness function (poolsize 50, mutation-rate 0.5, max. generations 20, random mutation and 1-point crossover). We found an approximately linear correlation between the poolsize and the performance.

15.3.4 ZEBRA

The problem is to decide which person lives in which house (5 persons, 5 houses). Information is supplied on the nationality of the inhabitant, his/her favourite beverage (drink), pet and cigarette (smokes) of a particular, next or nearby house [9]. Furthermore information with respect to the colour of the houses is given. This problem is not only a common test case for classical methods, but it is also a challenge for GAs. The binary constraints are tight: for a given variable value, there is mostly one, or sometimes, there are two appropriate matching values of the other variable referred to by the constraint. Classical constructive methods can exploit this phenomenon (by filtering, by variable and constraint propagation), but GAs cannot. Thus a problem with such a strong coupling of variables is expected to be GA-hard. (This expectation was confirmed by the tests.)

We used two different representations in our tests. The first representation was order-based, in which case no genetic operator could find a solution in more than 4% of all runs. The second representation used two-dimensional individuals: a matrix of $5 * 5$ as illustrated in figure 15.5. Each row is a permutation of [1...5] denoting the possible nationalities, colours, etc.

House	1	2	3	4	5
Nationality					
Colour					
Drink					
Pet					
Smokes					

FIGURE 15.5. Matrix representation

For the matrix representation we found a significant improvement in performance. We designed a number of special genetic operators for this representation:

- row-swap: swap two randomly chosen rows in one individual.
- column-swap: swap two randomly chosen columns in one individual.
- $(1, b, r)$: the most critical row (the one for which the number of violated constraints is the maximal) is replaced by a random permutation.
- CPX: create two children from two parents reordering their columns by a permutation of [1,...,5]. The permutation applied for the first

(second) parent, equals a randomly selected row in the second (first) parent (the same row in each parent). The operator is demonstrated in figure 15.6.

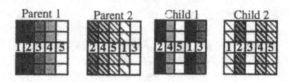

FIGURE 15.6. The CPX operator

In these tests we did some pre-processing and we introduced (some of) the implicit constraints explicitly in the fitness function. We also fixed the a-priori given values in the matrix. More details on these issues can be found in [15]. In these tests, the poolsize was set to 100 as was the maximum number of generations. When raising the poolsize to 300 we found better results; the column-swap operator achieved 46.4% effectivity (using learned weights to be discussed later). It is remarkable that in the cases when no solution was found, very often the same constraints were violated by the best candidate. We compared results obtained when each type of constraint is given a-priori weight (as an indication of the difficulty) as well as automatic learning of weight for individual constraints. We used three sets of weights for the HouseIs, SameHouse, NextHouse, NearHouse constraints, namely: *constant* (1,1,1,1), *ranked* (4,3,2,1) and *tightness-based* (10,6,5,1). The comparison of the results is shown in figure 15.7.

	Const.	Ranked	Tight.
(1,b,r)	20.8	24.4	26.0
column-swap	24.8	36.8	32.8
CPX	25.6	32.8	35.6

FIGURE 15.7. Effectivity without learning

We have also tested a GA that learned from its own mistakes. After each run it increased the weights of the constraints violated by the best individual and used these modified weights in the next run. We found that the results improved significantly in most cases. The results are shown in figure 15.8.

A very interesting fact is that the weights learned by the GA after 100 runs are to a big extent independent from the initially given weights (constant, ranked or tightness-based) as well as from the genetic operator applied. This independence from the GA specific components suggests that

	Const.	Ranked	Tight.
(1,b,r)	20.8	24.4	26.0
column-swap	24.8	36.8	32.8
CPX	25.6	32.8	35.6

FIGURE 15.8. Effectivity with learning

the learned weights reflect crucial features of the problem, without being corrupted by GA-related aspects.

15.4   Discussion and Further Issues

The main conclusion of our investigation is that GAs can be applied to solve CSPs. The GAs almost always found a solution for the N-queens (100-10000 queens), the graph 3-colouring (30-150 nodes) and the traffic lights problems. On N-queens, the performance of the best GA did not exceed that of the best hill-climbing method. However, for graph 3-colouring with more than 60 nodes GAs outperformed the corresponding local repair method, finding a solution in 93-100% of the cases versus 10-36% for local repair. This suggests that this otherwise tough problem is GA-easy. On the Zebra problem our best GA found a solution in 46.4% of the cases. This result was obtained using two-dimensional individuals, special matrix crossovers and problem-tailored tricks [15]; the straightforward approach with standard operators hardly worked. This suggests that Zebra is a GA-hard problem, but the performance of the GA could be improved by pre-processing the problem and by learning.

The observations above are especially attractive from a pragmatic point of view, i.e. in the case of CSPs where classical search methods and their extensions like local repair fail, a GA may offer a way out. In general, a categorisation of CSPs based on the analysis of the structure of the search space could provide some theoretical basis for the applicability of specific GAs to specific CSPs. The first steps in this direction has been taken in both fields [4, 16, 34].From a methodological point of view, the amalgamation of classical heuristics and evolutionary principles is a novel technique.

In the next stage of our research, we would like to explore GAs where individuals correspond to partial instantiations. Also, more sophisticated heuristics based on the structure of the problem can serve as a basis for further crossover operators.

We have not explicitly addressed an important issue: the detection of non-solvability of a given CSP. A GA can be trapped in a local optimum corresponding to a quite good candidate satisfying many of the prescribed constraints. In this case one cannot tell if there is a better candidate which the GA cannot produce, or if the problem has no solution. Possibly the penalty technique could be applied with success to avoid earlier found local optima.

Acknowledgements: The authors thank A. Corcoran, who made it possible for us to use the LibGA environment [5].

15.5   References

[1] Adorf, H. M. and Johnston, M. D., A discrete stochastic neural network algorithm for constraint satisfaction problems, In *Proc. of the International Joint Conference on Neural Networks*, San Diego, CA 1990.

[2] Back, T., Khuri, A., An evolutionary heuristic for the maximum independent set problem, In *Proc. of the First IEEE Conference on Evolutionary Computation*, Orlando, Fl. 1994, pp 531-535.

[3] Brassard, G. and Bratley, P., *Algorithmics – Theory and Practice*, Prentice Hall, Englewood Cliffs, NJ, 1988.

[4] Cheeseman, P., Kenefsky, B. and Taylor, W. M., Where the really hard problems are, In *Proc. of IJCAI-91*, 1991, pp 331-337.

[5] Corcoran, A. L. and Wainwright, R. L., LibGA: A User Friendly Workbench for Order-Based Genetic Algorithm Research, In *Proc. of Applied Computing: Sates of the Art and Practice-1993*, 1993, pp 111-117.

[6] Crawford, K.D., Solving the n-queens problem using genetic algorithms, In *Proc. ACM/SIGAPP Symposium on Applied Computing*, Kansas City, Missouri, 1992, pp 1039-1047.

[7] Davenport, A., Tsang, E., Wang, C. J. and Zhu, K., GENET: A connnectionist architecture for solving constraint satisfaction problems by iterative improvement, In *Proc. of AAAI'94*.

[8] Davis, L., *Handbook of Genetic Algorithms*, Van Nostrand Reinhold, New York, 1991.

[9] Dechter, R., Enhancement schemes for constraint processing: Backjumping, learning, and cutset decomposition, *Artificial Intelligence 41* 1990, pp 273-312.

[10] Dozier, G., Bowen, J., Bahler, D., Solving small and large scale constraint satisfaction problems using a heuristic-based microgenetic

agorithm, In *Proc. of the First IEEE Conference on Evolutionary Computation*, Orlando, Fl. 1994, pp 306-311.

[11] Dozier, G., Bowen, J., Bahler, D., Constraint processing using heuristic microgenetic algorithms, In *Proc. of the ECAI'94 Workshop on Applied Genetic and Other Evolutionary Algorithms*, Amsterdam, 1994.

[12] Eiben, A. E., Raué, P-E. and Ruttkay, Zs., *Heuristic Genetic Algorithms for Constrained Problems, Part I: Principles*, Technical Report IR-337, Dep. of Maths. and Comp. Sci., Free University Amsterdam, 1993.

[13] Eiben, A. E., Raué, P-E. and Ruttkay, Zs., Solving constraint satisfaction problems using genetic algorithms, In *Proc. of the IEEE World Conf. on Comp. Intelligence*, Orlando, 1994, pp 542-547.

[14] Eiben, A. E., Raué, P-E. and Ruttkay, Zs., Genetic algorithms with multi-parent reproduction, To appear in *Proc. of the 3rd Parallel Problem Solving from Nature*, LNCS Series, Springer-Verlag, 1994.

[15] Eiben, A. E., Raué, P-E. and Ruttkay, Zs., Repairing, adding constraints and learning as a means of improving GA performance on CSPs, In *Proc. of the BENELEARN-94*, Rotterdam, 1994.

[16] Forrest, S. and Mitchell, M., What makes a problem hard for a GA?, to appear in *Machine Learning* 1994.

[17] Fox, B. R. and McMahon, M.B., Genetic operators for sequencing problems, In *Proc. of Foundations of Genetic Algorithms-90*, Morgan Kaufman, 1991, pp 284-300.

[18] Freuder, E. C., A sufficient condition for backtrack-free search, *Journal of the ACM 29, 1* 1982. pp 24-32.

[19] Freuder, E. C., A sufficient condition for backtrack-bounded search, *Journal of the ACM 32, 4* 1985. pp 775-761.

[20] Goldberg, D. E., *Genetic Algorithms in Search, Optimization and Machine Learning*, Addison-Wesley, 1989.

[21] Hao, J., Dorne, R., A new population-based method for satisfiability problems, In *Proc. of ECAI'94*, Amsterdam 1994, pp 135-139.

[22] Haralick, R. M., and Elliot, G. L., Increasing tree search efficiency for constraint satisfaction problems, *Artificial Intelligence 14* 1980, pp 263-313.

[23] Holland, J.H., *Adaptation in Natural and Artificial Systems*, Ann Arbor: Univ. of Michingan Press, 1992.

[24] Hower, W. and Jaboci, S., Parallel distributed constraint satisfaction, In *Proc. of the Second International Workshop on Parallel Processing for Artificial Intelligence, IJCAI-93*, Chambery, 1993, pp 65-68.

[25] Huang, W., Kao, C., Horng, J., A genetic algorithm approach for set covering problems, In *Proc. of the First IEEE Conference on Evolutionary Computation*, Orlando, Fl. 1994, pp 569-574.

[26] Johnson, D. S., Aragon, C. R., McGeoch, L. A. and Schevon, C., Optimization by simulated annealing: an experimental evaluation, Part II, *Journal of Operations Research 39, 3* 1991, pp 378-406.

[27] Khuri, S., Bäck, T. and Heitkötter, J., An evolutionary approach to combinatorial optimization problems, In *Proceedings of CSC'94*, Phoenix Arizona, 1994, ACM Press.

[28] Manderick, B. and Inayoshi, H., The weighted graph bi-partitioning problem: an analysis of GA performance, To appear in Proc. of the 3rd Parallel Problem Solving from Nature, Springer-Verlag, 1994.

[29] Mackworth, A.K., Concistency in networks of relations, *Artificial Intelligence 8.* 1977 pp 99- 118.

[30] Meseguer, P., Constraint satisfactionproblems: an overview, *AICOM, Vol. 2. no. 1* 1989, pp 3-17.

[31] Michalewicz, Z. and Janikow, C. Z., Handling constraints in genetic algorithms, In *Proc. of Int. Conference on Genetic Algorithms-91*, Morgan Kaufman, 1991.

[32] Michalewicz, Z., *Genetic Algorithms + Data Structures = Evolution Programs*, Springer-Verlag, 1994.

[33] Minton, S., Johnston, M. D., Philips, A. and Laird, P., Minimizing conflicts: a heuristic repair method for constraint satisfaction and scheduling problems, *Artificial Intelligence 58.* 1992. pp 161-205.

[34] Mitchell, M., Forrest, S., and Holland, J., The royal road for genetic algorithms: fitness landscapes and GA performance, In *Proc. of the First European Conference on Artificial Life*, Cambridge, MA, MIT Press, 1991.

[35] Morris, P., On the density of solutions in equilibrium points for the n-queens problem, In *Proc. AAAI-92*, San Jose, CA 1992, pp 428-433.

[36] Paechter, B., Cumming, S., Luchian, H. and Petriuc, M., Two solutions for the general timetable problem using evolutionary methods, In *Proc. of the First IEEE Conference on Evolutionary Computation*, Orlando, Fl. 1994, pp 300-305.

[37] Paredis, J., Exploiting constraints as background knowledge for a case-study for scheduling, In *Proc. Parallel Problem Solving from Nature*, 1992, Elsevier.

[38] Sosic, R., Gu, J., A polynomial time algorithm for the n-queens problem, *SIGART 1 (3)*, 1990, pp 7- 11.

[39] Starkweather, T., Mc Daniel, S., Mathias, K., Whitley, D. and Whitley, C., A comparison of genetic sequenceing operators, In *Proc. of Int. Conference on Genetic Algorithms-91*, 1991, pp 69-76.

[40] Tsang, E. P. K. and Warwick, T., Applying genetic algorithms to constraint satisfaction optimization problems, In *Proc. of ECAI-90*, 1990, pp 649-654.

[41] Yamada, T. and Nakano, R., A genetic algorithm applicable to large-scale job-shop problems, In *Proc. Parallel Problem Solving from Nature*, 1992, Elsevier, pp 281-290.

Contributors

Christian Bessière
LIRMM, UMR 9928 University of Montpellier II/CNRS,
161, rue Ada, 34392 Montpellier Cedex 5, France
bessiere@lirmm.fr

Patrice Boizumault
Institut de Mathematiques Appliquées, Université Catholique de l'Ouest,
3 Place André Leroy, B.P. 808, 49008 Angers Cedex 01, France
boizu@ucoima.math-appli-uco.fr

Christian Codognet
LIENS, University of Paris XIII, 45 rue d'Ulm, 75005 Paris, France
Christian.Codognet@dmi.ens.fr

Philippe Codognet
INRIA Rocquencourt, B.P. 105, 78153 Le Chesnay, France
Philippe.Codognet@inria.fr

Yan Delon
Institut de Mathematiques Appliquées, Université Catholique de l'Ouest,
3 Place André Leroy, B.P. 808, 49008 Angers Cedex 01, France

Ágoston Eiben
Department of Mathematics and Computer Science, Vrije Universiteit
Amsterdam, De Boelelaan 1081a, 1081HV Amsterdam, The Netherlands

M. Anton Ertl
Institut für Computersprachen, Technische Universität Wien,
Argentinierstraße 8, 1040 Wien, Austria
anton@mips.complang.tuwien.ac.at

Gilberto Filé
Dipartimento di Matematica Pura ed Applicata, Università di Padova,
Via Belzoni, 7   I-35131 Padova, Italy
gilberto@hilbert.math.unipd.it

Eugene C. Freuder
Department of Computer Science, University of New Hampshire,
Durham, NH 03824, USA
ecf@cs.unh.edu

Jérôme Gensel
INRIA Rhône-Alpes – Université Joseph Fourier, LIFIA/IMAG,
46 avenue Félix Viallet, 38031 Grenoble Cedex 1, France
Jerome.Gensel@imag.fr

Andreas Krall
Institut für Computersprachen, Technische Universität Wien,
Argentinierstraße 8, 1040 Wien, Austria
andi@mips.complang.tuwien.ac.at

Guiseppe Nardiello
Dipartimento di Matematica Pura ed Applicata, Università di Padova,
Via Belzoni, 7   I-35131 Padova, Italy
guiseppe@hilbert.math.unipd.it

Laurent Péridy
Institut de Mathematiques Appliquées, Université Catholique de l'Ouest,
3 Place André Leroy, B.P. 808, 49008 Angers Cedex 01, France

Andreas Podelski
Max-Planck-Institut für Informatik, Im Stadtwald, D-66123 Saarbrücken,
Germany
podelski@mpi-sb.mpg.de

Patrick Prosser
Department of Computer Science, University of Strathclyde,
Glasgow G1 1XH, Scotland
pat@cs.strath.ac.uk

Paul-Erik Raué
Department of Mathematics and Computer Science, Vrije Universiteit
Amsterdam, De Boelelaan 1081a, 1081HV Amsterdam, The Netherlands

Jean-Charles Régin
GDR 1093 CNRS, LIRMM, UMR 9928 University of Montpellier II/CNRS,
161, rue Ada, 34392 Montpellier Cedex 5, France
regin@lirmm.fr

Francesca Rossi
Computer Science Department, University of Pisa, Pisa, Italy
rossi@di.unipi.it

Peter Van Roy
German Research Center for Artificial Intelligence (DFKI),
Stuhlsatzenhausweg 3, D-66123 Saarbrücken, Germany
vanroy@dfki.uni-sb.de

Zsófia Ruttkay
Department of Mathematics and Computer Science, Vrije Universiteit
Amsterdam, De Boelelaan 1081a, 1081HV Amsterdam, The Netherlands
zsofi@cs.vu.nl

Barbara M. Smith
Division of Artificial Intelligence, School of Computer Studies,
University of Leeds, Leeds LS2 9JT, U.K.
bms@scs.leeds.ac.uk

Adriano Tirabosco
Dipartimento di Matematica Pura ed Applicata, Università di Padova,
Via Belzoni, 7 I-35131 Padova, Italy
adriano@hilbert.math.unipd.it

Richard J. Wallace
Department of Computer Science, University of New Hampshire,
Durham, NH 03824, USA
rjw@cs.unh.edu

Author Index

Lecture Notes in Computer Science

For information about Vols. 1–848
please contact your bookseller or Springer-Verlag

Vol. 884: J. Nievergelt, T. Roos, H.-J. Schek, P. Widmayer (Eds.), IGIS '94: Geographic Information Systems. Proceedings, 1994. VIII, 292 pages. 19944.

Vol. 885: R. C. Veltkamp, Closed Objects Boundaries from Scattered Points. VIII, 144 pages. 1994.

Vol. 886: M. M. Veloso, Planning and Learning by Analogical Reasoning. XIII, 181 pages. 1994. (Subseries LNAI).

Vol. 887: M. Toussaint (Ed.), Ada in Europe. Proceedings, 1994. XII, 521 pages. 1994.

Vol. 888: S. A. Andersson (Ed.), Analysis of Dynamical and Cognitive Systems. Proceedings, 1993. VII, 260 pages. 1995.

Vol. 889: H. P. Lubich, Towards a CSCW Framework for Scientific Cooperation in Europe. X, 268 pages. 1995.

Vol. 890: M. J. Wooldridge, N. R. Jennings (Eds.), Intelligent Agents. Proceedings, 1994. VIII, 407 pages. 1995. (Subseries LNAI).

Vol. 891: C. Lewerentz, T. Lindner (Eds.), Formal Development of Reactive Systems. XI, 394 pages. 1995.

Vol. 892: K. Pingali, U. Banerjee, D. Gelernter, A. Nicolau, D. Padua (Eds.), Languages and Compilers for Parallel Computing. Proceedings, 1994. XI, 496 pages. 1995.

Vol. 893: G. Gottlob, M. Y. Vardi (Eds.), Database Theory – ICDT '95. Proceedings, 1995. XI, 454 pages. 1995.

Vol. 894: R. Tamassia, I. G. Tollis (Eds.), Graph Drawing. Proceedings, 1994. X, 471 pages. 1995.

Vol. 895: R. L. Ibrahim (Ed.), Software Engineering Education. Proceedings, 1995. XII, 449 pages. 1995.

Vol. 896: R. N. Taylor, J. Coutaz (Eds.), Software Engineering and Human-Computer Interaction. Proceedings, 1994. X, 281 pages. 1995.

Vol. 897: M. Fisher, R. Owens (Eds.), Executable Modal and Temporal Logics. Proceedings, 1993. VII, 180 pages. 1995. (Subseries LNAI).

Vol. 898: P. Steffens (Ed.), Machine Translation and the Lexicon. Proceedings, 1993. X, 251 pages. 1995. (Subseries LNAI).

Vol. 899: W. Banzhaf, F. H. Eeckman (Eds.), Evolution and Biocomputation. VII, 277 pages. 1995.

Vol. 900: E. W. Mayr, C. Puech (Eds.), STACS 95. Proceedings, 1995. XIII, 654 pages. 1995.

Vol. 901: R. Kumar, T. Kropf (Eds.), Theorem Provers in Circuit Design. Proceedings, 1994. VIII, 303 pages. 1995.

Vol. 902: M. Dezani-Ciancaglini, G. Plotkin (Eds.), Typed Lambda Calculi and Applications. Proceedings, 1995. VIII, 443 pages. 1995.

Vol. 903: E. W. Mayr, G. Schmidt, G. Tinhofer (Eds.), Graph-Theoretic Concepts in Computer Science. Proceedings, 1994. IX, 414 pages. 1995.

Vol. 904: P. Vitányi (Ed.), Computational Learning Theory. EuroCOLT'95. Proceedings, 1995. XVII, 415 pages. 1995. (Subseries LNAI).

Vol. 905: N. Ayache (Ed.), Computer Vision, Virtual Reality and Robotics in Medicine. Proceedings, 1995. XIV, 567 pages. 1995.

Vol. 906: E. Astesiano, G. Reggio, A. Tarlecki (Eds.), Recent Trends in Data Type Specification. Proceedings, 1995. VIII, 523 pages. 1995.

Vol. 907: T. Ito, A. Yonezawa (Eds.), Theory and Practice of Parallel Programming. Proceedings, 1995. VIII, 485 pages. 1995.

Vol. 908: J. R. Rao Extensions of the UNITY Methodology: Compositionality, Fairness and Probability in Parallelism. XI, 178 pages. 1995.

Vol. 909: H. Comon, J.-P. Jouannaud (Eds.), Term Rewriting. Proceedings, 1993. VIII, 221 pages. 1995.

Vol. 910: A. Podelski (Ed.), Constraint Programming: Basics and Trends. Proceedings, 1995. XI, 315 pages. 1995.

Vol. 911: R. Baeza-Yates, E. Goles, P. V. Poblete (Eds.), LATIN '95: Theoretical Informatics. Proceedings, 1995. IX, 525 pages. 1995.

Vol. 912: N. Lavrac˘, S. Wrobel (Eds.), Machine Learning: ECML – 95. Proceedings, 1995. XI, 370 pages. 1995. (Subseries LNAI).

Vol. 913: W. Schäfer (Ed.), Software Process Technology. Proceedings, 1995. IX, 261 pages. 1995.

Vol. 914: J. Hsiang (Ed.), Rewriting Techniques and Applications. Proceedings, 1995. XII, 473 pages. 1995.

Vol. 915: P. D. Mosses, M. Nielsen, M. I. Schwartzbach (Eds.), TAPSOFT '95: Theory and Practice of Software Development. Proceedings, 1995. XV, 810 pages. 1995.

Vol. 916: N. R. Adam, B. K. Bhargava, Y. Yesha (Eds.), Digital Libraries. Proceedings, 1994. XIII, 321 pages. 1995.

Vol. 917: J. Pieprzyk, R. Safavi-Naini (Eds.), Advances in Cryptology - ASIACRYPT '94. Proceedings, 1994. XII, 431 pages. 1995.

Vol. 918: P. Baumgartner, R. Hähnle, J. Posegga (Eds.), Theorem Proving with Analytic Tableaux and Related Methods. Proceedings, 1995. X, 352 pages. 1995. (Subseries LNAI).

Vol. 919: B. Hertzberger, G. Serazzi (Eds.), High-Performance Computing and Networking. Proceedings, 1995. XXIV, 957 pages. 1995.

Vol. 920: E. Balas, J. Clausen (Eds.), Integer Programming and Combinatorial Optimization. Proceedings, 1995. IX, 436 pages. 1995.

Vol. 921: L. C. Guillou, J.-J. Quisquater (Eds.), Advances in Cryptology – EUROCRYPT '95. Proceedings, 1995. XIV, 417 pages. 1995.

Vol. 923: M. Meyer (Ed.), Constraint Processing. IV, 289 pages. 1995.

Vol. 924: P. Ciancarini, O. Nierstrasz, A. Yonezawa (Eds.), Object-Based Models and Languages for Concurrent Systems. Proceedings, 1994. VII, 193 pages. 1995.

Vol. 925: J. Jeuring, E. Meijer (Eds.), Advanced Functional Programming. Proceedings, 1995. VII, 331 pages. 1995.

Vol. 926: P. Nesi (Ed.), Objective Software Quality. Proceedings, 1995. VIII, 249 pages. 1995.

Vol. 927: J. Dix, L. Moniz Pereira, T. C. Przymusinski (Eds.), Non-Monotonic Extensions of Logic Programming. Proceedings, 1994. IX, 229 pages. 1995. (Subseries LNAI).